MURDER
IN THE SHADOW
of
PIKES PEAK

MURDER IN THE SHADOW of PIKES PEAK

A Look at the Early Colorado Springs Police Department

Dwight Haverkorn

East of the Mountains  and West of the Sun ™

RHYOLITE PRESS LLC
Colorado Springs, Colorado

Copyright © 2024 Dwight Haverkorn

All Rights Reserved. No portion of this book may be reproduced in any form or by any electronic or mechanical means, including information storage and retrieval systems, without permission from the publisher, except by a reviewer who may quote brief passages in a review.

─────•❖•─────

Murder in the Shadow of Pikes Peak
A Look at the Early Colorado Springs Police Department

Haverkorn, Dwight, Author
Suzanne Schorsch, Editor
1st Edition, August 1, 2024

ISBN 978-1-943829-60-6
Library of Congress Control Number: 2024915537

Published by Rhyolite Press LLC
P.O. Box 60144
Colorado Springs, Colorado 80960
www.rhyolitepress.com   info@rhyolitepress.com

Publisher's Cataloging-in-Publication data

Names: Haverkorn, Dwight, author.
Title: Murder in the shadow of Pikes Peak : a look at the early Colorado Springs police department / Dwight Haverkorn.
Description: Includes bibliographical references and index. | Colorado Springs, CO: Rhyolite Press LLC, 2024.
Identifiers: LCCN: 2024915537 | ISBN: 978-1-943829-60-6
Subjects: LCSH Police--Colorado--Colorado Springs--History. | Frontier and pioneer life--Colorado--Pikes Peak Region. | Pikes Peak Region (Colo.)--History. | Colorado Springs (Colo.)--History. | BISAC HISTORY / United States / State & Local / West (AK, CA, CO, HI, ID, MT, NV, UT, WY) | TRUE CRIME / Murder / General | TRUE CRIME / Heists & Robberies
Classification: LCC F784.C7 .H38 2024 | DDC 978.8/56031--dc23

─────•❖•─────

Layout & design by Suzanne Schorsch
Cover design by Donald Kallaus
Cover photograph: Glenn W. Murray

The following is dedicated to all those who have served with CSPD, and will serve in the future. Even though often unrecognized, or understood.

Remember, you are the thin blue line!

Table of Contents

Chapter Number		Pages
	Acknowledgments	xi
	Introduction	xiii
1	The Downfall of Constable Foote	1
2	And the Reward Goes to . . .	11
3	The City Marshals Its Forces	15
4	Springs First Minority Hires	27
5	Officer Lost to Violence	35
6	Riot at the Opera House	43
7	Rules and the Question of Liquor	49
8	New Century, New Police Department, Old Style Corruption	57
9	Duff, The Rest of the Story	71
10	Explosive Case Unsolved	77
11	Dental Work Is Important	81
12	Death of Charles P. Essick, Suicide or Murder?	87
13	Bring on the Automobile: Regulations, Laws and Fines	95
14	Albert W. Marksheffel	105
15	Adventures of the Motorcycle	115
16	Serial Killer with an Axe?	119
17	Women have Arrived, Ever so Slowly	125
18	The Day the Chief of Detectives Died	133
19	Peyton Bank Robbery	143
20	International Association of Chiefs of Police Conventions	151
21	Wizards and Dragons	155
22	Manitou Bank Robbery	165

Chapter Number		Pages
23	Gidding & Kirkwood Department Store Burglary	177
24	Albert "Danny" Daniels	183
25	Lamar Bank Robbery	193
26	Pikes Peak or Busted	207
27	Colorado Springs Female Serial Killer	217
28	"The General"	227
29	"Dad"	239
30	Officer Richard Stanley Burchfield - Cold Case	249

Appendix 261

Incorporation of The Town of Colorado Springs September 2, 1872	262
City Organization March 16, 1876	263
Colorado Becomes a State July 1, 1876	263
City Reorganization April 1, 1878	264
City of First Class February 16, 1901	265
Nineteenth Century Officer List	266
Underworld Terms Glossary	271
Police Chief List	273
Colorado Springs First Police Department 1901	274
CSPD Firsts	275
Colorado Springs Police Department Fallen Officer List	278

Index 283

Acknowledgments

Commander Harry William Killa, Ret. and **Commander Robert L. Ownbey, Ret.** who made it possible to access the limited archives of the CSPD.

Cindy Conway, Assistant City Clerk, Ret. who gave me the opportunity to scan the old City Council minutes of the City.

Mary Davis, Pikes Peak Library District who helped me begin my journey on research in early 1990.

John Wesley Anderson, CSPD & El Paso Sheriffs Office Ret. for his advice and review of the Burchfield homicide case.

John Dwaine McKenna, author—my friend and a mentor on starting to write about this subject.

Kathleen Esmiol, author—*Everybody Welcome* by Fannie Mae Duncan with Kathleen Esmiol. Thank you for permission to reprint the Fannie Mae/"Dad" Bruce excerpt.

Nina Kuberski, Pikes Peak Library District

Jody Jones, Pikes Peak Library District

Chris Nicholl, Pikes Peak Library District

Tim Blevins, Pikes Peak Library District, all of the above people in *Special Collections* who spent many hours assisting me and giving help on research.

Jessy Randall, Colorado College, again, always there to help.

Grant Houston, Editor, *"The Silver World,"* Lake City, Colorado, was of unlimited assistance with information on our first constable.

Kathleen Scanton, Big Timbers Museum, Lamar, Colorado, was most generous and helpful with research on the Lamar bank robbery.

Lori Schmidt, Peyton, Colorado, asked a simple question about a possible crime which prompted my initial research into local homicides and history of the Colorado Springs Police Department.

Thank you one and all.

Introduction

The police are the public and the public are the police; the police being only members of the public who are paid to give full time attention to duties which are incumbent on every citizen in the interests of community welfare and existence. – Robert Peel

As a lover of history, learning about Colorado Springs and our nation has become my retirement pastime. As a retired police investigator, I noticed the lack of information written regarding the history of the Colorado Springs Police Department (CSPD). Colorado Springs has exceeded one and a half centuries. As I delved into CSPD's history, I learned one of the best ways to research the police was to study the early laws the police were to enforce and the crimes and criminals that got in the way. The purpose of this book is to record the growth of local law enforcement as the city and technologies grew and look at the criminals apprehended in the early days, making Colorado Springs safer for its citizens.

Police Departments, in general, are always looking at the future; what new technology is available, how can technology be used to network the needs of local and national police, how can the job be more efficient? When looking at the past, police look for things such as a criminal's past habits, places frequented and past associates, all in hopes of solving a crime. Writing down the history of a police department would be a timely effort, not afforded by police departments. That past lay hidden, until now.

Early police department's records were kept by the local government, many of which over the years have been destroyed. Some early records of Colorado Springs, founded in 1871, have not been located. Minutes recorded regarding city government actions started in 1875 and were maintained in the Office of the City Clerk. Unfortunately, they were kept in handwritten ledgers and are very hard to decipher. Typewriters were not manufactured until the 1870s. It wasn't until 1900 City Council records began to be typed in Colorado Springs.

One source used for researching the history of the police department and crimes they dealt with is the local newspapers. That too is problematic as most daily activity weren't reported. Crimes reported would appear as small notes in the "local happenings" section of the paper. An arrest might be given two lines found between "Mrs. Jones held a tea party at her home on Monday for the Ladies Home Improvement Society" and "Brown's Drug Store has a new cure for hair loss."

Microfilm of the local newspapers is on file in the Pikes Peak Library District's Special Collections area of Penrose Library, located at Cascade Avenue and Kiowa Street in downtown. These microfilms, like the handwritten records, vary in quality and readability depending on the person making the film and the quality of the newspaper archive. Not all the microfilm is decipherable.

Crimes of great magnitude such as murder, bank robbery, gun battles and serial killings would draw readers to the newspaper and were reported in greater detail. Reading between the lines, one gets a picture of the Colorado Springs Police Department, its outstanding officers, and its respect among national law enforcement. When following the dates of new technology such as fingerprinting and the use of automobiles, telephones and telegraphs, it can be noted the Colorado Springs Police Department was a leader with many firsts. The hiring of minorities and women, the collection of critical criminal information and education of police techniques on a national level are all part of CSPD's history.

The rich history of a department with a positive national reputation (with a few bumps along the way) should be told, and it is important the men and women of the CSPD and the general public learn a little about the great organization. And…who doesn't like a good crime thriller with many shoot-outs for a little entertainment? Enjoy.

Chapter 1

THE DOWNFALL OF CONSTABLE FOOTE

Sheriff Kelly survived four shoot-outs with outlaw gangs and had his horse shot out from under him twice. Kelly, respected for his honesty and fearlessness, served as El Paso County's first sheriff from 1861-1867 when the County was first established in the newly formed Colorado Territory in the heart of the American West. — Rankin Scott Kelly by John Wesley Anderson

The town of Colorado Springs' first appointed constable was Smith C. Foote. Appointed in 1872, Foote was a 29-year-old Indiana native who had gone to Rawlins, Wyoming, in Carbon County, after the Civil War and was appointed the county's first sheriff.[1] After his appointment an election was held and Foote lost the election.

Smith C. Foote moved to Colorado Springs in the summer of 1871 and began purchasing property.[2] He built a two-story building on the southeast corner of Cascade Avenue and Huerfano Street (renamed Colorado Avenue) known as Foote's Hall, which was recorded as being used as early as September 1871.[3] The main floor was rented out to a pharmacy, Barrett's Drug Store,[4] and the upper floor was a large open area where most of the churches, social organizations, dances, and gatherings of all sorts were initially held until other structures could be constructed in the new town.

It is unknown what prompted Foote to head to the new settlement east of the famous peak, but there was an article published in the July 28, 1871, Cheyenne Daily Leader extolling the benefits of the town as a fashionable resort, with a new narrow-gauge railway which was believed to carry throngs of people for health and pleasure. A new $18,000 hotel was to be built by the following spring. Maybe this could have been the catalyst for his move. Another reason could be his disappointment as the appointed sheriff in Wyoming, losing the position in the county's first election.[5] Interestingly, Foote was shown to be in Colorado Springs as early as August 6, 1871.[6]

Foote Hall in foreground.
Courtesy of Pikes Peak Library District,
Special Collections, Abby Kernochan Collection. 103-4095.

When the town was incorporated in September of 1872, Smith C. Foote was appointed as the town's first constable. There was no explanation for his selection, but it seems likely because he had previous law enforcement experience as a sheriff in Wyoming. The position of constable, for the most part, was handled by a single person. The only other law enforcement at the time was the county sheriff. There is nothing recorded that indicated that any of the town's constables were ever uniformed. The town of Colorado Springs was incorporated on September 2, 1872.

With the town's incorporation, came the town's first ordinances, for which the constable was responsible to enforce:

Ordinance No. 2 - Restrain running at large of certain animals.[7]

Ordinance No. 4 - Protection against fire.[8]

Ordinance No. 5 - Nuisances.[9]

Ordinance No. 6 - Protection of streets, fences, railings and trees.[10]

Ordinance No. 10 - Protection of trees, required in front of every building in the town, a hitching post had to be installed. This was so trees would not be damaged by tying horses to the trees. If anyone did not comply, it was the constable's duty to install said post and his expenses would be collected by a town justice of the peace.[11]

Although unclear as to how or what the constable was paid for his services, enforcement of the ordinances usually had a provision for money to go to the constable for their enforcement. For example; horses, mules, asses, cattle, sheep or swine were prohibited from running loose. If caught and impounded, the constable would receive fifty cents apiece and for every day that they were impounded, another seventy-five cents. Enforcement of the fire ordinance entitled the fire warden (at this time, the constable) $3.00 per day for time spent as a fire warden and one-half of all fines collected and paid to the city for violation of the fire laws.[12]

Part of the problem was knowing how the city operated and paid their few employees as no official records seem to exist for the operation of the town from 1871 to 1875, when the first City Council minutes began. Records had been maintained in the city clerk's office since the first ledgers were begun in 1875. This left the only unofficial "official" carrier of information as the local newspapers.

By January of 1873 the town did not have a place to maintain arrested prisoners. The newspaper noted the constable had arrested a couple of men and had to hire a guard to watch them overnight since the town did not have a calaboose.[13] The following month Constable Foote made up a room (unknown as to its location) as a calaboose and his expenses of $15 were paid by the town trustees.[14]

In April 1873, the town had its first election. Foote ran to maintain his appointed position, and he was pitted against Commodore Downing. This election was won by Downing by a margin of 43 votes out of a total of 233.[15]

Foote continued his business interests, which included purchasing and racing horses, purchasing businesses, starting a brickyard and renting Foote's Hall for events. In fact, November of 1873, found Foote's Hall being used as a court room. Colorado had three judicial districts at this time and El Paso County was part of the third district which included Fremont, Pueblo, Huerfano, Costilla, Conejos and Las Animas counties.[16]

The following year, Foote built an ice house near Fountain Creek where he had stored 250 tons of ice.[17] Being the entrepreneur he was, Foote became involved in mining with other men in the area of Hamilton (Chaffee County, west of Park and Fremont Counties) where placer mining was found to be successful, although it was not reported if Foote made a profit.[18] Foote even had a subdivision south of the downtown called the Foote Subdivision where several homes were constructed. This was an area south of Moreno Avenue between Cascade Avenue and Tejon Street, just a half block west and half a block north of today's location of the Police Operations Center at Rio Grande Street and Nevada Avenue. He purchased these eight lots in March 1875.[19] Regretfully, none of the structures constructed by Foote exist anymore, and as of 2024, the Tejon Street side is all businesses, and Cascade Avenue is an apartment building covering one half of the block called "The Mae" on Cascade. The name was used in honor of Fannie Mae Duncan, a local African-American operator of the famous "Duncan's Cotton Club," a mid-century-era establishment in Colorado Springs.

Everything was not all business oriented. Foote was involved in several court suits over properties and other things during his time in Colorado Springs. During February 1874, after a particular court case, there was a skirmish between Foote and a Judge Davidson. It seems that Foote believed he had hired Judge Davidson to represent him in a suit, and Foote did not believe the man properly represented him. On a Thursday afternoon, Foote was at the back of his hall on Colorado Avenue in the alley sitting on a plow. Judge Davidson crossed the alley a couple of hundred feet south of Foote's location, where, after hesitating, turned toward Foote and approached him. Davidson later complained that Foote had committed a brutal assault on his person, whereas Foote drew a pistol and threatened him. Davidson turned to walk away when Foote called to him, causing him to stop, and upon turning he was struck in the jaw by a large rock—weighing two pounds. The judge was removed to his room where he was confined.[20] Foote's reply was carried in a later newspaper—like the judge's version. However, the story had some variations. Foote said that as Davidson was approaching Foote, he denied representing Foote. Foote stated that Davidson did in fact represent him in the case and had treated Foote very poorly. Foote said he regarded the judge being no better than a thief.

The judge plunged his hand into a pants pocket while saying that Foote could not address him in such a manner. Foote expected the judge to pull a gun. The judge advanced on Foote, who rose from his sitting place and stepped back, where he found a heel of an old boot on the ground. Using this as a defensive device, he threw it at the judge striking him in the face. The judge then, holding a hand to his face, retreated toward Colorado Avenue. Foote went on to say he could not have pulled a gun on the judge as three months earlier after a trip to New Mexico, he had sold his pistol.[21] With nothing further being reported, it appears this was the end of any other actions with regard to this matter from either party.

July of 1875 found Foote and George Swain leaving for the San Juan area. Foote planned on opening a grocery and dry goods store in Silverton and Lake City.[22] He purchased $1,500 in groceries before leaving.[23] While in Lake City, it was reported that Foote planned to build a store there, plus he would engage in mining. He purchased a half-interest in the "Letter C" lode, located on Henson Creek, only a mile from Lake City.[24] Mid-August found Foote and Judge James H.B. McFerran of Colorado Springs obtaining a quit-claim deed to a portion of several mining properties in the Lake City area.[25] Three days later Foote, again with James H.B. McFerran, purchased partial ownership in more than one mining claim.[26] A third purchase of mining property occurred where the same partners purchased a 2/3 interest in the "Belle of the East" lode.[27]

Foote's further actions included the organization of about twenty leading citizens forming a corporation for construction of a wagon road over Cottonwood Pass. Foote was one of the nine trustees named in this undertaking.[28] Forty-nine people subscribed to the "Colorado Springs, Cottonwood and Lake County Toll Road," with the average investment of $100.

Even though his business interests were spreading across other areas of Colorado, Foote was not abandoning Colorado Springs. Along with two other parties, he built four brick buildings, two stories each, at the corner of Cucharras and Tejon Street known as the Dickey, Brown & Foote Block.[29] However, not everything was roses. In October of 1876 Colorado Springs suffered a disastrous fire. An empty building near the northwest corner of Cascade Avenue and Cucharras Street was ignited and the flames spread rapidly north along Cascade Avenue, taking all structures with it—including Foote Hall. The flames jumped across Huerfano Street(today Colorado Avenue) and engulfed most of the structures toward Nevada Avenue, before it was done.[30]

Foote continued to construct and run several businesses along with his mining interests around Lake City. Here he had another ice business where he put up 200 tons of ice during the winter.[31] For a second time a report was made that Foote was involved in a ruckus. In the latter part of October, 1878, Foote was in a saloon in Lake City and met with E.E. Eastman. Foote asked Eastman about some scandalous rumor of something that had occurred in Ouray, Colorado. Eastman, insulted, slapped Foote. Foote then obtained a warrant for the arrest of Eastman for the assault. Later that evening after the warrant had been served on Eastman, Foote was again in the same saloon, and was seated near a stove, a distance from Eastman who was playing cards. Suddenly, Eastman jumped up and assaulted Foote a second time, arming himself with a pistol. Eastman then exited the saloon. Foote believing that Eastman had left the area, went outside where Eastman again assaulted him. He held his pistol so close to Foote that when he fired the weapon, it singed Foote's clothes. The bullet passed through Foote's neck, but it was not fatal. Foote fired a shot at Eastman, but missed. The next morning a trial for the first assault was held where Eastman was found to be guilty and was fined $3.00. After that both parties were charged with discharging firearms in the city limits, Eastman pled guilty and Foote was discharged. Lastly, Eastman was charged with attempted murder. When court concluded, the case was thrown out due to conflicting testimony.[32] Apparently, some behaviors in saloons has not changed to this day.

The *Del Norte Prospector* of November 1878 published that S.C. Foote bore the reputation of a desperado, who at different times had put small chunks of lead into different individuals. While arriving from Lake City, Foote was involved in several quarrels, once shooting off his pistol twice at Bill Sawyer, but doing no damage. Other times he tried to draw his pistol, but was stopped by unidentified persons. The locals placed several bumps upon Foote's head, and when he left town the next morning, he had his head bandaged. It was thought those bumps were earned.[33]

Upon a visit to Lake City, I met the editor of the *Silver World* newspaper, Grant Houston. He had written a book about the area and was a wealth of information about our first constable and I was able to provide him with things of which he was unaware. I knew that Foote had never married, and romantic interests or such were never mentioned. A search of county records turned up a listing that Foote operated a saloon at Lake City. It was noted on the deed the saloon was "South of Henson Creek." Asking Grant Houston what that meant he laughed and said that meant it was located on "the wrong side of the tracks."

Drinking heavily and suffering delirium tremens during April 1883, Foote was in the habit of running to the Belle of the East Mine, and telling the miners that people were out to get him. The miners would calm Foote by telling him they would protect him and he would then stay until his hallucinations passed. The last time Foote did this, he seemed to believe the miners were out to get him also, and took off into the hills. Five men tried to follow Foote, and were able to as far as an area known as Lake Fork. It was noted that Foote had been a hard drinker for about two years.[34] At just 40-years-of-age Foote seemed pretty young to be suffering such a malady.

Residents of the town went in search of Foote in the hills for several days, but to no avail. Due to his condition many felt that Foote was thwarting their attempts to locate him. At times there were at least thirty people attempting to find the man.[35] Six years later, again in April, S.P. Robinson was on Hotchkiss Mountain prospecting. He was working along a gulch near the Golden Fleece Mine (about 5 miles south of Lake City) and was startled to find a skeleton, fully clothed, leaning against a small tree. In the pockets of the clothing Robinson found a purse, wallet and small memorandum book, which identified the man as Smith C. Foote. His remains were returned to Lake City and interred in the city cemetery. Foote was considered a pioneer of Hinsdale County and one of Lake City's most prominent businessmen. It was reported that Foote being a hard drinker, would go on prolonged sprees when he had money and would not sober up until the money was depleted.

During my visit with Grant Houston, he explained that the town had two cemeteries. There was the IOOF cemetery where all the past members of the Masonic orders, other social organizations and the more prominent citizens were buried. Then there was the city cemetery where Foote was buried. Grant explained this cemetery was where the prostitutes were buried and it did not contain many marked graves early on, Foote being an exception.

After finishing this research trip, I contacted El Paso County

Coroner Dr. David L. Bowerman. He had been the coroner during the time I worked in the crime lab and I attended many of his autopsies. Knowing him to be a forensic pathologist, I was certain he would be the person to ask for a medical opinion. I explained about Smith C. Foote and his strange behavior prior to his death. I asked the doctor if it was possible that if Foote had been fooling around with prostitutes and combined with the heavy drinking, could his strange behavior been caused by a venereal disease? The doctor believed that was a reasonable conclusion. The most likely venereal disease that would cause such conditions affecting the brain is syphilis.

In concluding, it can be wondered how different would Foote's life have been if he had won the election and continued in law enforcement in "dry" Colorado Springs. He was such a prolific entrepreneur. The man who took his place as constable would have an even greater downfall.

Notes

1 *Denver Rocky Mountain News,* 23 Dec 1871, Page 1.
2 El Paso County Clerk's Records, Article of Agreement between G. Banning, 3 J.M. Peninalt and S. Foote, August 6th, 1871,Book C, Page 302.
4 *Colorado Springs Out West,* 10 Oct 1872, page 3.
5 *Colorado Springs Out West,* 10 Oct 1872, page 3.
6 *Colorado Springs Out West,* 10 Oct 1872, page 3.
7 *Colorado Springs Out West,* 10 Oct 1872, page 3.
8 *Colorado Springs Out West,* 12 Nov 1872, page 1.
9 *Colorado Springs Out West,* 10 Oct 1872, page 3.
19 *Colorado Springs Gazette & El Paso County News,* 04 Jan 1873, page 2.
11 *Colorado Springs Gazette & El Paso County News,* 01 Feb 1873, page 2.
12 *Colorado Springs Gazette & El Paso County News,* 12 Apr 1873, page 2.
13 *Colorado Springs Gazette & El Paso County News,* 08 Nov 1873, page 2.
14 *Colorado Springs Gazette & El Paso County News,* 24 Jan 1874, page 2.
15 *Colorado Springs Gazette & El Paso County News,* 15 Aug 1874, page 4.
16 *Colorado Springs Gazette & El Paso County News,* 16 Mar 1875, page 2.
17 Colorado Springs Woodmen Edition, 15 Jul 2020.
18 *Colorado Springs Gazette & El Paso County News,* 28 Feb 1874, page 3.
19 *Colorado Springs Gazette & El Paso County News,* 07 Mar 1874, page 3.
20 *Colorado Springs Gazette & El Paso County News,* 17 Jul 1875, page 2.
21 *Colorado Springs Gazette & El Paso County News,* 24 Jul 1875, page 2.
22 *Lake City Silver World,* 07 Aug 1875. Page 3.
23 Hinsdale County Clerk Records, 14 Aug 1875, Book 1, page 83.
24 Hinsdale County Clerk Records, 14 Aug 1875, Book 1, page 96.
25 *Lake City Silver World,* 21 Aug 1875. Page 3.
26 *Colorado Springs Gazette & El Paso County News,* 18 Sep 1875, page 2.
27 *Colorado Springs Gazette & El Paso County News,* 17 Jul 1875, page 2.

28 *Colorado Mountaineer*, 11 Oct 1876, page 2.
29 *Colorado Springs Gazette & El Paso County News*, 19 May 1877, page 2.
30 *Colorado Springs Daily Gazette*, 03 Nov 1878, page 4.
31 *Colorado Springs Daily Gazette*, 01 Dec 1878, page 4.
32 *Laramie Weekly Boomerang*, 03 May 1883, page 5.
33 *Lake City Mining Register*, 04 May 1883, page 3.
34 *Hinsdale Phonograph*, 13 Apr 1889, page 1.

Chapter 2

AND THE REWARD GOES TO . . .

The Bertillon System, developed by French anthropologist Alphonse Bertillon in 1879, was a technique for describing individuals using photographs and measurements of specific physical characteristics. The system was used to track and identify suspects and criminals. — clevelandpolicemuseum.org

When Colorado Springs was founded, the first law officers were single constables. Then in 1878, the town became the City of Colorado Springs, officially, and a marshal's office was put into operation, with a marshal and some police officers. With the publishing of the 1900 United States Census, the population of Colorado Springs was large enough to be made a class-one city under the State's laws and the police department was installed with a chief and officers.

When Colorado Springs had its first election, the first man elected as constable was Commodore Perry Downing, taking over the position from the first appointed constable, Smith Foote. Downing only held the office for a month, from April 1873[1] until May. He was reported in the newspaper as being appointed as an El Paso County deputy sheriff and jailer at that time. Two other men followed as constables and then in October, Downing was again appointed as the town constable at a salary of $80 per month. The following April, when elections were held, he was again made the town constable for another year, but the following year his bid for the office was unsuccessful and he was rehired by the sheriff's office serving as a deputy.

In December of 1876, U.S. Detective Lewis E. Thaw was in Colorado Springs with his son. His title made people believe he was a government employee; however, he was employed by a private investigation service. Frank Flannigan, a rancher, posted a reward of $75 for the recovery of his horse and gear which had been stolen by William Klowen, a recent escapee from jail. Deputy Downing hired the private detective and the future constable, John E. Clark, to help locate the escapee. Thaw located Klowen and a second party, Mr. Crist, near the west border of El Paso County, in Manitou Park. Woodland Park was originally known as Manitou Park and was 19 miles west of Colorado Springs. Thaw brought the prisoners and Flannigan's property to the city and had the culprits locked up. For some unexplained reason, Deputy Downing decided he should be included in consideration for some of the reward as he had hired Thaw, even though he was not involved in the actual arrest of the two miscreants.

Later, Thaw and Downing had a chance-meeting on Tejon Street where an argument commenced. The meeting continued to escalate until Downing became so enraged he drew his revolver and pistol-whipped Thaw. John Clark, being near, was able to separate the two combatants. While Clark was struggling with Downing, the revolver discharged and a bullet struck Thaw. Before the shot was fired, a crowd had gathered, so there was no lacking for witnesses.

Downing retreated down the street where he put himself in the custody of Town Constable Frank Lombard. Thaw was carried to Robinson's drug store where Willie Thaw, his son, was employed and he was treated by doctors. At this time there was no hospital. Thaw had a head wound, not the result of the pistol shot, but from being struck on the head with the pistol. Thaw had been struck by the bullet in the lower back and it had passed through the bowels. He was taken to his home where he could be cared for. The following day, Thaw asked that Downing be brought to him, where Thaw wrote a note forgiving Downing for what happened. He died that same day.

Downing testified at the coroner's jury saying Thaw and Clark had been the parties that found the horse and gear and arrested Klowen. Since Downing had hired the two men, he believed he was entitled to part of the reward. That opinion was not shared by the two men. A fist fight ensued, and Downing felt he was at a disadvantage due to a weakened condition from a recent illness and Thaw was physically bigger and stronger. So, when Clark tried to hold Downing back, he took his pistol out and struck Thaw more than once. While continuing to struggle with Clark, the pistol discharged.

The coroner's jury decision was Downing was responsible for the death of Thaw. Bail was set at $4,000 and several prominent citizens posted his bail. Downing was free and did not show any signs of being a flight risk. A grand jury was finally convened the following February to take up the incident. As reported in the newspaper, when Downing was called to report to the grand jury, no one was able to locate him. This was the first recorded homicide in the city limits of the town.

In March, Downing's wife had left town going east to an unknown final destination. While trying to figure out what had happened to Downing, I considered he might have gone back to his wife's home in the east and possibly was using her maiden name, but I was unable to find any further information. Several years later, while going through the national fallen officer's data base, Downing's name popped up. It turned out that he had gone to Montana.

Downing was working as a miner before he was reported as being appointed as the sheriff of Cascade, Montana in 1887. Interestingly, the *Great Falls Weekly Tribune*, in December 1887, reported that "For six or seven years he was undersheriff in Colorado, where he made the reputation of being a cool and careful officer, and fearless when the occasion required." It was very apparent that the citizens of Montana were unaware that Downing was wanted for murder in Colorado Springs. In the late 1880s it was not very easy for information to pass from one place to another and there would have been no reason for authorities in Colorado Springs to have notified officials in Montana to be on the lookout for Downing.

In May of 1895, Downing was made city marshal of Great Falls, Montana. The following August, Downing was a victim of a serious accident. Officers were on their way to a casino across the street from Johnson's beer hall. A person was observed riding a bicycle and was having problems controlling it. The man fell off the machine almost in front of the trolley. Marshal Downing, himself standing within a few feet of the trolley rail line was also dangerously close to the tracks. Downing jumped, not away from the trolley, but toward it. The car being unable to stop, Downing was knocked down and pushed along the tracks about 15 or 20 feet by the trolley's bumper. Taken to his home, he was examined and it was found that his right leg was broken between the knee and hip. Two months passed while Downing was at home recovering. However, on Thursday, November 7, 1895, he suddenly passed away. It never came to light that he was wanted for the homicide of Lewis E. Thaw.

Notes

1 *Colorado Springs Weekly Gazette* and El Paso County News, 17 May 1873, Page 2.
2 *Colorado Springs Weekly Gazette* and El Paso County News, 25 Oct 1873, Page 2.
3 *Colorado Springs Weekly Gazette* and El Paso County News, 30 May 1874, Page 3.
4 *Colorado Springs Weekly Gazette* and El Paso County News, 06 Dec 1876, Page 2.
5 *Colorado Springs Weekly Gazette* and El Paso County News, 17 Feb 1877, Page 2.
6 *Colorado Springs Weekly Gazette* and El Paso County News, 17 Mar 1877, Page 2.
7 Great Falls Weekly Tribune, 21 Dec 1887, Page 1.
8 Great Falls Weekly Tribune, 17 May 1895, Page 5.
9 Great Falls Tribune, 23 Aug 1895, Page 4.
10 Great Falls Tribune, 07 Nov 1895, Page 4.

Chapter 3

THE CITY MARSHALS ITS FORCES

The first burglar alarm, invented in 1853 by Augustus Pope, used electromagnets to ring a bell with a hammer when a door or window opened. It wasn't until 1918, after World War I ended, that consumer demand for home security systems truly took off. — Home Security: The History of Evolution and the Future, originwirelessai.com November 8, 2021

Following the two original constables, four other individuals served in that capacity. Edward C. Sandell lasted less than four months before being replaced by Thomas Hughes who made it one month before the second term of Constable Downing. After Downing's deprivation, there were only two more constables before the reorganization of the Colorado Springs government. Delos Durfee, who had run against Downing for constable in 1874 and lost, was this time his replacement and stayed for almost a year.

The last person to serve as a constable was Frank P. Lombard, elected in April 1876. Lombard served until the reorganization of Colorado Springs when the town was officially declared a city in 1878.[1] The City Council that April, selected Loren C. Dana to be its first City Marshal, along with John N. Beall as a policeman. Dana's monthly salary was set at $40.00 per month,[2] but by July, Dana's monthly salary was increased to $60.00 per month (2024 equivalent of $1,900). According to Colorado Springs' first city directory of 1879, the population was estimated to be around 5,000 persons.[3] The city's limits were unchanged since its incorporation until 1880, when at least two additions were added to the city. This meant that the police officers were tasked with patrolling a little over five square miles.

Dana, a native of Illinois, arrived in Colorado Springs in March 1873, at the age of twenty-four.[4] In August of 1874, Dana and his wife managed the "Hotel at the Lake on Pikes Peak Trail,"[5] where they worked and lived for about two years before moving into Colorado Springs. Dana became a special policeman for the town of Colorado Springs.[6]

In April 1878, Dana was named the city's first marshal. Six months into his tenure, uniforms were ordered for the officers: blue coats, brass buttons with caps and pants to match.[7] By mid-December the officer's uniforms arrived on a Saturday and the Marshal and the Captain were wearing them on the street by the next day.[8]

At the end of 1880, the city annexed two parcels into the city. The first being Roswell City, located north of the town roughly at

CSPD Officers 1888: Standing Left to Right: Robert Martin, Horace Shelby, John Chapman & James McCabe. Sitting: Left to Right: Marshal Loren Dana, Joel Atkinson, John W. Garthright, unknown and Thomas Michaels. Courtesy of Pioneer Museum A84.1.62a

today's Fillmore Street and Nevada Avenue and the North End Addition, located just north of Colorado College. With this addition, the city grew almost one extra square mile to patrol, bringing the total size to just under six square miles.[9]

Near the end of the first year of being appointed to the position of City Marshal, Dana resigned just prior to the 1879 elections which would be conducted that April.[10] Interestingly, three weeks later he put himself to run for the position of City Marshal, however, he was not elected by the council. The position went to John N. Beall.[11] After Beall was selected, Dana was made a special policeman through September of that year, before being moved to day police officer.[12]

Mid-October, Dana became an El Paso County Deputy Sheriff. working in the jail for Sheriff Walter Smith.[13] During January 1880, Dana was made Undersheriff of El Paso County.[14] Apparently, he was not satisfied being a deputy, because the newspaper recorded on February 1881, Dana was Deputy U.S. Marshal and was out summoning jurors.[15] Now, in April of 1882, the El Paso County Commissioners appointed Loren C. Dana as Sheriff, replacing Sheriff Smith who had left the office to be a U.S. Marshal.[16]

After completing Smith's term, Dana was elected by the voters to continue in the position of Sheriff. He held the office into 1886, and in January of that year, when selecting people to be his deputies, he appointed his younger brother, Lamont E. Dana as a deputy.[17] This brother died during December of that year.[18]

April 1883, found the city offices moving into their new headquarters at 18 South Nevada. The building contained the Fire Department and its equipment, City Council chambers and the Marshal's office.[19] So by the time Dana was again Marshal, he was in new quarters. City Marshal William Saxton tendered his resignation to the City Council during January 1888 and Loren C. Dana was put in as City Marshal to serve out the term,[20] however, he was to continue administrating the Sheriff's Office until the newly elected Sheriff Len Jackson took possession of the office a week later.[21]

With the increase of the minority population of Colorado Springs, the city looked to recruit a minority officer. With the seating of the new City Council in April 1888, Horace Shelby was hired as the first black officer. He was one of the seven officers chosen at that time along with City Marshal Dana.[22]

1883 City Hall, 18 South Nevada Avenue.
Courtesy of Denver Public Library.

Thou Shalt Not Sell Intoxicating Liquors!

Due to the town restricting the sale or making of alcoholic beverages, the constables were harangued by the local print media. It was often reported the constables weren't doing enough to stop liquor from being sold. Colorado Springs stipulated in all of the original deeds issued for properties in the town, a clear provision: if liquor laws were flaunted, property would return to the Colorado Springs Company. This was continually a contentious situation between factions that wanted liquor and those that did not.

It 1873, the Colorado Springs Company, the owner of the lands to make up Colorado Springs, filed a lawsuit against David A. Cowell, operating a business on the Southeast corner of Pikes Peak Avenue and Tejon Street, for the selling of intoxicating liquor in violation of the deed provision forbidding the same.[23] After Cowell was found to be in violation, he appealed the case to the Territorial Supreme Court of Colorado. Prior to the law suit, Cowell had several arrests for the selling of intoxicating liquors: twice[24] in October 1873,[25] April 1874,[26] May 1874,[27] September 1874,[28] June 1875,[29] July 1875,[30] and March 1876.[31] Apparently assessing him fines of $50 or $100 and up to 20 days in jail for his violations had not deterred him.

The trial of the suit brought by the Colorado Springs Company against David A. Cowell began in the District Court in Colorado Springs on the 24th of April, 1874. After three days of trial and deliberation, the jury were unable to arrive at a verdict.[32] Cowell asked for a retrial and change of venue, which was granted. The trial was moved to Pueblo, and on June 18th, the court found in favor of the Colorado Springs Company.[33]

After three years, the Colorado Supreme Court affirmed the verdict of the lower courts on Tuesday, March 21, 1876.[34] Not to be deterred, Cowell appealed to the highest court in the land. The case was taken up by the United States Supreme Court in 1879. It was finalized and published as Cowell v. Springs Company, cited 100 U.S. 55 (1879). The decision is only six pages long and very interesting to read. When all was said and done, the Colorado Springs Company prevailed. This was the only time that the reversion clause was ever taken to court and amazingly all the way to the U.S. Supreme Court to finally complete the issue.

On Monday, February 2, 1880, a writ issued by the Pueblo County Court addressed to El Paso County Sheriff Loren Dana, commanded to deliver to the Colorado Springs Company possession of the property and its appurtenances.[35] When Cowell moved into the building at Pikes Peak Avenue and Tejon Street, he installed a water line, so now he believed he had the right to remove the line and was going to have it dug up. Again, the Colorado Springs Company had to go to court and were awarded an injunction. [36] More on this trial will be covered in a later chapter.

Henry George Starr—Bank Robber Extraordinaire

During 1890 the city made three annexations—West Colorado Springs, East End and North End No. 3. This enlarged the city by almost two square miles. The west city limits now extended from Limit Street to almost 21st Street—abutting Colorado City. The East End annexation extended the east side of town from Hancock Avenue to Main Street later renamed to Union Boulevard, its largest annexation to the time. Even with this increase in the size of the town to patrol—on foot—the marshal only had a captain and seven police officers,[38] and the population had increased to over 11,000.[39]

Another event that occurred during the time Loren Dana was marshal happened during 1893. An infamous bank robber, Henry George Starr, was arrested by the local officers and Marshal Dana.[40] Starr was part Cherokee who seemed to love robbing banks. Born on December 2, 1873, near Fort Gibson in Indian Territory (later to become Oklahoma), he was one of three children.[41] After being arrested in 1891 and jailed after being falsely accused of stealing a horse,[42] he was sentenced to prison, but jumped bail. In a shoot-out with a deputy, who died, Starr's life went wrong, [43]

Starr was involved in over 35 robberies of banks, trains and railroad depots from 1892 through 1921. His robberies were mostly in Arkansas, Kansas, Missouri, and Oklahoma. July 11, 1908, a small bank in Amity, Colorado, (near Lamar) in the southeastern part of the state was robbed by Starr.[44] For the robbery in Colorado, he was captured and spent time in the penitentiary at Cañon City. After going through a list of robberies in which Starr was accused of participating, the approximate total of loot taken was around $110,000. He was captured several times and spent time in prison.

He had the luck to often be released early, even once being pardoned by President Theodore Roosevelt. Because of this release Starr's son was named after the President—Roosevelt Starr. [45]

Arriving in Colorado Springs, Sunday, July 2, 1893, on the Santa Fe Railroad, two men and a woman, went to the Spaulding, a hotel located just west of Tejon Street on Cucharras Street. They registered as Frank Jackson, Mary Jackson and John Willison (being uneducated he did not know the correct spelling of Wilson), of Joplin, Missouri. The clerk being from Joplin, tried to engage the trio in conversation, but was unsuccessful. The following morning the two men went to Oppenheimers at 19 East Colorado Avenue and purchased new clothing. The men were haphazard in flashing a large amount of money, and both were carrying heavy revolvers. Finding William & Joe Oppenheimer friendly, Jackson asked the brothers to join them on a tour of the area. Accepting the invitation, they picked up the woman at the hotel, rented a buggy, and toured the Garden of the Gods and Manitou.

In the meantime, information was presented to Marshal Dana that two of these visitors, were none other than, members of the Starr gang of robbers—Henry Starr, his wife and Kid Wilson. Knowing that Starr was dangerous and had professed to say he would not be taken alive, Dana did not want to end up in a gun fight with the bandits. Officers, donning civilian clothing, began to surveil the trio, hoping to get them in a position where they could be taken without incident. After playing tourists, Starr and his wife, were dropped at the Spaulding hotel, and Kid Wilson and the Oppenheimers returned the buggy to the stable. It being late in the afternoon, Starr was hungry, but his wife just wanted to lie down at the hotel. Wilson wanted to visit a sporting house in Colorado City.

About 8 o'clock that evening, Henry Starr left the hotel and stopped at a restaurant, the Café Royal at 15 East Colorado Avenue. Starr seated himself at the counter and was in the process of eating his food when Marshal Dana approaching from behind, grabbed Starr's right arm as Captain Garthright grabbed his left. Detective

Atkinson, covered the bandit with two revolvers while two other officers covered from the sides. Starr was taken without any fight.[46] Starr wrote of his arrest in Colorado Springs in his biography and said, "I, the 'Bear Cat' of a bunch of sure bad hombres, had been arrested without a shot being fired, by four or five pot-bellied policemen!"[47] When Starr was captured, Dana's police force included a captain and eight patrolmen.[48] The town had about 11,000 residents.[49]

Wilson having gone to Colorado City was at Lulu Belle's sporting house on West Cucharras Street. Colorado City (today west side of Colorado Springs) allowed the sale of liquor. Captain Garthright and Marshal Dana arrived at Colorado City and engaged the assistance of two Colorado City officers before going after Wilson. Getting the drop on him, they were able to disarm Wilson of his Colt .45-caliber revolver and take him back to Colorado Springs and place him in jail.[50] The two main arrests being accomplished, the officers went to Mrs. Starr's room at the Spaulding hotel and woke the 19-year-old Mary Starr. A search of the room turned up $1,400-plus in cash and about $500 in gold.[51] In the next few days, U.S. Marshals arrived and removed the prisoners to Fort Smith, Arkansas, to stand trial.[52]

After getting out of prison, Henry Starr participated as the star in a movie about one of his bank robberies. Pan-American Motion Picture Company of Tulsa, began filming by staging a bank robbery in Boynton, Oklahoma in March 1920.[53] The film, *A Debtor to the Law*, about Henry Starr was completed in April 1920, and was planned to be distributed soon.[54] Apparently, being a movie actor did not take care of Starr's continued straying into banks and robbing them, because Friday, February 18, 1921, Starr and three others went into the People's State Bank, at Harrison, Arkansas, and attempted a robbery. While Starr was directing bank employees into the vault, the bank president, entered the vault through a secret door at the rear and taking up a loaded Winchester rifle hidden in the vault, shot Henry Starr striking him in the right side just below the ribs. The bullet pierced his spinal cord. Starr's confederates abandoned their leader and fled the area.[55] Henry George Starr died at Harrison, Arkansas Tuesday, February 22, 1921, on his first wedding anniversary to Hulda Starr.

First Bank Robbery Attempt in Colorado Springs

In September of 1893, Colorado Springs banks had alarms installed allowing them to signal each other and the police station.[56] There had never been an attempt to rob a bank in Colorado Springs—until Wednesday, June 19, 1895. Fred George, a 42-year-old man down on his luck, decided that he needed money and schemed to rob a bank in Colorado Springs. He had last worked at the Kentucky Stable, 108 East Cucharras Street. Approaching an acquaintance, George asked if he would be interested in a plot to make a lot of money. Edward Hutchinson listened to the plan, but the bank George was planning to rob was not identified to Hutchinson. The description convinced him it was the Exchange National Bank, located on the Southwest corner of Pikes Peak Avenue and Tejon Street.

George decided this bank would be easier to rob than either of the two other banks on the same intersection—El Paso County Bank (Northeast corner) or the First National Bank (Northwest corner). Hutchinson did not tell George he would not participate, but did immediately contact Sheriff F.M. Bowers, and a plan was put together to catch the bandits in the act. Hutchinson returned to George and assented to participating in the robbery. George needed a couple more men, which took some time. Eventually, he located Mike Kennedy and Bob McFarland. They were in a similar state as being without money. In fact, the robbers were so poor, it is unknown how George came up with a gun so he could do the robbery.

It was decided to hit the bank at noon, as it was the habit of the bank to only leave one person working in the lobby. On the day the robbery was planned, the sheriff and a deputy were hidden in the Exchange bank and every employee was armed. A sharpshooter was placed in a store across the street. Marshal Dana and Detective Atkinson were stationed in the El Paso Bank. Irving Howbert, the President of First National and others were in the First National Bank, all armed and waiting.

A horse and buggy had been rented from George's old employer, the Kentucky Stables. Mike Kennedy was mounted and waiting at the rear of the bank. McFarland was to watch outside at the front door, and George was to go in and hold up the cashier Ed Heron. At 12:30 p.m., Hutchinson followed George into the bank. George drew his pistol and approached the cashier while Hutchinson was to go to the rear and grab the loot. As soon as George drew his gun, the alarm button was pushed, which set off bells at the three banks and at the police station. George found himself covered by many people with guns and quickly surrendered. No shots were fired and no one was injured.

As soon as Kennedy arrived at the rear of the bank, he was arrested. During all the excitement, McFarland watching the front of the bank, just faded away. He was arrested later in the day. To add insult to injury, the bandits were forced to ride on their rented buggy to the county jail after their arrest.[57]

Trial was held in September 1895, and George was sentenced to the penitentiary for a term of eight years, after confessing to the crime and his two cohorts testifying against him. Both Kennedy and McFarland were released. Hutchinson, who had reported the planned robbery to the police, was not arrested.[58]

Notes

1 Colorado Springs City Council Minutes, 06 Mar 1878, Book 1, Page 215.3
2 Colorado Springs City Council Minutes, 01 July 1878, Book 1, Page 255
3 *Colorado Springs, Manitou and Colorado City Directory*, 1879-80, Published by W.H.H. Raper & Co., August 1879, page 4.
4 *Colorado Springs Gazette*, 10 Sep 1882, Page 2.
5 *Colorado Springs Gazette & El Paso County News*, 01 Aug 1874, Page 2.
6 Colorado Springs City Council Minutes, 07 Jul 1876, Book 1, Page 102.
7 *Colorado Springs Gazette & El Paso County News*, 26 Oct 1878, Page 4.
8 *Colorado Springs Gazette & El Paso County News*, 17 Dec 1878, Page 4.
9 Colorado Springs City Planning Records.
10 *Colorado Springs Weekly Gazette*, 08 Mar 1879, Page 6.
11 Colorado Springs City Council Minutes, 05 Apr 1879, Book 1, Page 309.
12 Colorado Springs City Council Minutes, 01 Sep 1879, Book 1, Page 346.
13 *Colorado Springs Weekly Gazette*, 11 Oct 1879, Page 6.
14 *Colorado Springs Daily Gazette*, 23 Jan 1880, Page 4.
15 *Colorado Springs Daily Gazette*, 24 Feb 1881, Page 4.
16 *Colorado Springs Daily Gazette*, 25 Apr 1882, Page 1.
17 *Colorado Springs Daily Gazette*, 31 Jan 1886, Page 4.
18 *Colorado Springs Daily Gazette*, 30 Dec 1886, Page 4.
19 *Colorado Springs Daily Gazette*, 05 Apr 1883, Page 1.
20 Colorado Springs City Council Minutes, 02 Jan 1888, Book 3, Page 75.
21 *Colorado Springs Daily Gazette*, 04 Jan 1888, Page 4.
22 *Colorado Springs Evening Telegraph*, 09 Jul 1897, Page 11.
23 *Colorado Springs Weekly Gazette* & El Paso County News, 05 Jun 1875, Page 2.
24 *Colorado Springs Weekly Gazette* & El Paso County News, 25 Oct 1873, Page 2.
25 *Colorado Springs Weekly Gazette* & El Paso County News, 01 Nov 1873, Page 3.
26 *Colorado Springs Weekly Gazette* & El Paso County News, 02 May 1874, Page 2.
27 *Colorado Springs Weekly Gazette* & El Paso County News, 30 May 1874, Page 2.
28 *Colorado Springs Weekly Gazette* & El Paso County News, 12 Sep 1874, Page 2.
29 *Colorado Springs Weekly Gazette* & El Paso County News, 17 Oct 1874, Page 2.
30 *Colorado Springs Weekly Gazette* & El Paso County News, 10 Jul 1875, Page 2.
31 *Colorado Springs Weekly Gazette* & El Paso County News, 05 Jun 1875, Page 2.
32 *Colorado Springs Weekly Gazette* & El Paso County News, 02 May 1874, Page 2.
33 Pueblo Daily Chieftain, 19 Jun 1874, Page 4.
32 *Colorado Springs Weekly Gazette* & El Paso County News, 25 Mar 876, Page 2.
35 *Colorado Springs Weekly Gazette*, 07 Feb 1880, Page 6.
36 *Colorado Springs Weekly Gazette*, 06 Mar 1880, Page 6.
37 City of Colorado Springs Annexation map.
38 Colorado Springs City Council Minutes, 18 Apr 1890, Book 4, Page 5.
39 1890 United States Census of Colorado.
40 *Colorado Springs Daily Gazette*, 04 Jul 1893, Page 1.
41 "Thrilling Events Life of Henry Starr," by Henry Starr, Publisher: Creative Publishing Co., College Station, Texas, 1982, Page 7.
42 "Thrilling Events Life of Henry Starr," by Henry Starr, Publisher: Creative Publishing Co., College Station, Texas, 1982, Pages 14 — 18.
43 "Thrilling Events Life of Henry Starr," by Henry Starr, Publisher: Creative Publishing Co., College Station, Texas, 1982, Page 26.
44 Grand Junction Daily Sentinel, 11 Jul 1908, Page 3.
45 Fort Gibson Post, 28 Jul 1904, Page 5.
46 *Colorado Springs Weekly Gazette*, 06 Jul 1893, Page 5.
47 "Thrilling Events Life of Henry Starr," by Henry Starr, Publisher: Creative Publishing Co., College Station, Texas, 1982, Page 51.

48 Colorado Springs City Council Minutes, 01 May 1893, Book 5, Page 7.
49 1890 United States Census of Colorado.
50 *Colorado Springs Free Press*, 01 Mar 1970, Page 11.
51 Pueblo Daily Chieftain, 04 Jul 1893, Page 2.
52 *Colorado Springs Daily Gazette*, 09 Jul 1893, Page 1.
53 Boynton Index, 12 Mar 1920, Page 10.
54 *Muskogee Times Democrat*, 13 Apr 1920, Page 10
55 Fayette Daily Democrat, 22 Feb 1921, Page 1.
56 *Colorado Springs Daily Gazette*, 08 Sep 1893, Page 4.
57 *Colorado Springs Daily Gazette*, 20 Jun 1895, Page 1.
58 *Colorado Springs Daily Gazette*, 13 Sep 1895, Page 5.

Chapter 4

SPRINGS FIRST MINORTY HIRES

By 1878, word had spread far and wide that William Jackson Palmer, a former Union Army general and the founder of Colorado Springs, had decreed that All children—black and white—would attend school together.
— Pikes Peak Library District

After the Civil War, many African Americans moved away from the South, seeking industrial and manufacturing jobs in large cities. Although some came west, without large industrial centers in Colorado Springs, the numbers were relatively small. The 1870 census recorded only one African American in El Paso County. The town of Colorado Springs was founded in 1871, but El Paso County did have many small towns such as Fountain and Colorado City. By 1910 the black population numbered 1,009 according to the article "African Americans in Colorado Springs" found on the Pioneer Museum's website.

As early as 1888, the City Council noted the large Negro population in the town and thought it should appoint someone to the police department from that community.[1] April 1888, Horace Shelby, who was black, was elected as a policeman along with six other men.[2] He became well-known and was liked by the populace. Shelby often was in charge of the hobos that were arrested and placed on the street gang.[3] Prior to 1888 only a small amount is known about the man.

Shelby, a native of Henry County, Missouri, was 44-years-old at the time he was hired as an officer.[4] An account in the Henry

County, Missouri, newspaper dated September 1879, written by a visitor to Colorado Springs, stated the writer met Horace Shelby, a thrifty man earning $2.50 a day as an auxiliary stone mason.[5] Shelby had been a general laborer in Colorado Springs until 1888.

Officer Horace Shelby, Circa 1888.
Courtesy of CSPD.

Horace was involved in local politics and was part of the organization of the Garfield and Arthur Club. He was voted to be one of the three vice-presidents of the organization when it was formed September 1880.[6] They wanted to show support for Garfield and Arthur's run for the presidency. James Garfield, the Republican candidate, became the 20th president. In the early days of the Civil War, when the Union wasn't very successful in battle, Garfield led a successful brigade. Upon Lincoln's request he returned to Washington to serve in Congress. In 1880, Garfield was elected President but would only serve 200 days in office before an attorney, unhappy and not receiving a desired appointment, assassinated him.

During the summer of 1890, a large contingent of blacks from Denver arrived in Colorado Springs where they held a parade to celebrate baseball. Horace Shelby was the marshal of the day. The day's events concluded that afternoon, when the Stillman Giants of Colorado Springs played the Denver's Colored Nine for the colored championship of Colorado baseball.[7]

Considered a good officer, Shelby served the city well for close to three years. Then on the 17th of July, 1891, Officer Shelby was accused of assisting two women to escape from the city jail. Marshal Dana filed charges against the officer with the City Council, and he was discharged by the council.[8] During that same meeting the second black officer, Henry Cornell, was hired to replace Shelby.[9] Little was reported about this incident and nothing revealed as to the reason why Shelby helped the ladies escape, nor the identity of the ladies. If there was a relationship with either lady, it was never revealed.

The following April, when the new employees were elected to office by the City Council, Horace Shelby was again among the members of the police department. No explanation was found for deciding to return Shelby to the force. He did not replace Henry Cornell, who continued his service as a mounted officer.[10] Shelby was again in charge of the chain gangs working on the streets of the city. April 1894, the chain gang made a break for freedom on North Nevada Avenue. Officer Shelby stopped the attempt when he fired his pistol in the air.[11] A few years later, Officer Shelby, while working, spied a man wearing a kilt which showed his bare knees. The officer believed this was an indecent exposure violation, so arrested the man. After Marshal Garthright explained to Shelby the man was wearing his native costume to celebrate the diamond jubilee of Queen Victoria and was also playing a bagpipe. It was not sure if Shelby approved of such a sight or maybe it really was the playing of the bagpipe![12]

When examining the Colorado Springs City Council minutes, book 3, page 123, April 30, 1888, shows the hiring of Horace Shelby as one of the seven policeman and a marshal was recorded. This is the first entry found about the career of Shelby. Then in March of 1891, City Council minutes recorded that Shelby submitted his resignation, but nothing to explain the reason for this happening. The council did not accept his resignation, but did suspend him from duty for a period of ten days without pay. This was before the incident where Shelby was fired for helping with the escape of female prisoners.[13] Even more interesting, when the city elections occurred the following April, it was reported that Shelby was back on the department along with Henry Cornell.[14] It has been reported that Shelby was a 22-year serving officer and was proposed to be the first police officer to receive a retirement.[15] Shelby being almost 60 years old[16] was in poor health and it was believed he could not continue the physical rigors of being a policeman. Alderman Carl Albin introduced a resolution to pay a half-pay retirement, for life, to any police officer serving 20 consecutive years. Another alderman recommended that the resolution be put aside to be considered at a later date by the full council.[17] Shelby continued to be employed as an officer through 1906. Even if the proposed ordinance had passed, Horace would not have qualified for a retirement as he had only served for 18 years, not 22 as previously believed.

By 1907 Shelby and his wife, Anna, moved to Los Angeles, California where he was listed in the city directory of that year as being a laborer. The directories showed he continued as a laborer through 1927. Shelby was then listed as a janitor through 1934 when he was age 86![18] Los Angeles County Death Records recorded Horace Shelby died on June 17, 1938—Age: 89 years, 10 months and 2 days.[19] One week later, to the day, his wife Anna Shelby died —Age: 67 years, 1 month, 9 days.[20]

Henry Cornell arrived in Colorado Springs about 1872 and spent much of his time on the plains. He was known as one of the finest horsemen. Upon the city hiring Cornell in 1891, and because of his horsemanship, it was decided that the best use for him was as a mounted officer to work on the outskirts of the city. Henry was described as five foot ten, 210 pounds and very strong.[21] Henry was a native of Missouri, where he was born in 1854.[22] He served as a policeman until 1899 when he decided to try mining, which he did for three years. Then in 1903, he was again listed as an officer through 1909. In 1906 his wife of 21 years passed away, leaving him with two children, a son and step-daughter, 18 and 13, respectively.[23]

Officer Henry Cornell,
Circa 1888.
Courtesy of CSPD.

During 1895, before entering the police service, Henry was definitely a cowboy. At the Western Carnival being held in the southern part of the city, a wild west show was presented with all the things that come with such a show: shooting, racing chariots, staged cavalry battle, etc. One event the newspaper didn't describe pitted three cowboys against one another for a $90 prize. Henry Cornell entered this competition. Nothing was printed to tell what the event consisted of or who won the prize.

Officer Cornell was on patrol in downtown Colorado Springs during the night of Thursday, February 25, 1904. A fire occurred in a feed store on the southwest corner of Cascade and Colorado Avenues around 12:30 a.m. The flames, due to strong winds, were fanned into the rooming house next door. In moments, the house was aflame. People yelling there was a fire, turned out most of the tenants of the building. Firefighters arrived quickly and began using ladders to help residents of the second floor escape the fire. However, the landlady, Mrs. Smith, jumped from the second floor into the arms of Officer Henry Cornell, followed by Frank Spears. The officer was able to safely dampen their falls. He was described in the paper as being a very strong man—this says it all.[24]

The 1910 *Colorado Springs City Directory* listed Henry Cornell as a teamster, residing at 524 South Wahsatch Avenue. It is unknown where Henry moved or what became of him after 1910.

John C. Cooper a resident of Colorado Springs from the early 1890s, was a general laborer until he was hired as the next minority officer near the end of 1909.[25] He served as an officer until 1924, when he requested retirement due to age (71) and disability.[26] The officer, known as Jack, passed away three years later at his home on North Corona Street. Two years later the officer's widow appeared at a meeting of the Policemen's Relief Fund Association requesting some relief due to her financial position. The board made an investigation and after the matter was reviewed by the City Attorney and finding that she had moved to California, no further action was taken.[27] At this time the Relief Fund had been established for seventeen years. Requests by retiring officers and requests by family members did not arrive very often. Also, the rules did not cover many things that would become a standard practice in future years.

Only one more black officer was hired, who lasted just one year, then there was a gap of forty-three years before another black officer was hired. When I entered the CSPD there was one black officer on the force. He resigned in 1969. Another black officer was not hired until March of 1973. Now black officers regularly serve on the force.

In 1973 women were beginning to be brought into the department and in 1974, the first black woman was hired. She was my rider for most of a year. She stayed on the department for three years. Today the police force hires qualified personnel of all races, sexes and religions.

Notes

1 *Colorado Springs Evening Telegraph*, 09 Jul 1897, Page 11.
2 Colorado Springs City Council Minutes, 30 Apr 1888, Book 3, Page 123.
3 *Colorado Springs Evening Telegraph*, 09 Jul 1897, Page 11.
4 Los Angeles County, California Death Records, 18 Jun 1938 Page 8204.
5 *Henry County, Missouri, Democrat*, 11 Sep 1879, Page 1.
6 *Colorado Springs Gazette*, 28 Sep 1880, Page 4.
7 *Colorado Springs Gazette*, 06 Aug 1890, Page 6.
8 Colorado Springs City Council Minutes, 20 Jul 1891, Book 4, Page 190.
9 *Colorado Springs Gazette*, 22 Jul 1891, Page 3.
10 Colorado Springs City Council Minutes, Book 4, Page 295.
11 *Colorado Springs Gazette*, 15 Apr 1894, Page 4.
12 *Colorado Springs Weekly Gazette*, 24 Jun 1897, Page 4.
13 Colorado Springs City Council Minutes, 20 Jul 1891, Book 4, Page 190.
14 Colorado Springs City Council Minutes, 21 Apr 1891, Book 4, Page 152.
15 *Henry County Democrat*, 16 Aug 1906, Page 8.
16 Los Angeles County Death Records, 18 Jun 1938, Volume 386, Page 8204.
17 *Colorado Springs Gazette*, 04 Dec 1906, Page 1.
18 *Los Angeles City Directories*, 1907 through 1934.
19 Los Angeles County Death Records, 18 Jun 1938, Volume 386, Page 8204.
20 Los Angeles County Death Records, Volume 386, Page 8480.

21 *Colorado Springs Evening Telegraph*, 09 Jul 1897, Page 11.
22 1900 Colorado United States Census, 06 Jun 1900.
23 *Colorado Springs Gazette*, 13 Sep 1895, Page 5.
24 *Colorado Springs Gazette*, 25 Feb 1904, Page 1.
25 Colorado Springs City Council Minutes, Book 12, Page 54.
26 Letter to the Police Relief Fund, 21 May 1924.
27 Colorado Springs Policemen's Relief Fund Association Records, 18 Jun 1930.

Chapter 5

OFFICER LOST TO VIOLENCE

The Colorado Springs Police Department has lost thirteen officers in the line of duty. "All that is necessary for the triumph of evil is that good men do nothing."
—Edmund Burke

During the last year of Marshal Dana's term as City Marshal, the city lost an officer to violence for the first time since its beginning. On Sunday, June 28, 1896, Officer Benjamin Franklin Bish was walking his beat on Pikes Peak Avenue, just east of Cascade Avenue; after reporting for duty at 10:00 p.m. At approximately, 10:20 p.m., citizens downtown heard three to four gunshots in the alley which ran north and south between Pikes Peak Avenue and Huerfano Street (Colorado Avenue), west of Tejon Street. A man was seen running toward Pikes Peak Avenue out of the alley. People rapidly ran toward the sounds, which emanated from behind the Gazette building, located west of the alley entrance. The running man saw people approaching, turned, and ran behind the Gazette building. This area was enclosed and did not have another way out.

Marshal Dana, who was in his office, at the City Hall, 18 South Nevada Avenue, heard the shots and immediately ran to the area. A quick search in the alley found Officer Bish lying at the rear of the Wilbur Dry Goods store, 22 South Tejon Street. The officer's hand was clutching a .45-caliber Colt revolver which was smoking. The Colt was found to have been fired two times. About forty-five minutes later Bish died. When the officer's body was moved, another

Colt revolver was found under his body. This second weapon was one that had been taken from Officer Samuel Agard during an assault a couple of weeks earlier.

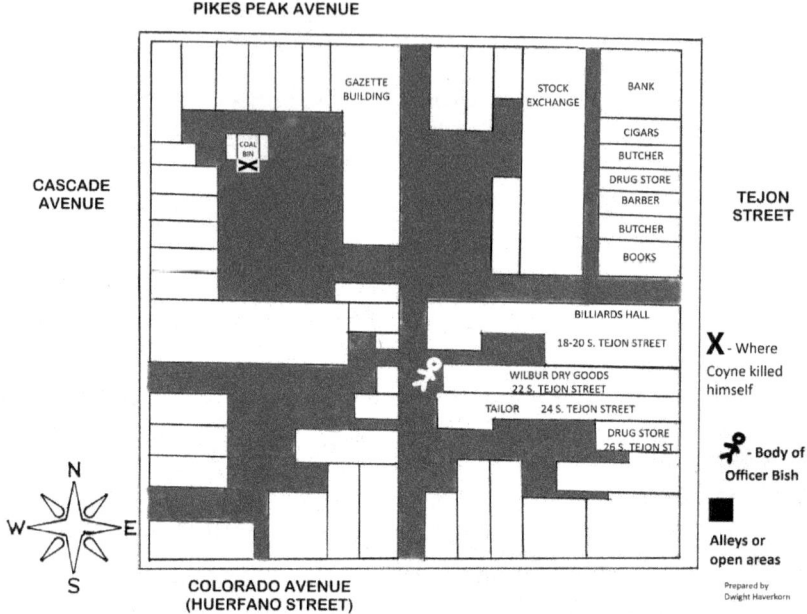

Colorado Springs crime diagram.

People began searching in the dead-end area behind the businesses, checking doorways, and coal houses. During this search a shot rang out and a man was found dead. He had shot himself while hiding in one of the coal-houses. The dead man was William H. Clark, a local teamster. His weapon had been fired two times—it was believed one shot had been fired at the deceased police officer and the second to end his life. A search of Clark's clothing revealed a second revolver of .38-caliber in his coat.

When Clark's body was taken to a funeral home, many people crowded in to see the remains. Several people said that he had a companion named Coyne, and they both worked as teamsters for the same employer. Some bystanders said the two men, Clark and Coyne roomed at Mrs. Green's, 216 South Cascade Avenue. This was next door to the home of Officer Bish! Marshal Dana, Captain Garthright and Detective Atkinson went to Mrs. Green's rooming house and found Patrick Coyne in bed. He was arrested and the officers searched his room. A coat was found which was torn and had burn marks caused by firing a gun. Coyne denied having had anything to do with the death of Officer Bish and stated he had been in bed since nine o'clock that evening. A satchel was located which contained two cloth masks, a ring that had been reported stolen and a watch of unknown ownership.

Otis S. Kimball, a freight transfer operator, was contacted and said he had seen Clark and Coyne about eight o'clock that evening when they left work together. When Coyne was questioned, he confessed to being involved when the officer was slain. He explained that he and Clark had met when in the Colorado penitentiary, where Coyne was sent for doing a holdup. After being released they both went to work for Kimball in Colorado Springs. They had been committing robberies in the area recently.[1] A couple of weeks earlier they tried to rob Officer Agard. Unaware that he was a police officer, they assaulted Agard and took his revolver in the process.[2]

Before the killing of Bish, the men only used their guns to intimidate people, and never intended to hurt anyone. Earlier Bish confronted the two men in the rear of the May Clothing store, 20 South Tejon Street. The officer, while in the process of arresting Coyne, found and confiscated a weapon found in his coat pocket. Clark standing about ten feet away, drew his revolver and shot the officer. After the shooting occurred both men ran. Coyne walked quickly toward Pikes Peak Avenue and then west toward Cascade Avenue. From there he ran to his room and waited for Clark to join him.[3]

Officer Bish, a 35-year-old native of Missouri, was relatively new to the force.[4] He had been hired the previous April—just two months earlier.[5] The officer was married and had a small daughter.[6] They were married at Scotland County, Missouri, 10-years earlier.[7] Following the officer's death, the City Council passed a resolution:

RESOLUTION

WHEREAS, on the 28th day of June 1896 Police Officer Benjamin F. Bish while in the discharge of his duty was assassinated by highwayman; and

WHEREAS, the City Council of the City of Colorado Springs desiring to show its appreciation of the services of those who watch over the welfare of its citizens, by day and by night, through sunshine, storm, ever faithful in the discharge of their duties imposed upon them, and recognizing in Officer Bish a faithful and conscientious servant of the people, offer the following:

RESOLVED, that in the death of Officer Bish, the City has lost a brave and efficient officer, the community a true and loyal citizen, the wife a noble and generous husband, the daughter a kind and indulgent father.

RESOLVED, that these resolutions be spread upon the records of the City, and a copy of the same be furnished the bereaved family and City Press.

                Signed: W.H. McIntyre
                                H.C. McCreery
                                J.A. Leech, Committee[8]

Officer Benjamin Bish gravemarker Colorado Springs, Evergreen Cemetery.

There was no pension fund or state benefits for a fallen officer at this time, so a benefit performance was held by the Elks minstrels and almost $800 (2024 would be $29,900) was raised for Bish's family. A large parade was held in the fallen officer's honor, which included not only the officers of the Colorado Springs Police Department, but those of Colorado City, and members of the paid fire departments of the area, plus two different groups of the state militia.[9]

Patrick Coyne prisoner photo.
Courtesy of Colorado State Pennitentiary.

On Wednesday, July 4, 1896, Patrick Coyne pled guilty to his involvement in the death of Officer Frank Bish. Even with the plea, a hearing had to be conducted, and the case was set to be held before a jury. The following Wednesday, Patrick Coyne was sentenced to the Colorado penitentiary for life, on the charge of second-degree murder. He was transported to the penitentiary in Cañon City, just eight months after having been released from the prison for a previous offense. This had to be one of the fastest cases ever: one week after the killing the suspect was in prison!

Eight years later, Patrick Coyne appealed his sentence and was granted a new trial after making a complaint that evidence in aggravation and mitigation had been not allowed in the original trial. Evidence in the aggravation and mitigation means after the finding of guilty, the prosecutor could put before the judge in aggravation, past convictions and other wrong doings in the prisoner's past. On the other hand, the defense attorney can give information in mitigation, things in the prisoner's favor that could also be put before the judge prior to declaring the sentence.

Friday, September 2, 1904, Coyne appeared in district court, where he tried to change his plea to not guilty, but the judge would not allow the change and testimony was taken. After the conclusion of the new trial, Coyne was again sentenced to life in prison. However, Coyne was not to serve life. On June 24, 1912, his sentence was commuted to 35 years to life; then July 1, 1913, again, his sentence was commuted to 17 years, 11 months and 14 days to life. On Friday, July 7, 1913, Coyne was paroled. He was 30 years old when he was first sentenced for this crime and when released was 51 years of age.

Officer Bish's passing opened the eyes of many on the needs of our police department, especially for those killed in the line of duty. It took many years before changes came. In 1913, the Colorado State Legislature decided that firefighters needed a relief or pension fund, so they passed a law requiring cities to provide such a vehicle, but without any funding. It was then decided that police should also be included in this plan. The plans were to be administered by a local board in each city. When I served on the Pension Board it consisted of three people: a permanent member, the city manager and two police officers elected by the officers to serve two-year terms. What money was in the fund was invested, according to state & federal law, by the city, after approval of the board members. When an officer applied for retirement, they were required to have 25 years of service and be the minimum age of 50 years.

By this time, the state was providing some funding to the cities, depending on the number of police officers. The main problem was there were more liabilities to come in the future than the pension could handle. Because the state mandated the fund—without funding—it was in the hole from day one.

After a period where some of the funds' discretionary monies was being handled by one of the, then, big three local banks, as was the fire fund and the cemetery fund. After some research, I found we could get out of this vicious cycle, by going to outside management. We were able to hire Funds Advisory out of Houston, Texas, to handle our investments. Before, we were unpaid volunteers, with the help of the city's financial advisory board, making recommendations for investments. We were making about 6% income each year. After going outside, we were paying E.F. Hutton as our advisors and Funds Advisory to manage the money. We were then making close to 10% on our investments, but were still in the hole on the needs in the future to pay pensions. Officers were paying into the pension 3½% of our salaries, which was ridiculous. The state was contacted asking that we be allowed to increase our funding, but were turned down because it was spelled out in state law.

An officer in 1978, applied for his retirement in a small southeastern Colorado town, only to find that the city had not been saving the state money, or the officer's contributions into a fund, but placing the money into their general fund as operating money. He sued the city and the State of Colorado. The legislature took notice and decided that police and fire pensions were "of state wide concern." Shortly after this, the state took over all the city's pension funds, increased the state funding, increased the officer's contributions, changed the retirement to 25 years of service and minimum age of 55.

If an officer dies, there is $10,000 for duty-related death for active sworn and civilian members; $2,500 for an active member's off-duty death; and a $1,500 death benefit to the listed beneficiary upon a retired member's death.

If an officer is killed on duty, the spouse receives 70% of the member's base salary. These benefits are payable for life and for dependent children until age 23, as long as the child remains a dependent. The federal government created the Public Safety Officers' Educational Assistance Program. Financial assistance is available for spouses and eligible children—until their 27th birthday.

Notes

1 *Colorado Springs Gazette*, 29 Jun 1896, Page 1.
2 *Colorado Springs Evening Telegraph*, 29 Jun 1896, page 1.
3 *Colorado Springs Gazette*, 29 Jun 1896, Page 1.
4 1880 U.S. Census,
5 Colorado Springs City Council Minutes, 20 Apr 1896, Book 6, Page 3.
6 *Colorado Springs Gazette*, 30 Jun 1896, Page 1.
7 Scotland County, Missouri Marriage Record, 16 Mar 1886, Book1, Page 361.
8 Colorado Springs City Council Minutes, 21 Jul 1896, Book 6, Page 44.
9 *Colorado Springs Gazette*, 09 Jul 1896, Page 5.
10 *Colorado Springs Gazette*, 04 Jul 1896, Page 5.
11 *Colorado Springs Gazette*, 09 Jul 1896, Page 5.
12 *Colorado Springs Gazette*, 03 Sep 1904, Page 1.
13 Colorado State Prison Records, Prisoner 6125.

Chapter 6

RIOT AT THE OPERA HOUSE

In 1835 Henry Goddard linked a bullet recovered from a victim to the gun of the murderer. This was the first documented case of the use of ballistics in forensics. —Incognito Forensic Foundation

John Walter Garthright served as a police officer in Colorado Springs as early as 1887.[1] He was promoted to rank of captain of the night force in 1890;[2] a position he held through April of 1897. At the age of 40,[3] the Missouri native, was appointed to the office of City Marshal serving from May 1897[4] until April of 1900.[5] As marshal he started with a force consisting of a captain, a detective and 10 uniformed policemen.[6] Colorado Springs jumped from 4,000 people in 1880 to 11,000 in 1890.

Garthright, was described as a big man at six feet, two inches in height and two hundred pounds[7] During the time that he had served as an officer for the city, he had been involved in little controversy. Events in the Colorado elections of 1898 would be very controversial for Garthright and the police department.

In 1897 Congress changed to a gold standard for backing currency in the United States. Previously the United States had a bi-metal standard, both gold and silver. In the mid to late 1800s the government began purchasing silver for its reserves through the Bland-Allison Act and the Sherman Silver Purchase Act. The change to the gold standard was an attempt to match other international economies. It was very detrimental for areas where silver mining was a major source of income for its residents, like Colorado. New alliances were made in the political party system, with people forming "fusion" tickets to promote voting for a group of individuals who would support silver. Fusion tickets held Republicans, Democrats and Progressives joining together for the common goal of saving the use of silver. Another group to emerge was Silver Republicans who were stepping away from the gold standard. A bill was sent to congress to change the country to a bi-metal standard from the money supply being backed by gold.[8] In Colorado the state Silver Republican Convention was to be held in Colorado Springs.[9]

One faction, known as the "Tellerites," was led by the Colorado senior Senator Henry Moore Teller.[10] The other faction, known as "Wolcott's," was led by Edward Oliver Wolcott. Each group demanded to be the ones to lead the party during the convention. Charles S. Sprague, leader of the fusion faction of the Tellerites, told the *Rocky Mountain News* that immediately after the selection of Colorado Springs for the state convention, he telegraphed the manager of the Colorado Springs Opera House to rent it for the convention, guaranteeing that their group would control the site. Sprague paid the manager $100 to rent the facilities. However, at some time later, the former chairman of the Silver Convention Republican party, Richard Broad, Jr., arrived in Colorado Springs and told the house manager, Simeon Nash Nye, that he was state chairman and he should be the one to secure the facility for the party. Nye, believing Broad, sent Sprague's check back and accepted payment from Broad. Broad was really representing the Wolcott group.[11] The feelings were so strong among the groups they seemed willing to do anything to get their way.

Conflict over the use of the Colorado Springs Opera House, at 18 North Tejon Street was about to cause all kinds of problems. Sprague's group (Tellerites) learning of this treachery, took physical possession of the building, putting armed guards inside and sleeping there on the night of September 6.[12] Rumors had been bandied about that the Wolcott faction from Denver would attack the Opera

House and force the first group out of the building. Sheriff Winfield Scott Boynton was aware of this and about 3:00 a.m. Wednesday morning, he had one of his deputies wake Marshal Garthright and he was asked to meet at the Alta Vista hotel (located at the Northwest corner of Kiowa Street and Cascade Avenue, 112 Cascade Avenue). The two officers discussed this rumor, but did not think that anything really would happen; yet the sheriff and Garthright had men grouped to act if there was trouble.[13]

About 4 o'clock the following morning, a group breached the Opera House and occupants began shooting. Charles E. Harris, part of the intruders, was shot and killed on the steps to the second floor. The police officers and deputies were gathered nearby and upon hearing gunfire, the officers, quickly stormed the building, took control and held everyone inside until it could be investigated. After inspection of the front entrance to the building, the sliding doors were found to have been struck by two bullets at head height, fired from inside the structure. One of these bullets had struck the deceased man.

Many of the attackers entered through the front door of the building and at the rear door, it was found that 15 to 20 sledge hammer marks were left by the attackers which allowed their entry to the building. All the bullet holes located at the Opera House were fired from the inside of the building.[14]

Officers searched the hall and located two loaded Winchester rifles and 10 revolvers. Three-quart bottles of whiskey were found inside, two empty and the last holding about one inch of liquid. Many of the attacking group had dispersed before control of the crowd could be accomplished. It was found that attackers had arrived from Denver and were hired for the purpose of wrenching control of the Opera House from the lessees.[15]

Thursday evening the coroner convened a jury to look into the death of Charles E. Harris. The jury decided that Harris had been killed at the Opera House by shots from within the hall, but identity of the shooter was unknown.[16]

The *Rocky Mountain News*[17] and the *Colorado Springs Evening Telegraph* vehemently accused the sheriff and marshal, along with their officers of being involved with the attacking group. Numerous articles published in both papers caused enough of a stir the City Council appointed a committee to investigate the officer's, of involvement in the fray. Completion of the council investigation did not uncover any improper actions on the part of the local law enforcement, but did chastise them for not being sufficiently prepared to prevent the incident.[18] The murderer was never found.

One thing fascinating about the case was the police ability to prove that all gunshots were from within the building and those attacking the building did not fire a shot. Ballistics is the study of flight path of projectiles. Police departments were using new and improved methods by the 1800s to solve crimes. Ballistics and forensic firearm examination helped to understand a crime scene that involved guns. It relies on gunpowder residues, shell casings and bullets found at the location to help solve a crime. The study of weapons used, where it was shot from, angles and even the gun barrel that fired a shot was all new scientific methods for the police in the early days of Colorado Springs.

In 1902, Oliver Wendell Holmes, who later became the justice of the US Supreme Court, is said to have used a magnifying glass to examine a test bullet that he fired into cotton wool to compare its striations with those found on the bullet recovered from the victim during an autopsy. Later in Paris (1912), Professor Balthazard took numerous photographs of the circumferences of the bullet found at the crime scene. He then enlarged these photographs to compare the markings with those obtained on the bullet that he had test-fired from the suspect's weapon.— Incognito Forensic Foundation ifflab.org.

Notes

1. Colorado Springs City Council Minutes, 25 April, 1887, Book 3, Page 3
2. Colorado Springs City Council Minutes, 18 Apr 1890, Book 4, Page 5.
3. 1900 Colorado U.S. Census, 10 Jun 1900.
4. Colorado Springs City Council Minutes, 03 May 1897, Book 6, Page 169.
5. Colorado Springs City Council Minutes, 16 Apr 1900, Book 7, Page 250.
6. *Colorado Springs Weekly Gazette*, 09 Jul 1897, Page 11.
7. *Colorado Springs Weekly Gazette*, 09 Jul 1897, Page 11.
8. *Cripple Creek Morning Times*, 01 Jun 1898, Page 2.
9. *Denver Rocky Mountain News*, 04 Sep 1898, Page 1.
10. *Denver Rocky Mountain News*, 03 Sep 1898, Page 1.
11. *Denver Rocky Mountain News*, 07 Sep 1898, Page 4.
12. *Denver Rocky Mountain News*, 07 Sep 1898, Page 4.
13. *Colorado Springs Daily Gazette*, 08 Sep 1898, Page 1.
14. *Colorado Springs Daily Gazette*, 08 Sep 1898, Page 1.
15. *Colorado Springs Weekly Gazette*, 07 Sep 1898, Page 1.
16. *Colorado Springs Daily Gazette*, 08 Sep 1898, Page 1.
17. *Denver Rocky Mountain News*, 09 Sep 1898 through 18 Oct 1898, numerous articles.
18. *Colorado Springs Weekly Gazette*, 19 Oct 1898, Page 2.

Chapter 7

RULES AND THE QUESTION OF LIQUOR

The Colorado Springs Company issued land deeds to early settlers. These deeds contained a clause which expressly prohibited the sale, production, and consumption of alcohol in any form. Anyone found violating this clause would forfeit their deed, which would revert to the Company. — The Pioneer Museum

As Colorado Springs grew in population, the scope of the job for a policeman grew along with the rules to be followed while conducting the job. Not only were police to uphold the law, prevent crime, and apprehend criminals, there were also rules on how to conduct themselves on and off duty.

In 1887, the local newspaper printed the seventeen rules that governed the behavior and duties of a police officer. The first two rules explained the city marshal was the head of the police force and was responsible for keeping records of the members of the force, stolen property reports, and violations of the law. The third rule was, all on-duty officers would be uniformed.

Officers had to wear their star or shield on the outside garment, over the left breast, so it could be easily observed. However, detectives would be clad in citizens garb and their shields would be concealed, but readily available to show. Every arrestee was to be searched prior to being jailed and the said officer would be responsible for any property of the prisoner so removed.

The officers rank would be shown by a respective number worn on the hat or cap, number one being the top-ranking officer. Officers were not allowed to substitute another person to perform their sworn duties. Though they were not expected to work 24-hours a day, they were still considered to be on duty at all times and subject to call up.

At fires, the first officer was to locate the exact point of the fire, attempt to discern the cause and upon the arrival of the firefighters, control any crowds. At fires and all other places, an officer was expected to be aware of any crime. Crime detected required immediate notification of the marshal. There was also a requirement of the marshal to report any conduct violating the department rules to the City Council. These rules were to be rigidly enforced.

The tenth rule was one that would cause problems; NO OFFICER SHALL DRINK any kind of alcoholic drink! Understandable, knowing alcohol was not allowed in Colorado Springs. It was a dry town. This would cause some problems when rules for first aid would be given to the police depart.

The last rule, explained in 1887, was an officer could be discharged or punished for any violation of the rules.[1]

In 1905 another set of rules was found to exist under the direction of Chief of Police Alexander Adams. Instead of just one page of rules, it had expanded to sixteen pages! First, it was that the distribution or posting of circulars, etc. were prohibited. Officers were expected to see that the alleys on their beats were kept clean or unblocked by any horse team. Please note, the ruling was under A, for alleys.

The second rule was regarding A for automobiles. Officers were expected to see that said vehicles were licensed and their license number openly displayed. The rules were set out alphabetically, so next was A for awnings. Awnings were to be seven feet or more above the sidewalk. Then on to B for bicycles. People were not to ride a bicycle on the sidewalk, except mail carriers and newsboys. Also, under the B rules was, buildings were not to be moved on the streets without a permit. Interesting, were buildings being moved often enough and of a problem to include in the rules?

Still a problem to this day is C, concealed weapons were not allowed without special permission. E's rule stated expectoration was not allowed! The rules continued to M, no minors were allowed in pool halls. Under S rules; sidewalks will have no beggars and in regards to streetlights, officers were to report all streetlights that were inoperative.

In a latter part of the manual, there was a list of the 48 churches by denomination, with addresses, so if a person inquired of an officer, he could direct the questioning citizen. And, lastly, a list of the 75 street names with hundred blocks.[2] Everything an officer ever needed to perform his duties!

Once again, 1914 brought more rules. By the time James Howard Stark was the Police Chief, it was time to update the departments rules and regulations. The conduct of an officer was covered in much more detail, even though much of it was common sense.

> In making an arrest do not use undue force and do not restrain the prisoner unduly. The laying of your hands upon the shoulder, arm or other part of the body of the person to be arrested, together with the statement, "You are my prisoner," or "You are under arrest," or other similar expression, constitutes an arrest. Whether or not the person resists, it is essential that you keep your temper. Nothing is to be gained and much is to be lost by a display of temper or excitement on your part.

Then there is my favorite: something every police officer has heard at one time or another:

> If you are in the right in any action you take, be assured that your superior officers and the Commissioner of Public Safety will support throughout. No citizen, however influential he or she may be, will be able to "get your job" if you have been in the right. Therefore, when you are discharging your duty

according to instructions from headquarters, do not permit threats of this nature to intimidate you. First make sure you are right, then go ahead.

Colorado Springs was considered a "dry" town where intoxicating beverages were frowned on and especially when it came to its police force. Under "Duties of the Patrolmen," part 4 stated "Any patrolman is hereby forbidden to drink intoxicating liquors on duty. Patrolmen who shall become intoxicated while on duty or in uniform shall be peremptorily dismissed from the force." The reader must keep this in mind as the story progresses.

Another area the police were to be familiar with was the giving of first aid. For instance, there is a section labeled "First Aid to the Injured."

FOR USE OF PATROLMEN IN EMERGENCY CASES BEFORE THE ARRIVAL OF A PHYSICIAN OR THE POLICE SURGEON

Every member of the department should memorize the following methods of treatment:

First call the ambulance.
Keep cool at all times.
Act promptly but not hastily.
Always keep the crowds back, and when necessary, detail one or more of the bystanders to assist you in doing this.
Give the patient an abundance of fresh air and do not move the patient unnecessarily.
Always have a sick or injured person lie on the back unless the character of the injuries forbid.
All tight or binding articles of clothing, such as belts, collars, **corsets**, etc., should be loosened.
In case of thirst, give water—cold water in summer and warm in winter.
Do NOT give liquor unless hereinafter especially prescribed or advised.

[Author's Note: It is okay madam, I determined that your corset was too tight and I am loosening you up! I'll have that corset off in a second . . . don't worry, no one is looking. It is okay—I am a police officer!]

Below are other basic first aid rules, remember the rule about officers having liquor.

ARTIFICIAL RESPIRATION

If or when a person such require this action:

Place the person on the back, the shoulders resting on a roll of clothing. Grasp the tongue with a handkerchief, or dry cloth, and pull it out of the mouth, and let a bystander hold it.

Press the arms firmly downward and inward against the chest. Then repeat the movements, but do not do this oftener than twenty times per minute. Keep this up an hour and a half, if necessary.

DROWNING

Wrap the limbs in dry clothes. ***Give liquor***, if able to swallow. Expose the shoulders and chest to the wind.

If breathing has not commenced, throw cold water on the face and chest, or tickle the nose with a feather or straw; a quick slap over the pit of the stomach with the open hand may start breathing. If none of these methods are successful use artificial respiration.

ELECTRIC SHOCKS

May be of any degree of severity from a slight shock to death.

Lay the person down, put a cold wet cloth on the brow and give ***a drink of liquor,*** if able to swallow.

If necessary, use artificial respiration.

SHOCKS FROM WOUNDS OR INJURIES

A person who has sustained a severe accident, a bad burn, or even a sudden fright, is liable to suffer from the shock.

If there is severe bleeding, it must be stopped. Lay the person down, raise head slightly, give a ***drink of whiskey*** in hot water, put hot cloths on chest and abdomen, cover the patient with a blanket.

SUNSTROKE, OR HEAT PROSTRATION

Loss of consciousness may occur suddenly without warning. If the face, head and body are burning, hot and dry, with no perspiration, or the face is red and flushed, give the patient fresh air, wet the hands and face and back of the neck with cold water and loosen the clothing.

If the face is pale, and the skin moist and even cool, let the patient rest, and *give some liquor* as a stimulant, and wrap patient to keep warm.[3]

[Authors note: Where does this NON-DRINKING police officer obtain all this "illegal" liquor to perform the first aid? It would not be in an illicit flask . . . um?!]

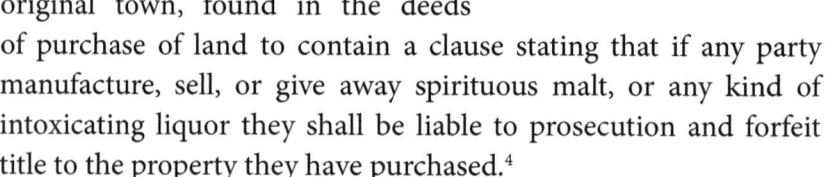

When Colorado Springs was first platted and lots sold to persons that would become the residents of the original town, found in the deeds of purchase of land to contain a clause stating that if any party manufacture, sell, or give away spirituous malt, or any kind of intoxicating liquor they shall be liable to prosecution and forfeit title to the property they have purchased.[4]

As with any rule or law requiring a citizen to do (or not do) is always of two camps. The above clause in property deeds was no different. From 1873 through 1875, a property located on southeast corner of Pikes Peak Avenue and Tejon Street, was purchased by David A. Cowell from the Colony's developer, The Colorado Springs Company. Cowell was arrested and charged with the selling of intoxicating liquors. A plea of guilty was entered by the defendant and he was fined $25 and costs. At that time the first attempt was filed to have the defendant removed from the property, per the deed clause.[5] In November Cowell was again charged with selling intoxicating liquors. For second time, pled guilty and was fined $50.[6] Later in the month, a trial was held with regard to the removal of Cowell from his property and it reverting to the Colorado Springs Company. The trial judge told Cowell that since he had accepted the deed to the property, then he was bound by its contents. Because under the territory's laws, Cowell was allowed to demand a new trial, which had to be granted. This trial was held April, 1874.[7] The trial was ended with a hung jury.

A change of venue was made and the retrial was held in Pueblo County. This jury found for the Colorado Springs Company.[8] By October David Cowell was again arrested for selling intoxicating liquors and was fined $50.[9] Cowell, one not to give up was arrested the following July for allowing the sale of liquor at his property and was fined $100 and twenty days in jail.[10]

David A. Cowell, appealed the Pueblo County's District Court decision to the Supreme Court of the Territory of Colorado, which was heard during the February Term, 1876. The court affirmed the Pueblo County court decision.[11] One more time this case was appealed to the ultimate court—The Supreme Court of the United States. The case was taken up by the Court at the October Term, 1879. In a short, six-page opinion, which was prepared by Justice Stephen Johnson Field, again the judgment was affirmed.

Simply laid out Cowell purchased the property in May, 1873 for $250. The court found that Cowell sold intoxicating liquors in violation of his deed. Cowell contended that the condition as "repugnant to the estate conveyed." The court said that just because a deed had restrictions, did not invalidate those restrictions.

> The defendant . . . went into possession of the premises in controversy under the deed of the plaintiff. He took his title from the company, with a condition that if he manufactured or sold intoxicating liquors, to be used as a beverage, at any place of public resort on the premises, the title should revert to his grantor; and he is therefore stopped, when sued by the grantor for the premises, upon breach of the condition,

from denying the corporate existence of the plaintiff, or the validity of the title conveyed by its deed. Upon obvious principles, they cannot be permitted to retain the property which he received upon condition that it should be restored to his grantor on a certain contingency, by denying, when the contingency has happened, that his grantor ever had any right to it.[12]

The U.S. Supreme Court decision was sent back to the, now, Colorado Supreme Court, who returned the decision to the Pueblo County District Court where Judge Henry directed the clerk of the court to issue a writ of possession.

This is the only time that a property was repossessed by the Colorado Springs Company for violation of the liquor clause. As is obvious today, just within two blocks of Tejon Street located within the original Colony Plat, there are numerous bars selling intoxicating liquors. This just proves nothing lasts forever.

Notes

1 *Colorado Springs Daily Gazette*, 26 Apr 1887, Page 1.
2 Colorado Springs Police Department Archives copy of Rules and Regulations, 1905.
3 Rules & Regulations of the Colorado Springs Police Department, 1914.
4 *Pueblo Chieftain*, 16 Jun 1874, Page 4.
5 *Colorado Springs Weekly Gazette* & El Paso County News, 25 Oct 1873, Page 2.
6 *Colorado Springs Weekly Gazette* & El Paso County News, 01 Nov 1873, Page 3.
7 *Colorado Springs Weekly Gazette* & El Paso County News, 25 Apr 1874, Page 2.
8 *Pueblo Chieftain*, 19 Jun 1874, Page 4.
9 *Colorado Springs Weekly Gazette* & El Paso County News, 17 Oct 1874, Page 2.
10 *Colorado Springs Weekly Gazette* & El Paso County News, 10 Jul 1875
11 Supreme Court of Colorado Territory, Cowell vs Colorado Springs Company, February, 1876, (Need real cite)
12 United States Supreme Court, 100 U.S. 55, 25 L. Ed. 547, October, 1879. (Need correct way to cite)

Chapter 8

NEW CENTURY—NEW POLICE DEPARTMENT OLD STYLE CORRUPTION

Gold found in El Paso County had "caused a steady deterioration of the moral climate." Every smart mine owner had a judge or two on his payroll if a favorable decision was needed in a mine dispute. The citizens of the Springs were complacent about the operations of someone like Adolph Duff and his gang operating openly in areas like Stratton Park, the Opera House and the Roswell racetrack. Duff's gang were highly active at the railroad depots looking for suckers to their confidence games or just straight pocket picking.
— Newport in the Rockies by Marshall Sprague

After several months of disagreement among the City Council during 1899, a motion was made by Councilman Woodland granting officers of the marshal office and fire department vacation of ten days each year without the loss of pay. The motion passed on a 6 to 3 vote.[1] Considering officers only received one day a month off from duty, this was quite an accomplishment.

John Walter Garthright, then the marshal, completed his term in April 1900. John Oliver Henry appointed by the City Council, was the last serving city marshal. Henry had been a resident of Colorado Springs since 1892 and by 1894, had become a police officer.[2] He continued as a patrolman until his promotion to the rank of captain at the annual hiring of officers in April 1896.[3]

Because the Colorado Springs population was officially determined in the 1900 United States Census, and met the requirements of the State Constitution, it was declared a First-Class City in February 1901. This set in motion replacing the marshal's office with that of a police department. Following the annual election of council members, a police chief was selected. Rumors had been circulating, that the new chief would be Len Jackson, formerly an El Paso

County sheriff. Right up to the night before the selection those in the know were ready for Jackson to step into the position. As a first-class city the mayor had the power to appoint certain department heads, such as police and fire heads. This would be done with approval of council. A newspaper reported an effort was being made to secure the position of police chief for Vincent King. The newspaper was in favor of Len Jackson and said that King was offered the position of street supervisor but declined.[4]

However, the next morning, Mayor John R. Robinson announced that Vincent King had been selected, council approving 9 to 1 for the appointment.[5] One would expect a man with law enforcement experience or at least a background in running a company to be named as the head of the new police department. Before being selected as the first police chief of Colorado Springs, he had been a collector for the Union Ice & Coal Company for the previous eleven years.[6]

Tuesday's evening newspaper wrote they believed Mr. King to be above reproach, but unqualified as a chief of police, having no experience in police work. The paper expounded the appointment seemed to be wholly political. They could not understand why John O. Henry, the last marshal, who had an excellent record in that position, and was totally non-political had not been selected. Mayor Robinson was accused of lacking political independence and unable to defy the political bosses.[7]

Len Jackson, a Republican, had been an El Paso County deputy sheriff from about 1882 through 1888, when he was elected sheriff, for about four years. After that he was the manager of a mine in Cripple Creek, called the "Sheriff." He continued to do this until his name was put up on the republican ticket for the chief of police. It was a forgone conclusion that he would be appointed, however, he had been a Silver Republican, and this did not sit well with some, and may have been the impetus making him persona non grata. King also was a Republican, as was most of the city administration. Apparently, King was more politically acceptable than Jackson, causing the sudden, middle of the night switch. Without the appointment, Len Jackson appeared to continue his involvement with the mine in Cripple Creek.[8]

King began his career with a cadre of officers numbering a captain, sergeant (a new position), two detectives and fifteen uniformed officers.[9] A group of nineteen men were appointed as special police, who worked without pay. This work today would be referred to as security guards. If there was compensation, it would come from owners/operators of businesses. At the same meeting of the council, it was approved that $280.00 be used to pay for a team of horses for the patrol wagon.[10] An ordinance was passed by the council ordering the right-of-way on the streets and public places for the police patrol wagon and the ambulance. This is one of the early traffic ordinances.[11]

A patrol wagon had been ordered for the use of the police department which was also to act as an ambulance. It contained a stretcher that could be stored under the driver's seat. It arrived by train April 19 and after installing its wheels, was taken to city hall for storage until the new city hall was constructed.[12] In the year following, attorney Frank J. Baker sued the city for the destruction of a chainless bicycle belonging to Ford Edwards, after it was run down by the patrol wagon on August 9, 1902. Damages amounted to $68.[13]

Kings career would be tarnished due to accusations he could not stop the notorious con man Adolf W. Duff. Duff's activities were destructive to early El Paso County, its citizens, and the police department. El Paso County originally was larger than it is today and included the town of Cripple Creek. Gold discovery in Cripple Creek in 1891 brought a new level of crime to the area.

Little is known about the early life of Adolph William Duff, born in Iowa around 1871. The first mention I could find of Duff was a Texas newspaper reporting that he was arrested along with three other men in September, 1891 in San Antonio. They were accused of drugging and robbing a man of $200. They were fined $10.00 by the judge and turned loose.[14]

Duff was first reported to be in the Colorado Springs area in an article of the *Cripple Creek Morning Times* the first month of 1896. He and R.S. Washburn were arrested as bunco-steerers.[15] They had been warned a week earlier Cripple Creek did not want con games going on and were trying to rid the town of such riffraff.[16] By August Duff and James Neil would find themselves jailed in Colorado Springs for a bunco worked upon a Kansas City train passenger.[17]

In 1901 Duff again was jailed, this time by the El Paso County sheriff's deputies who had been chasing him for about two months. They believed him to be a very clever bunco-steerer operating in the Pikes Peak Region. It was believed he had criminal records in several large cities in the West. The deputies were successful in locating him in Colorado City.[18]

During 1901, Earl E. Teeple, visiting from Iowa, was separated from $500. A warrant was issued for con-man Adolf W. Duff, but he had left town. Upon returning at the end of September to Colorado City, Deputy Sheriff Allward clamped the bracelets on the wanted man. Duff had been working in the local area for more than six years by the time of this arrest.[19] Duff and two other members of his group were caught during April 1902 using bellhops at some hotels to steal luggage or other things of value. The three men were fined, but the fine would be stayed if they would leave the area.[20]

That October Adolf W. Duff was arrested in Colorado City and incarcerated in the county jail. He had been plying his trade upon passengers of trains between Denver to Pueblo. Information was obtained that Duff and his cohorts had set up shop in Colorado City. His "steerers" would find a gullible tourist, guide the person to the gang's rented room where he would be shown mineral specimens, the idea was to sell these as valuable commodities. At other times the gang resorted to the use of drugs on the victims and cheating at cards.

By 1903 Duff was successful in roping the Colorado Springs police chief and its long-time detective into his web, or so the newspaper reported. The newspapers did not state the deprivations of the compromised officers. Even more interesting is the mayor would not take any action about the officers even after they were indicted and/(or) convicted of their crime.

May 9, 1903, Police Chief King and Detective Joel Atkinson, were indicted by the grand jury and arrested for assisting the confidence man of Colorado City—Adolph Duff. Seven counts were among the indictments charging that they allowed the gang members to escape to keep from being charged with crimes. Some of the department's officers had complained there was no use arresting certain thieves or bunco men as they seemed to be released without cause. A $3,500 bond was required, at $500 per count, but Judge Cunningham made the decision that the officers post only $500 on one count and be released on the other six on their own recognizance.[21]

The officers were accused of allowing the following to escape:

Joe Bailey, R.R. Rose, and Adolph Duff, April 1902;
Ed Clancy, R.R. Rose, and Adolph Duff, October 1902;
Arlo Aleshire, March 1903.

Chief King remarked to the *Gazette* that he was innocent of all these charges. He said Aleshire, a witness against Duff, and other malefactors, was a cripple, so he was sent to his home for convalescence; whenever he was needed by the officers, he made himself available. Many of the people considered criminals, those involved with Duff, were known as floaters. This meant instead of trying the people for suspected crimes, they were run out of town —floated. Chief King explained the people were all taken to the courts and turned loose from there. The officers were also accused of taking bribes to protect the bunco men.[22]

It was alleged evidence was against the officers and the police magistrate Earl C. Hammond. The newspaper located Adolph Duff in Colorado City, where he had just returned from out of town. Duff was a property owner in Colorado City for several years and his employment was that of a gambler. The district attorney alleged that Duff was in charge of a group of men called "bunco steerers" and confidence men, who ran some of their games on people by working the railroad between Denver and Pueblo. Also, this area was a prime location to con the many tourist passing through.

When the press asked Mayor Ira Harris what was going to happen to Chief King and the detective, he replied that he had not considered suspending either, as the matter had not been put before him officially. Duff stated he would be a witness for the officers, when needed.[23] With the grand jury's term expiring the following week, much more investigation was required.[24] It was anticipated a new jury would be impaneled to complete the investigations.[25] Corruption in the city government was not limited to the police department as the president of the City Council was indicted for having interest in contracts being let by council.[26]

Suddenly, following the indictments, several men suspected of being pickpockets were arrested. These men worked the trains from Denver to Pueblo, usually in a group of three. Their method involved crowding a victim into a corner and while the victim was being bumped around by the motion of the train and the crooks, they would relieve the victim of his wallet and valuables.[27]

Both local papers wrote that a new grand jury was needed to be impaneled to continue its investigation of the local corruption. District Attorney Henry Trowbridge agreed, but he was not in control of this as the court had to make that call.[28] As the current grand jury was on their way out they reported it was their belief the police department had not been operated in such a manner as to protect the city and its citizens, and this allowed bunco steerers, pickpockets, and confidence men to operate while being protected by certain members of the police department. The outgoing jury made it clear another jury was needed to finish the work started.[29]

The morning newspaper was beside itself that the Chief of Police and the long time serving detective had not been suspended after indictment by a grand jury, considering these men were in positions expected to be above suspicion or reproach.[30] Even though the district attorney requested, the chief judge of the local district court, Judge William P. Seeds, refused to sit another grand jury and proceedings were in the works to quash the existing indictments.[31] Interestingly, no mention of Chief of Police King and Detective Atkinson's indictment was recorded in the City Council minutes of the time.

In a similar situation, the *Gazette* reported that a Washington City police officer charged with a crime of fraud, was suspended almost immediately until the charges were disposed. The paper wrote with seventeen indictments against Colorado Springs officials, without anyone being suspended, the citizens had a right to know why no action had been taken.[32]

For over a week the defendants' attorneys fought to have the indictments quashed. It took about ten days, but Judge Seeds quashed the indictments accusing the officers of helping in the escape of Aleshire because the indictment did not state the charge against Aleshire. The remaining charges were then set for trial. Again, the *Gazette* listed the three charges remaining. The first charge was the officers took bribes. Second, they were charged with hiding the witness, Patrick McNellis, who was to testify against Duff and his gang.[33] Finally, they were charged with assisting with a confidence game. The paper asked what was the real motive behind the mayor not taking any action against the indicted officers.[34]

Patrick McNellis, victim of the gang robbing him of $150, was to be the major witness in any upcoming trial. Also, several former police officers and one current officer were to testify that Detective Atkinson obtained $25 from the robbers and was to tell McNellis that was all he could recover, so he should be satisfied and leave the city. McNellis then complained to the D&RG Railway attorneys, McAllister & Gandy, that he still wanted the rest of the money taken from him while riding the railroad.[35]

The trial of Police Chief King and Detective Atkinson was set and postponed several times before being held in mid-July. Friday,

July 16, the trial was to finally begin. The district attorney, however, requested that the court again postpone its start. This time due to the absence of the main witness, Patrick McNellis. District Attorney Trowbridge was not successful in getting the victim of the crime to return to give testimony, but did have an affidavit about the facts he presented to the court. Interestingly, the defense did not object to its admission. Then, on Tuesday, July 28, 1903, the case was called. Railway attorney Newton S. Gandy testified that after McNellis complained to the railway attorneys, Chief King and Detective Atkinson told him they had obtained $25 which was given to the victim. When that was not acceptable, the officers were sent back to get the remaining stolen amount of money, which they obtained from Adolph Duff. It was odd that Duff would just hand over the money to the officers. The total amount was given to the victim after which he was ushered from the city. This was to have been a quid-pro-quo, in that if the money was returned there was to be no prosecution by the victim.[36]

VINCENT KING, Chief of Police.
Chief of Police 1901, 1902.
First Chief of Police of the City of Colorado Springs.

JOEL ATKINSON, City Detective.
City Detective 1891, 1892, 1893, 1894, 1895, 1896, 1897, 1898, 1899, 1900, 1901, 1902.

Chief of Police Vincent King and Detective Atkinson.
Colorado Springs Annual Reports and Financial Statements, 1901.

Gandy testified when King and Atkinson arrived at his office with the remaining $125, he was told the money would be given to McNellis but there were conditions. The conditions presented were if the money was returned, there would be no further issues and it would be the end of the matter. Gandy said that the money and conditions were presented to the railway's council by mail. The railway would not accept these terms. His firm then returned the money to King and Atkinson. King and Atkinson, asked this information not be communicated to the newspapers. Finally the railway having no further objections, accepted the cash.[37]

Two days later, the jury returned a verdict of guilty in the matter of Chief of Police Vincent King and Detective Joel Atkinson. The maximum sentence that could be imposed was a fine of $1,000 and confinement in county jail for up to a year. King, when confronted by the press, said he still had his self-respect! Alderman Albert L. Patton, who was the chairman of the police committee, said the mayor would have to appoint an acting chief until the court's final decision.[38] But even after the guilty verdict, the mayor was undecided as to what action he would take.[39]

July 31, 1903, William Sullivan Reynolds and Stanley Dean Burno were appointed to take the place of the chief and detective respectively. Chief King and Detective Atkinson turned in their resignations to Mayor Ira Harris.[40] Within a week the department's sergeant, Sherman Ellsworth McNew and the other detective, James R. Gregory, both resigned. The morning paper surmised it was because they knew too much. Apparently, the mayor believed information about the Duff case came into public view because of McNew, and the mayor wanted him to resign. McNew stated he had gone to Chief King shortly after his appointment as chief and told him of Atkinson's misconduct when it came to the Duff gang, and this turned out to be a mistake. King and Atkinson's policy regarding the gang was to suppress facts about crimes the gang were involved in. Atkinson had been a member of the department for 16 years.[41]

August 14, 1903, District Court Judge William P. Seeds denied the request of King and Atkinson for a new trial and sentence was then imposed. The court fined each defendant $100 and court costs. The fine was suspended, but the court cost of $65.20 were still required. After a strong message of how the court would not stand for such conduct on the behalf of the city's highest positioned law enforcement officers, the defense did not find it necessary to appeal the case further. The judge believed the defendants had an excellent reputation and the punishment imposed would prove in time to be ample![42] Unbelievable! It sure made the appearance that Mayor Ira Harris, District Court Judge William P. Seeds, plus unnamed others, were involved in the cover up of Duff's crimes.

William M. Banning,[43] alderman and owner of the Union Ice and Coal Company, welcomed Vincent King back to his firm by employing him again as he had in years past. Atkinson said he would be a private detective for the Short Line Railroad. It did seem the conviction for dishonesty didn't harm them.[44] Meanwhile, Adolph Duff was arrested in Pueblo and sent to the El Paso County jail awaiting trial on matters of operating confidence games and participating in the fleecing of passengers on the trains. District Judge Cunningham had his bond raised to $5,000 hoping it would hold him in the jail until his trial.[45]

Appearances did not make the local government and some of its officials look upstanding and forthright. The chief and his detective had been complained about by department officers for some time. Atkinson's apparent unquestioned ability to just go visit Duff at his haunts in Colorado City and obtain money for the asking to get a problem to go away did not sit well with Colorado Springs citizens. The decision of Judge Seeds, making it look as if the crimes were no big deal, smacked of at least political involvement and possibly direct involvement with the actors.

Vincent King continued to work for the Union Ice & Coal Company until 1926[46] and died in 1928 at the age of 71.[47] Joel Atkinson stayed in Colorado Springs after his resignation through

1911. He worked as a watchman for the Portland Mill in Colorado City.[48] Atkinson and his family moved to Long Beach, California, where he was employed as a merchant policeman until he started his own company, Atkinson Merchant's Police & Fire Patrol.[49] After 1922, he employed his son Jesse, who carried the rank of captain.[50] Wednesday, February 18, 1931, Joel Atkinson was sleeping when his wife called him to the phone. He spoke to an unidentified man for a few minutes, walked back to his bedroom and shot himself to death, the reason unknown.[51] He was 73-years-old.[52] His son Jesse, continued to run the merchant patrol business until June of the following year when he too committed suicide.[53] He was 38.[54]

During May following the arrest of the officers, five more of the pickpockets were arrested at the D&RG depot. The complaining witness, Perry Osgood, told officers he was in the process of exiting the train with a small grip in each hand and found the exit blocked by a man. This caused people to be crowded at the exit. Someone brushed passed him and another person removed his wallet from his pocket. Upon reaching for his wallet to get a baggage check, he realized the pocketbook was gone.[55] Corruption was not just in Colorado Springs, but apparently was suffered by the Denver Police Department as well. When the pickpockets were tried, two Denver police detectives testified the men could not have participated in the robbery as they were in jail at the time in Denver. This was at odds with the victim and another witness positively identifying the men as the robbers.[56]

Seventy-six-year-old D.F. Deskin, of Lawrence, Kansas, complained of being robbed, just like Osgood, of $175.00. This time by three young men and a woman.[57] Two days later Reverend James B. Gregg was similarly robbed at the Santa Fe depot of $20.00.[58] The railroad companies realizing there was little assistance from police had put more of their own detectives on the trains and at the depots in an effort to stop the fleecing of their passengers.[59] Two weeks passed before another man, Walter A. Stauffacher, of Houston, Texas, reported being robbed as he was boarding a street car. The next day, Colorado City Marshal George Birdsall arrested a suspect, but the victim could not positively identify the man.[60]

Duff was still operating his crew from Colorado City, but because of the indictments of Colorado Springs police officers, he had been doing his "work" in Cripple Creek. Recognized there by Special Agent Wilson, Duff was arrested on a warrant out of Pueblo.[61] It was obvious that the gang was not deterred by the arrest and accusations as they continued to operate in the area.

The work of the pickpockets did not end with summer, because Joseph M. Keener, reported that his wallet had been "picked" at Busy Corner (Pikes Peak Avenue & Tejon Street) during September, but it contained no money.[62]

Duff, still confined at the county jail, was interviewed by a newspaper reporter and told of his fascination for the roulette wheel, which he could watch for hours. He would stay and play until he had no money. His criminal life began by gambling, working his way into picking pockets and later overseeing such activities, as he was not very good at the actual work himself. To help his ability to stay awake for hours to play roulette, he began using cocaine and morphine. He bragged he had not served time in prison, but always worked out a way to get off from any charges brought against him. This time it was believed the man was going to be sent to prison for his actions.[63]

Since the exit of Chief King and Detective Atkinson, several pickpockets had been arrested, tried, fined and/or floated.[64] September 1904, found Adolph Duff being arrested by Police Chief George Birdsall for operating a policy wheel in Colorado City.[65] A policy wheel was a way to take bets for as little as a penny, making gambling easy for the down and out. So much money was made by this means, con-men could pay off politicians to pass policy that would favor the con-men. For the first time, Duff was sentenced to county jail for a crime. At the end of his jail term, he said that his plan was to start for Mexico, he was going to mend his bad behavior, avoid his old companions, and begin life anew.[66]

Notes

1. Colorado Springs City Council Minutes, 04 Sep 1899, Book 7, Page 114.
2. Colorado Springs City Council Minutes, 30 Apr 1894, Book 5, Page 169.
3. Colorado Springs City Council Minutes, 20 Apr 1896, Book 6, Page 3.
4. *Colorado Springs Evening Telegraph*, 14 Apr 1901, Page 1.
5. Colorado Springs City Council Minutes, 15 Apr 1901, Book 8, Page 2.
6. *Colorado Springs City Directories*, 1890 through 1901.
7. *Colorado Springs Evening Telegraph*, 16 Apr 1901, Page 4.
8. *Denver Rocky Mountain News*, 16 Apr 1901, Page 7.
9. Colorado Springs City Council Minutes, 18 Apr 1901, Book 8, Page 12.
10. Colorado Springs City Council Minutes, 22 Apr 1901, Book 8, Page 15.
11. Colorado Springs City Council Minutes, 07 Aug 1901, Book 8, Page 112.
12. *Colorado Springs Daily Gazette*, 19 Apr 1901, Page 5.
13. Letter of Frank J. Baker to City of Colorado Springs, 22 Aug 1902, files of the City Clerk, file No. 83, Record No. 8, Page 392.
14. *San Antonio Daily Light*
15. Bunco-steerer is someone who tricks or deceives others to get their money or property. They might use illegal methods or schemes to do this. They are also known as bunco operators or bunco men. This is similar to a confidence man or woman, who gains someone's trust and then tricks them into giving them money or property.
16. Cripple Creek Morning News, 21 Jan 1896, Page 1.
17. *Denver Rocky Mountain News*, 15 Aug 1896, Page 3.
18. *Denver Rocky Mountain News*, 02 Oct 1901, Page 6.
19. *Colorado Springs Daily Gazette*, 03 Oct 1901, Page 11.
20. *Colorado Springs Daily Gazette*, 30 Apr 1902, Page 5.
21. *Colorado Springs Gazette*, 10 May 1903, Page 1.
22. *Colorado Springs Gazette*, 10 May 1903, Page 1.
23. *Colorado Springs Gazette*, 11 May 1903, Page 1.
24. *Colorado Springs Gazette*, 12 May 1903, Page 1.
25. *Colorado Springs Gazette*, 13 May 1903, Page 3.
26. Colorado State Journal, 16 May 1903, Page 32.
27. *Colorado Springs Gazette*, 16 May 1903, Page 7.
28. *Colorado Springs Evening Telegraph*, 18 May 1903, Page 5.
29. *Colorado Springs Gazette*, 19 May 1903, Page 1.
30. *Colorado Springs Gazette*, 23 May 1903, Page 4.
31. Colorado State Journal, 30 May 1903, Page 28.
32. *Colorado Springs Gazette*, 31 May 1903, Page 14.
33. *Colorado Springs Gazette*, 10 Jun 1903, Page 1.
34. *Colorado Springs Gazette*, 12 Jun 1903, Page 4.
35. Colorado Springs Telegraph, 28 Jul 1903, Page 3.
36. *Colorado Springs Gazette*, 19 Jul 1903, Page 12.
37. *Colorado Springs Gazette*, 28 Jul 1903. Page 1.
38. *Colorado Springs Evening Telegraph*, 30 Jul 1903. Page 1.
39. *Denver Rocky Mountain News*, 31 Jul 1903, Page 1.
40. *Colorado Springs Gazette*, 01 Aug 1903, Page 4.
41. *Colorado Springs Gazette*, 08 Aug 1903, Page 1.
42. *Colorado Springs Gazette*, 15 Aug 1903, Page 1.
43. William M. Banning was the father of Ruth Banning, who married Raymond "Pinkie" Lewis in 1921. They owned 30,000 acres east of Colorado Springs, which was annexed in 1988 by Colorado Springs, known as the Banning-Lewis Ranch Development. At the time of annexation, it increased the size of the city by almost 25%.
44. *Colorado Springs Gazette*, 06 Sep 1903, Page 11.
45. *Colorado Springs Gazette*, 03 Oct 1903, Page 5.
46. Colorado Springs City Directory, 1926, Page 259.
47. Colorado Springs City Directory, 1929.
48. Colorado Springs City Directory, 1905 through 1911.
49. *Long Beach City Directories*, 1913 — 1931.
50. *Long Beach City Directories*, 1924, Page 162.
51. *Long Beach Sun*, 19 Feb 1931, Page 2.

52 *Long Beach Sun*, 17 Jun 1932.
53 *Fighting the Underworld*, Philip S. Van Cise, 1936, The Riverside Press, Cambridge, Page 16.
54 Vincent King, "The City of Colorado Springs Annual Reports and Financial Statements — 1901-2, Page 184.
55 *Colorado Springs Weekly Gazette*, 21 May 1903, Page 12.
56 *Colorado Springs Gazette*, 04 Jun 1903, Page 5.
57 *Colorado Springs Gazette*, 10 Jul 1903, Page 1.
58 *Colorado Springs Gazette*, 12 Jul 1903, Page 3.
59 *Colorado Springs Gazette*, 15b Jul 1903, Page 6.
60 *Colorado Springs Gazette*, 21 Jul 1903, Page 1.
61 *Colorado Springs Weekly Gazette*, 23 Jul 1903, Page 12.
62 *Colorado Springs Gazette*, 07 Sep 1903, Page 1.
63 *Colorado Springs Gazette*, 04 Oct 1903, Page 6.
64 *Colorado Springs Weekly Gazette*, 25 Aug 1904, Page 7.
65 *Colorado City Iris*, 23 Sep 1904, Page 3.
66 *Colorado Springs Gazette*, 01 Mar 1905 Page 5.

Chapter 9

DUFF, THE REST OF THE STORY

The United States has a current recidivism rate of 70% within five years (U.S. Prison Population, 2019). This means, within five years of their release, 70% of prisoners will have re-offended. — Western Michigan University wmich. ed April 18, 2023

Duff may have left the area, but he was not in Mexico. November of 1909, found him to be partnering with another known con-man, R.S. Richardson, in Portland, Oregon. Again, this was reported because of an investigation of police corruption involving the con-men and their operations.[1] The Duff gang was reported as operating a fake bookmaking operation, which included at least 16 members. The operation was being conducted from the Selling-Hirsch Building, in room 26, and had been working for over two months.[2] Duff, never one to sit on his laurels, next was reported in Juarez, Mexico, operating a bar with two other men. Again, he was running a con game in January 1913. A man playing a game at the bar was told that he had won $500, but before he could collect, he had to produce a like amount. The man, produced checks in his possession totaling near the amount, and placed them on a table. A man grabbed the checks and ran from the building.[3]

October 1917, Adolph Duff was arrested in Denver as a bunco steerer and confidence man. At that time, he was offered 60 days in jail or leave town—he left town. In 1917, he claimed to be a real estate dealer and was carrying around over $4,000.[4]

Duff was wanting to be behind the scenes, so he made contact with Louis Herbert Blonger, a saloon owner in Denver. Blonger was the operator of many scams and con-games in the area. Duff was hired by Blonger to run all the operations letting Blonger stay in the background. The con-games were run in Denver's summer months with Duff and the actual operators working their way east during the fall. Upon becoming the favored employee of Blonger, Duff's criminal record in Denver was "lost." The crew operated offices in the American National Bank Buildings third floor, downtown Denver. Blonger's office was listed as being involved with mining, while Duff's was insurance.[5]

From 1916 to 1920, Blonger's crew numbered as many as 500 grifters.[6] They ran as many as 40 men in Colorado Springs and Manitou to locate "suckers," but took them immediately to Denver to work their schemes. This information was provided to the Denver district attorney in a series of five letters from someone who signed as "A. Friend."[7] Colorado Springs Chief of Police Hugh D. Harper and Detective Captain Irvin B. Bruce were no friends to these people, so Duff had the "suckers" brought to Denver.

Philip Sidney Van Cise, a local attorney in Denver, returned from military service during WWI as an intelligence officer, and decided that he would run for district attorney. He, like most of the Denver citizenry, were well aware of the corruption of the local government officials and decided that he wanted to try to do something about it. Running as a Republican in 1920, he was selected as their candidate. He had practiced law in Denver for eleven years, was an officer in the National Guard for five years, and in the military was a Lieutenant Colonel as an assistant chief of staff and intelligence officer for the Eighty-First Division. With his known dislike of the confidence gangs and the local corruption, he was much disliked by city hall. Van Cise was directed to meet a man who was said could help with his election as district attorney. The man he met with was Lou Blonger. Van Cise was well aware of this man, as early in life he was a reporter and knew of Blonger's reputation as head of the local rackets. Blonger, 71 at the time, spoke of being a soldier in the Civil

War and knew Van Cise's father. After some talk, Blonger offered to put up $25,000 to help with the Van Cise's political campaign. He said he recently had made some money in mining. Van Cise, less than politely, turned the gangster's offer down flatly.[8]

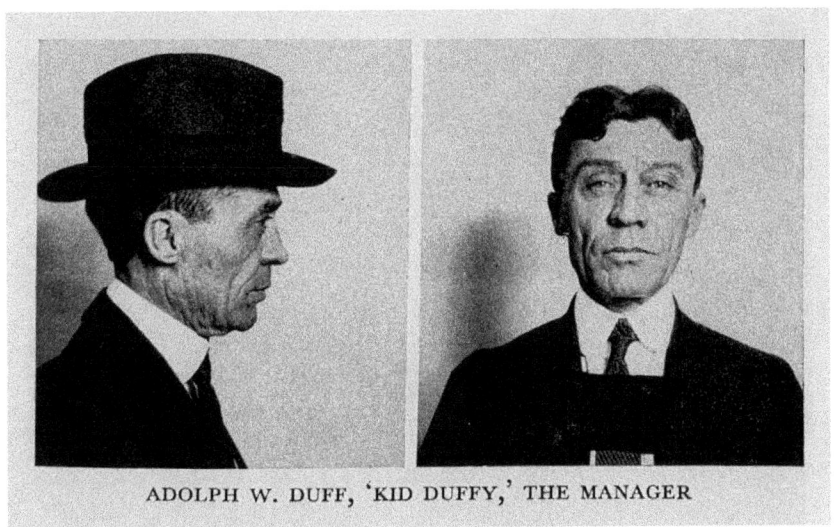

ADOLPH W. DUFF, 'KID DUFFY,' THE MANAGER

Adolph Duff, mug shot photo.
Photograph public domain.

Van Cise was elected to the office of district attorney and began his education on the operations of the local government. For one example, it was learned early on Blonger had a telephone line installed in the office of the Denver police chief and would tell the chief who he could arrest and those he could not.[9] The new district attorney began looking into pending criminal cases and found one. E. Nitsche, a Dallas florist had been scammed of $25,000 in fall of 1919, but the Denver police were unable to find the crooks. Not giving up, Nitsche had flyers printed about the crime and one was received by the Colorado Springs Police Department. The suspect, Robert Ballard, was arrested the following year in the Springs. Van Cise wrote that "Colorado Springs had an excellent force, and its officers were honest. At their head was Chief of Police Hugh D.

Harper and his Captain of Detectives was Irvin B. "Dad" Bruce. They were relentlessly on the trail of the con-men, because Blonger's gang frequently dropped into Colorado Springs to pick up a sucker and take them to Denver to trim."[10]

LOU BLONGER, THE FIXER

Lou Blonger, mug shot photo. Photograph public domain.

Many members of the Denver police department, the Denver County sheriff's office, the mayor, some council members, and judges were all receiving money and other "gifts" from the boss, Lou Blonger. This was how he could control the criminals and their activities.[11] In August 1922, the district attorney was able to break up the gang by making raids which netted 34 bunco men.[12] Blonger and Duff were successfully tried and convicted for their activities and sentenced to the Colorado State Penitentiary to serve seven to ten years.[13] Blonger went to visit District Attorney Van Cise after his conviction to plead for mercy because of his age (73) and poor health he believed he would die in jail. District Attorney Van Cise asked Blonger what leniency had he shown to those he bilked over the years. Had he helped a preacher's family or parish after taking the preacher's trust funds, when afterwards the preacher, out of shame, committed suicide? Another elderly man from New Orleans was reduced to living as a pauper. Had Blonger done anything to ease the man's last months of his life?[14] Five months after his meeting with Van Cise, Blonger died in prison, Sunday, April 20, 1924.[15]

District Attorney Philip Van Cise.
Denver Public Library.

Before being sent to the penitentiary, Duff gave his wife close to $200,000 in securities to hold for him. Soon after entering prison, Duff became a trustee and took over the operation of the prison's curio shop. Eventually, he was able to make a contract with a large curio company in Denver and supply them with "genuine" Navajo rugs (made by the prisoners—you know—those Cañon City Navajos) in a large production.[16] Because, he was a model prisoner, he served a minimum time and was released in 1929.

He returned to Denver and tried to restart the con-games and large operations, but was frustrated with how things were working and began to drink heavily. His wife divorced him. He was gambling and losing large amounts of money. Even though he was out of Colorado prison, he still had a federal charge hanging over him in Cleveland, Ohio.

L.A. Chapin wrote in a *Denver Post* article, that Adolph William "Kid" Duff, was found dead in the front seat of his car, while it was parked in his garage. The "field marshal" of Denver's million-dollar bunco ring, had died of carbon monoxide poisoning. Walter Erickson, while on his milk delivery route, heard a car running about 2:30 a.m. November 25, 1929. He went to the door of the garage but did not receive any response from anyone inside. He then entered the structure and found Duff lying sprawled across the front seat with the door of the coupe standing open.

It appeared that Duff had driven into the garage about 10:00 p.m. the previous night. It was not possible to determine if the death was caused because of heavy drinking, and Duff just passed out in the garage with the car running or if it was suicide, due to the unsuccessful struggle to restart the cons.[17]

Notes

1. *Portland Oregon Daily Journal*, 09 Nov 1909, Page 1.
2. *Portland Oregon Daily Journal*, 14 Nov 1909, Page 6.
3. *El Paso Herald Post*, 03 Jan 1913, Page 7.
4. *Des Moines News*, 15 Oct 1917, Page 10.
5. "Fighting the Underworld," by Philip S. Van Cise, 1936, Riverside Press, Cambridge, Pages 10-11.
6. Grifter might be a pickpocket, a crooked gambler, scammer, or a confidence man. Grift may have come from graft, a slightly older word meaning "to acquire dishonestly."
7. "Fighting the Underworld," by Philip S. Van Cise, 1936, Riverside Press, Cambridge, Pages 54-55.
8. "Fighting the Underworld," by Philip S. Van Cise, 1936, Riverside Press, Cambridge, Pages 15-16.
9. "Fighting the Underworld," by Philip S. Van Cise, 1936, Riverside Press, Cambridge, Page 4.
10. "Fighting the Underworld," by Philip S. Van Cise, 1936, Riverside Press, Cambridge, Page 25.
11. "Fighting the Underworld," by Philip S. Van Cise, 1936, Riverside Press, Cambridge, Pages 48-52.
12. *Denver Post*, 25 Aug 1922, Page 1.
13. *Fort Worth Star-Telegram*, 02 Jun 1923, Page 7.
14. "Fighting the Underworld," by Philip S. Van Cise, 1936, Riverside Press, Cambridge, Page 346.
15. Henryetta Oklahoma Daily Free-Lance, 21 Apr 1924, page 1.
16. "Fighting the Underworld," by Philip S. Van Cise, 1936, Riverside Press, Cambridge, Page 347.
17. *Denver Post*, 25 Nov 1929, Page 1.

Chapter 10

EXPLOSIVE CASE UNSOLVED

On January 12, 2024, at 10:10 PM, CSPD received a report of an explosion near 548 East Costilla Street in Colorado Springs, Colorado. Patrol officers responded to the scene and found several items that pointed toward the use of an improvised explosive device. The CSPD Regional Explosives Unit (REU) subsequently took over the investigation. — coloradosprings.gov

Colorado was at an explosive time in its history. In 1903 and 1904 mine laborers desired better pay and working conditions. Mine owners and management's interest were supported by state government. This period would be known as the Colorado Labor Wars. One of the only ways that workers could get noticed was to strike. With strikes came violence. Colorado City, now the west side of Colorado Springs, contained the reduction mills, which processed the ore mined in the Cripple Creek District, and in early 1903 strikes occurred. It is not known if the incident that happened in July of 1903 was connected with labor problems, but the timing and location seem to connect the two.

The *Gazette* reported on July of 1903, the city experienced an explosion at the city's power plant on the northern outskirts of town. One hundred-fifty sticks of dynamite (75 pounds) were placed against the north wall of the plant. The north side of the building was selected it was believed, as being less likely to be observed. Being the day after July 4th, the noise heard in town was thought to be just more celebrating the holiday.

The power plant was the main supplier of power to three cities—Colorado Springs, Colorado City, and Manitou. It also supplied the Standard, Telluride, and Portland plants located in Colorado City.[1]

The evening newspaper reported the explosives were 40 percent Hercules gelatin dynamite. It was surmised the guilty party was unfamiliar with use of dynamite and must have placed the fused stick under the pile of dynamite and not on top. The explosive force of dynamite goes down, and therefore would not ignite the other sticks piled on top. Ninety-two complete sticks of dynamite were recovered scattered around the area. If the miner's union was responsible for the explosion, they should have received the proper instruction from their workers with backgrounds in explosives. This explosive, when used properly, was used extensively in the mining district of Cripple Creek. Undersheriff Grimes reported that the California Powder Company at Denver was broken into on the 4th but only caps and fuse were taken, so it was not known if this was related to the crime at the power plant.[2]

Five employees were on duty in the plant at the time of the explosion. However, in a nearby cottage another twelve employees were sleeping when the one stick of the dynamite was set off at 2:00 a.m. However, the plant did not totally escape damage—twenty some window panes were blown out on the side of the building where the explosive charge was left.

The power plant's general manager, George B. Tripp, told the newspaper he was unaware of any grievance against the company. The plant was situated almost four miles north of the Colorado Springs Post Office. The following day the Colorado Springs Electric Company said they would pay $5,000 for information leading to the arrest and conviction of the party or parties that caused the explosion.[3] On the seventh of July, the City of Colorado Springs also offered a reward of $1,000.[4]

At this time, the union trouble in the mining district was not at its peak. A few months later, on November 21, 1903, someone placed an explosive at the 600-foot level of the Vindicator Mine which killed two men. The situation was so pronounced that Colorado Governor Peabody sent 400 infantrymen to the area to keep peace.[5] Then on June 6, 1904, fifteen men were killed while awaiting the train at the Findley station on Bull Hill. The men killed were non-union miners.[6]

Problems between the miner's unions and the mine owners continued. During a large gathering tempers got out of hand when the secretary of the Mine Owners Association blamed the Western Federation of Miners for the explosion. Two men, Roscoe McGee and John Davis were killed and five more wounded during the gathering.[7]

The mining at Cripple Creek reached its peak between 1900 and 1901. "The decline after this period can be attributed in most part to a combination of labor unrest and the complexities of deep mining."[8] By 1903 Cripple Creek was a union camp. The eight unions in the area included porters and dance hall girls. The unions all grouped themselves into one controlling unit. Trouble at Colorado City then cropped up. The reduction mills had been able to hold off unionization. During March 1903 the Western Federation of Miners got the mill employees to go on strike. The militia was called in to quell the possibility of violence. A truce was made at the beginning of April and everyone went back to work. In July another strike was called because one of the mills was accused of violating the truce. A black list was kept by the unions of those non-union agencies, to include the mills.[9] Considering the Colorado Springs power plant supplied power to the non-union reduction mills, it seems a good bet that it was the motivation behind the attempt to destroy the power plant. Besides, owners of the reduction mills were wealthy men who lived in Colorado Springs.

No one was ever arrested for the blast at the power plant in Colorado Springs. If the power plant had been destroyed, it would have direct effect on many of the mine owners who lived in Colorado Springs and could have stopped the processing of the ores from Cripple Creek at the reduction plants. Maybe its purpose was to put pressure on the mine owners to meet some of the mining unions demands.

Notes

1 *Colorado Springs Gazette*, 06 Jul 1903, Page 1.
2 *Colorado Springs Evening Telegraph*, 06 Jul 1903, Page 3.
3 *Colorado Springs Gazette*, 06 Jul 1903, Page 1.
4 *Colorado Springs Gazette*, 07 Jul 1903, Page 5.
5 *Colorado Springs Gazette*, 22 Nov 1903, Page 1.
6 *Colorado Springs Gazette*, 07 Jun 1904, Page 1.
7 *Colorado Springs Gazette*, 07 Jun 1904, Page 1.
8 *Cripple Creek Mining District*, by Robert Guilford Taylor, 1973, Published by Filter Press, Palmer Lake, CO, Pages 96.
9 *Cripple Creek Mining District*, by Robert Guilford Taylor, 1973, Published by Filter Press, Palmer Lake, CO, Pages 97.

Chapter 11

DENTAL WORK IS IMPORTANT

Enamel is the hardest substance in the human body; teeth and dental work are vital to forensic dentistry. Paul Revere identified his friend Dr. Joseph Warren, killed in the Revolutionary War, through dental work he had fabricated for him.— dentalcare.com

In mid-December 1904, while surveying a 40-acre tract on Mount Cutler, between North and South Cheyenne Cañon the county surveyor William P. Woodside and property owner, Dr. Frank C. Chamberlain discovered the body of a nude woman laid across a log. The body, lying face down, had been set afire, apparently in an attempt to prevent identification. All of the woman's clothing was missing from the scene. She appeared to be a woman about 17 years of age, 5-foot, 2-inches, 125 pounds. An empty bottle was found that had contained an inflammable liquid; liquid was poured over the body and set ablaze. The complete destruction of the body had failed.[1] Her face had been burnt with acid, making it impossible to identify the woman.

Quickly the coroner David F. Law was contacted, who, along with sheriff's deputies and police officers arrived to start investigating the murder scene. After the body was removed to the morgue, it was noted the woman had dental work performed at some time. Officers from other cities viewed the body and then checked their missing persons' cases in the hope of identifying the woman.[2]

After the body thawed, an examination revealed the woman had been shot in the head with what was believed to be a .38 short-caliber bullet. The bullet was discovered inside the skull. Dr. Isaac Burton, a dentist, made a cast of the woman's teeth and produced a description of the dental work that had been done.³ This report stated the woman was between 25 and 35 years old, much older that the first reports.

Toward the end of November, officers were contacted by Mrs. Ellen E. Jack, who owned mining claims in the area. She reported finding pieces of clothing that might belong to the victim. She also said she had seen what she thought was a German man climbing in the mountains nearby, carrying a bundle in a gunny sack, He seemed somewhat excited.⁴

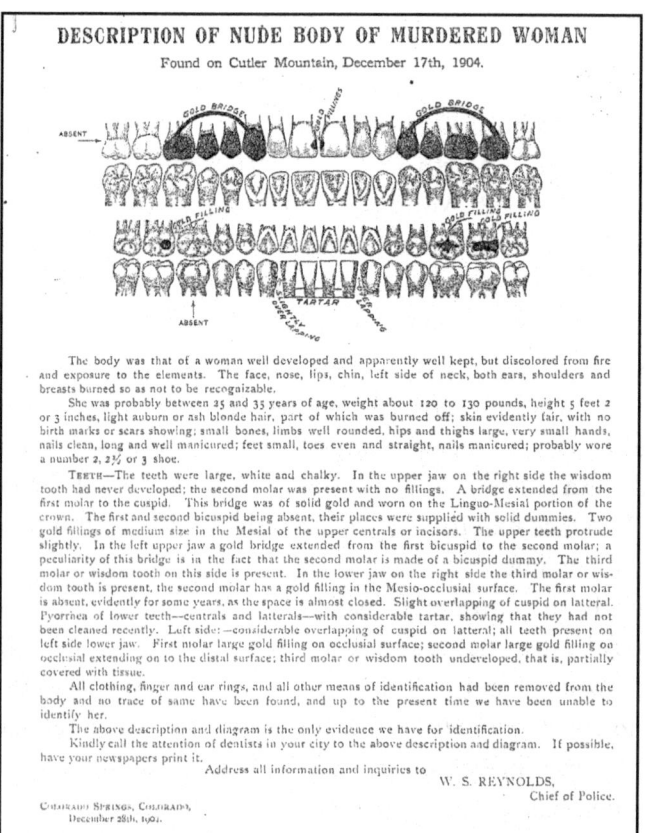

Bessie Bouton's dental record.
Courtesy of CSPD.

Continuing searches in the area where the woman's body was discovered, Detective Clyde C. McReynolds found a bottle of Carbolic Acid, a poison.[5] The label had been damaged, but some of the label was legible. Also, a fine linen handkerchief with a laundry mark was located.[6] After sending out inquires to many larger cities regarding the murder, the police had received numerous inquiries, but none worked out.

On Sunday evening, December 25th, Police Chief William S. Reynolds received a telegram from Syracuse, New York, stating it was believed the murder victim was a woman with the last name of Kempter.[7] When contact was made with parties in Syracuse, the victim was thought to be Bessie Bouton, daughter of a Mrs. Kempter. Flyers had been sent to major cities with the dental work description of the murdered woman and it appeared that the records matched that of the Bouton woman.[8]

A piece of hair was examined by a Mrs. H.R. Crooks, a local hairdresser. She said the hair looked like the hair belonging to a woman that represented a manufacturing chemist, Dr. J. Parker Pray of New York City. This same day, Chief Reynolds received a telegram from Santa Barbara, California Police Chief James Ross saying the victim was the sister of Mrs. Charles R. Nelson of Santa Barbara and she had been traveling in the company of a man by the name of Milton Franklin. The victim had written to her sister on stationery of the Antlers Hotel, but no record of Bouton was found having her registered at the hotel. However, police determined several druggists had been in contact with Bouton as a saleswoman during September and October. Her father, Charles R. Kempter said he last received a letter from his daughter stating that she was stopping in Colorado Springs. The letter was dated October 2, and related she would be home in Syracuse by December 24.[9]

Mrs. Charles Nelson, of Santa Barbara, California, was sure the homicide victim was her sister and she related that in August Bessie and Milton Franklin toured the Pacific coast and spent a month with her. Franklin was said to have given Bessie three to five thousand dollars in jewelry and paid the expenses for both of them. A three-week trip to the Catalina Islands followed before the couple left for the East. She received a communication from her sister a few weeks before December stating Bessie had quarreled with Franklin and their engagement was ended. The sister's thoughts were Franklin murdered the girl to regain possession of the jewelry. Mrs. Nelson described Franklin as a man 6-foot-3 inches and about 23-years-of-age.[10]

Although victims of fires, wars and accidents had been identified by their dental records for many years prior to Bessie's death, Bessie Bouton was believed to be one of the first homicide victim to be positively identified by dental records in the United States with a joint effort between police departments in multiple states. Two leading dental publications *The Dental Cosmos* and the *Dental Summary* editorialized that dental work should lead to positive identification of the body.[11] Dr. Sherman Williams of Denver was shown the above flyer of Mrs. Bouton's teeth and positively identified them as belonging to Mrs. Bouton.[12]

Police learned from several sources that Bouton had been in the company of one Milton Franklin Andrews (aka: Milton Franklin; aka: George Bouton; aka: George Barnett). During Chief Reynolds investigation, he found Andrews was constantly traveling and was believed at that time to be in the company of an unidentified woman, posing as his sister.[13]

It was discovered Andrews was married and had a daughter six years of age. Contact was made with the former Jennie Walsh, current wife of Andrews, described as one of the prettiest girls around. He had married in about 1897, and then in 1902, left her. She did not hear from him until October, 1904, when he wrote to her saying he was in a sanitarium in Battle Creek, Michigan and asked for her to come. She did go and stayed until he was able to rob her of all her money and jewelry—about $1,100 value. Yet she did not believe he would kill Bouton.[14] Just another nice guy!

In October 1905, it was reported that William Brush (aka:

Milton Franklin Andrews; aka: William Curtis; aka: Clayton Hill), had planned to murder William E. Ellis, an Australian turfman, in Berkeley, California, with the help of a "stunning" young woman, posing as Andrews' wife.[15] Andrews and his "wife" had traveled to Australia and were returning to America[16] when they met Ellis on their ship.

Ellis, had been in the hospital after suffering an attack by Andrews and being robbed. Prior to leaving the hospital, he swore out warrants for the arrest of Andrews and his companion. Then Ellis left for Australia. Colorado Springs Detective Charles Schultz, traveled to Berkeley, California, to assist in finding Andrews. It was learned that Andrews was also wanted in Troy, New York, suspected of killing a woman there.[17]

On Sunday, November 7, 1905, police trapped Andrews in his rooms in San Francisco. When four officers dispatched to make the arrest, did not receive a response at the door, the officers forced the door and found Andrews had shot his companion Nulda Olivia, and then shot himself in the head, using a .45-caliber handgun.[18]

Today it is not uncommon for dental records to be used if fingerprints are not sufficient to make an identification. This is done by the county coroner, who is responsible for the victim's body, until full identification has been made and the body released for burial.

Notes

1. *Colorado Springs Gazette*, 18 Dec 1904, Page 1.
2. *Colorado Springs Gazette*, 19 Dec 1904, Page 5.
3. *Colorado Springs Gazette*, 20 Dec 1904, Page 2.
4. *Colorado Springs Gazette*, 21 Dec 1904, Page 5.
5. Highly poisonous chemical substance made from tar and also found in some plants and essential oils. Today it has many uses, including its being a precursor to polycarbonates and epoxide resins.
6. *Colorado Springs Gazette*, 22 Dec 1904, Page 1.
7. *Colorado Springs Gazette*, 26 Dec 1904, Page 5.
8. *Telluride Daily Journal*, 26 Dec 1904, Page 1.
9. *Colorado Springs Gazette*, 27 Dec 1904, Page 5.
10. *San Francisco Chronicle*, 27 Dec 1904, Page 1.
11. *Colorado Springs Gazette*, 15 Feb 1905, Page 5.
12. *Colorado Springs Gazette*, 10 Dec 1972, Page E13.
13. *Leadville Herald Democrat*, 31 Jan 1905, Page 1.
14. *Colorado Springs Gazette*, 02 Feb 1905, Page 1.
15. *Oakland Tribune*, 13 Oct 1905, Page 1.

16 *Golden Transcript*, 19 Oct 1905, Page 7.
17 *Leadville Herald Democrat*, 02 Nov 1905, Page 1.
18 *Colorado Springs Gazette*, 07 Nov 1905, Page 1.

Chapter 12

DEATH OF CHARLES P. ESSICK—SUICIDE OR MURDER

According to FBI statistics, approximately half of the murder cases in the United States ever get solved. — Federal Bureau of Investigations

The Essick family suffered more than one tragedy. In December of 1905, the fifth child of Charles Pittman Essick was arrested for being involved in the murder of Frank L. Scott. Charles Harrison Essick, age 17, and Leslie Francisco, aka: Leslie F. Foster, accosted Mr. Scott on his way to the Santa Fe Railroad Depot, where he was planning to take a train to California.[1] The two suspects approached the victim. Essick supposedly accidentally shot the man. The man was rushed to St Francis Hospital, where the bullet was removed. He survived for four days, but on Christmas Eve he succumbed to his injuries.[2]

Three years later and four days after Christmas in 1908, Charles Essick, 67, was found in a room at the front of his home at 313 South Wahsatch Avenue, around 8:30 a.m. by his wife. She knocked on the door but did not get a reply. She entered the room and found the deceased body of her husband in a sitting position, a bullet wound in his forehead and a revolver lying on the bed beside the body. Authorities soon arrived including Coroner David Freeman Law and Chief of Police William Sullivan Reynolds. Upon examining the revolver, it was found to be fully loaded and one fired cartridge remained in the weapon. Mr. Essick had laid out a clean shirt before going to bed and there wasn't any note or instructions left by the victim. Authorities found this somewhat confusing, but it appeared to be a suicide.[3]

One reason it was believed to be a suicide was three years earlier, one of his sons, Charles H. Essick, a teenager at the time, and an accomplice had tried to rob a man and shot the man to death. After confessing to the crime, he was sentenced to a life sentence at Cañon City. The theory at that moment was the father might have been despondent, over the situation. Also, the previous January, he lost his favorite grandson, Arthur Miller, 18-months-old.[4]

After the removal of the body to the morgue, however, the victim was found to have suffered two knife wounds in his left side. It was determined that the blade of the weapon was just over three-inches in length. One wound penetrated between the fourth and fifth ribs and managed to puncture the heart, and the other wound was a little lower. Authorities returned to the victim's home but were unable to locate the stabbing weapon. The victim had a small pocket knife in his trousers' pocket, that was closed and there were no signs of blood. Further examination of the bullet wound showed the bullet traveled downward, from where the revolver had been placed against the forehead, lodging itself in the jawbone just under the left ear. If the victim had fired the weapon, it would have been necessary for him to use his thumb to fire it and would have been a very odd angle. It was beginning to look more like a homicide. In the victim's office/bedroom, a large amount of cash was on the desk, discounting the theory of robbery.[5]

Initially, the coroner theorized the victim, had stabbed himself, hid the knife, and since he was unsuccessful at ending his life, took up the handgun and shot himself in the head, completing his task. After the examination of the body, it was shown to be very unlikely the victim could have stabbed himself, completed physical tasks, returned to the bed and then shot himself to death. Now, the problem became a "who-dun-it." There was a $4,000 life insurance policy (2024 value of over $136,500), which could have been a motive for a family member to have killed the victim.[6]

To complicate matters, Mr. Essick's room had four entrances, the outside door on the west was locked, as was the outside screen door; a north door exiting into the parlor was locked from inside; a door on the east, which allowed entry into the victim's son's room was locked; leaving only the south door unlocked leading into the hall. When family members were contacted by the news media, they were "satisfied" that the incident was a suicide.[7]

The media's reporting of the killing caused the coroner's room to quickly overflow the seating area for witnesses to view the operation of the coroner's inquest, which had to be adjourned and reconvened in courtroom one at the courthouse. It appeared everyone in town wanted to know more, and watch the coroner and district attorney in action plus the opportunity to view the witnesses during their testimony.[8]

For the many years when coroners impaneled juries, reporting indicates that often people other than the family and jury were in attendance. When I was attending autopsies, I don't ever remember a coroner's jury being called. And at the morgue, only the coroner and police officers were usually in attendance. I am not aware of a law allowing or disallowing anyone else to attend.

Following the examination of the body by County Physician Harry L. Richardson and having completed the autopsy, he reported the knife wounds possibly were inflicted as much as two hours prior to the gunshot wound. The time of death was estimated to be around 5:00 a.m. The coroner impaneled a jury of five men to handle the coroner's investigation. The victim was buried that afternoon at Evergreen Cemetery in Colorado Springs. The actual inquest was delayed so an investigation could be more complete before its session was necessary.[9]

January 1, 1909, the victim's son-in-law, Arthur Davis was taken into custody and was held pending the completion of the coroner's inquest. The murder weapon was found in Essick's overcoat pocket. Chief Reynolds, stated the room where the death occurred had been thoroughly searched following the crime. Therefore, the knife had to have been placed in the pocket almost 36 hours after the death. The knife was found by the victim's son-in-law, Reverend George Cook. This belief was bolstered by the fact, even though the knife blade was covered with blood, there was no blood transfer to the inside of the pocket where it was found.[10]

Saturday, January 2, 1909, the coroner's jury met to begin the inquest into the death of Charles Pittman Essick. Five witnesses were examined. It was determined the knife used to kill the victim had been purchased from Lowell-Meservey Hardware, two weeks earlier.[11] At the inquest the knife was identified as a Henckels brand by Ray Lowell of the hardware store and was sold exclusively by them locally. It was sold between December 16 and 18, at a cost of $1.50, by Charles Baggs, a store clerk, who was presently out of town.[12]

The night prior to the crime, the inhabitants of the dwelling included the victim's wife, Flora Ina (Pierce) Essick; Arthur E. Davis, son-in-law; his wife Mrs. Ella W. Essick-Davis, victim's daughter; and Paul S. Essick, victim's son. The son was physically closest to the victim at the time of the killing, being in an adjoining room to the scene of the crime. When questioned as to the gun shot, he testified that he did not hear anything after he went to bed at 9:30 p.m. the night before. He regularly slept with bedclothes over his ears. The Davises' room was adjoining Paul Essick's room, but they too did not hear a gun being fired during the night. Mrs. Essick, the victim's wife, slept at the rear of the home and did not hear anything out of the ordinary. However, the victim's other son-in-law, Dr. George Cook, testified that when the telephone rang in the victim's room, it could be heard through two closed doors easily. This did not help the testimony that other tenants of the residence could not hear a gunshot.[13] The weapon was said to be a .38-caliber.[14]

When the victim's wife found her husband deceased, she screamed which awakened her daughter Ella. Dressed in only her night clothes, she went to the front door and yelled for the neighbors—the Halstead's and Dyers—who soon joined the family members in the room of the tragedy.[15] Neighbors at 317 South Wahsatch Avenue, Mrs. Alfred Halstead and Mrs. Thomas Hall said they heard the report of a gunshot at 5:00 a.m. on the morning of December 29. The two ladies also said they were kept awake around midnight because of loud voices quarreling at the Essick home. This arguing was also reported by Mrs. Jacobs living in the house north of the Essick's, 309 South Wahsatch Avenue.[16]

The victim was employed by the Woodmen of the World, at the Pike's Peak camp No. 5, in the Colorado Springs area. For fourteen years he had collected dues of members and would regularly turn collections over to the organization's treasurer, Charles F. Aldrich[17] who owned Colorado Monumental Works, 331 South Wahsatch Avenue.[18] The treasurer told authorities that the victim handled between $2,500 to $3,000 a month. After the treasurer arrived and went through records of the organization, he found some money was missing. The last remittance to Aldrich was on December 22.[19]

The coroner's jury returned a verdict on Friday, February 5, 1909. The report stated Charles P. Essick was killed on December 29, 1908, at his home succumbing to a stab wound to his left side between the fourth and fifth ribs, which penetrated the heart. The wound was done with felonious intent. It was also concluded that a bullet was fired into the head of the victim using a .38-caliber revolver after the victim was dead. With no evidence to indicate someone entered the residence from the outside, it was concluded the 16-year-old son, Paul S. Essick and the son-in-law, Robert Edward Piper (aka: Arthur Davis) were responsible for the death. The two men were arrested and placed in jail. The motive was believed to be the theft of money from the victim, amounting to $594.00 of Woodmen of the World funds.[20]

The coroner's jury also believed that Paul Essick was more guilty than Davis. They were of the mind that initially Essick stabbed his father and Davis hid the weapon. Both men were taken before Justice Orville R. Dunnington where they pled not guilty and were returned to jail without bond.[21] The attorney for the pair, James Alexander Orr, Sr., at the preliminary hearing, told the court that Paul was only 16-years old and therefore should be taken before the juvenile court. However, the prosecutor, Assistant District Attorney Michael William Purcell, revealed a Colorado Supreme Court decision—Gibson vs. the People of Colorado—which stated "A person is 16 years old only one day in law, the day of his sixteenth birthday." This decision was only a few weeks old at the time.[22]

The case was continued for some time, but finally on Saturday, April 3, 1909, Assistant District Attorney Michael W. Purcell moved for the dismissal of all charges against the two defendants, after they had been incarcerated for over two months. No one was expecting this result. The prosecutor told the public that he believed the victim was a homicide victim and the work of the coroner's jury was justified in returning the verdict they presented. However, there was not sufficient evidence to obtain a conviction. Defense Attorney Orr requested the defendants be taken before a jury so they might be acquitted by the court, which would assure they could never be tried for this crime again. The request was denied by the court. The prosecutor would not make any insinuations, and this decision would allow his office to pursue the matter in the future should better evidence be found.[23]

Forensic science was still in its infant stage where fingerprinting was used. In 1892 Francis Galton published *Fingerprints*, the first comprehensive book on the nature of fingerprints and their use in solving crime. It wasn't until 1903 when the New York State Prison system began the first systematic use of fingerprints in United States for criminal identification.

In this case, the problem with trying to locate fingerprints in the victim's room, which was used by all members of the family at one time or another, combined with the theory that one of the family was responsible for the killing, would make looking for fingerprints useless. The age of fingerprints cannot be determined and if prints of a family member were found, unless on the gun or the knife, they would prove nothing. Obtaining usable fingerprints on a knife or a gun is often not easy to do. Today, there are processes that were not available during my time that might allow usable results.

Notes

1	*Colorado Springs Gazette*, 21 Dec 1905, Page 1.
2	*Colorado Springs Gazette*, 25 Dec 1905, Page 1.
3	*Colorado Springs Gazette*, 30 Dec 1908, Page 1.
4	*Colorado Springs Evening Telegraph*, 29 Dec 1908, Page 1.
5	*Colorado Springs Gazette*, 30 Dec 1908, Page 1.
6	*Colorado Springs Evening Telegraph*, 30 Dec 1908, Page 1.
7	*Colorado Springs Evening Telegraph*, 30 Dec 1908, Page 1.
8	*Colorado Springs Gazette*, 05 Jan 1909, Page 1.
9	*Colorado Springs Gazette*, 31 Dec 1908, Page 1.
10	*Colorado Springs Evening Telegraph*, 02 Jan 1909, Page 1.
11	*Colorado Springs Gazette*, 03 Jan 1909, Page 1.
12	*Colorado Springs Gazette*, 05 Jan 1909, Page 1.
13	*Colorado Springs Gazette*, 05 Jan 1909, Page 1.
14	*Colorado Springs Evening Telegraph*, 05 Jan 1909, Page 1.
15	*Colorado Springs Gazette*, 05 Jan 1909, Page 1.
16	*Colorado Springs Evening Telegraph*, 06 Feb 1909, Page 1.
17	*Colorado Springs Evening Telegraph*, 04 Jan 1909, Page 1.
18	R.L. Polk Colorado Springs City Directory, 1908, Page 70.
19	*Colorado Springs Evening Telegraph*, 04 Jan 1909, Page 1.
20	*Colorado Springs Evening Telegraph*, 05 Jan 1909, Page 1.
21	*Colorado Springs Evening Telegraph*, 06 Feb 1909, Page 2.
22	*Colorado Springs Evening Telegraph*, 12 Feb 1909, Page 9.
23	*Colorado Springs Evening Telegraph*, 03 Apr 1909, Page 1.

Chapter 13

BRING ON THE AUTOMOBILE REGULATIONS, LAWS AND FINES

On June 17, 1994, just two days after the brutal murders of his ex-wife Nicole Brown Simpson and her friend, Ron Goldman, Orenthal James (O.J.) Simpson would lead police on a 90-minute-long pursuit which ultimately ended in his arrest at his home in the affluent neighborhood of Brentwood, California.
— foxnews.com

The year 1899 found the city invaded by the first gasoline automobile to arrive in Colorado Springs. Edward J. Cabler, an electrician and electric appliance salesman, commissioned Robert Temple, operator of the Temple Machine Company in Denver, to create a gasoline powered vehicle that he could use to do his selling and delivering. The vehicle was a long wooden wagon with a two-cylinder gasoline engine installed under the floorboards. The vehicle had four solid rubber tires on the wooden spoked wheels. Its empty weight was at one-ton and it was capable of carrying fourteen people. There were two gears, one capable of half a mile per hour to three miles per hour and the faster gear capable of up to fifteen miles per hour.

Cabler's plan was to show, that unlike autos in eastern parts of the country where it was basically flat, this vehicle would be able to climb the hills of the Rocky Mountains. He loaded up his wife and Mr. Temple, the builder, packed about a thousand pounds of clothing and necessities, then took off from Denver toward Colorado Springs very early in the morning. His plan was to follow the Denver & Rio Grande railroad rails south.[1] He believed this mode of transportation a better and cheaper method of getting around instead of train fares. The fifteen-horsepower machine was to travel to Colorado Springs, through the Ute Pass and finally arrive in Victor, Colorado. The auto would carry about eight gallons of fuel. He calculated that this amount would be needed to operate for eight to ten hours.[2]

The Cabler's plan was to arrive at Cripple Creek the following day. As with many best laid plans, things did not quite occur as expected. First, the car became mired in the sand near Sedalia, Colorado still about 25 miles north of Palmer Lake.[3] After finally getting free of the soft earth, they made it to Palmer Lake on Sunday, two days after the start of the adventure. Secondly, they had used up all of their fuel. Palmer Lake did not have such solvents and it was necessary for gasoline to be shipped to Palmer Lake on the rail lines.[4]

Monday, July 24, 1899, the Cablers and their automobile arrived in Colorado Springs in the afternoon. The third minor problem was the engine was not receiving its supply of gasoline and had to be repaired before an exhibition of the car's abilities could be seen around town. The couple was set to start up Ute Pass the following morning and continue to Victor.[5] An observer reported that afternoon the automobile was progressing nicely, with little difficulty with the steep grades of the pass.[6]

They arrived in Victor Thursday morning, with everything working in a proper manner.[7] Mr. Temple was so pleased with the new automobile he decided he would begin working on a machine for city use. His prediction was the auto would be the new mode of transportation and powered with gasoline.[8]

August found the Cablers in Leadville, Colorado, exhibiting their automobile. However, they did not drive it from Victor, but had it shipped by train. The reporter for the *Herald Democrat* was not impressed with the vehicle's fifteen mile per hour capability on level ground. He remarked that it appeared to him that Cabler was always going uphill, because the car never exceeded its slowest speed.[9]

It wasn't too long following the visit of Mr. Edward J. Cabler's gasoline powered wagon to Colorado Springs and Victor, until automobiles started showing up in Colorado Springs. However, it was not the first non-horse powered vehicle in the Colorado Springs area. On October of 1892, Luther B. Hammond, 76 years of age, being startled by an electric car near the Broadmoor casino, was thrown from his wagon and died.[10] Possibly the first pedestrian death by a car in Colorado Springs?

By 1900, William C. Anthony, taking more than a year, constructed his own vehicle. George Dana Boardman Bonbright, member of a brokerage, ordered a vehicle from the Stanley Automobile Company, which was brought by the railroad.[11] In July of 1900, an automobile livery company was organized in Colorado Springs. The company was planning on purchasing twenty-four vehicles to be used as rentals. The autos were to be of six styles: runabouts, Victorias, drags, phaetons, surreys and enclosed. Fees for the rentals were to be compared with that of renting horse drawn vehicles of the same size.[12] At the same time Miss M.E. Crowell gifted to the city a horse-drawn ambulance; a $900 dollar gift.[13] Cars were becoming more common.

General Palmer was not initially a fan of gasoline powered contraptions, saying "that they smelled too bad and made too much noise to appeal to civilized people."[14] But this did not stop the opening of the first auto rental in the State of Colorado in September 1900. It was operated by Douglas Bernard at 17 East Cucharras Street,[15] where he had three vehicles for rent. Purchased from the American Bicycle Company of Indianapolis, Indiana, the electric cars were of three different sizes and styles. Unlike their gasoline powered cousins, they produced little or no noise during operation. A reporter, after half-an-hours' training, took the largest of the vehicles for a test drive and was promised the battery would last up to 45 miles. The reporter was quite impressed when the battery actually lasted for over 70 miles.[16]

During July of 1903 an automobile club was formed for the

purpose of organizing vehicle owners to conduct a parade through downtown. At the time it was estimated there were about 100 cars in town. The purpose of the parade was so Harry H. Buckwalter, a motion-picture photographer, and Orion Lawrence Foster, an official photographer of the Rock Island Railroad, could take photos for brochures used by the railroad to promote Colorado Springs. The parade was to form in front of the Antlers Hotel on Thursday morning, July 29, 1903. The parade was to travel north on Cascade Avenue to Madison Street, east to Nevada Avenue, then south. At Costilla, the parade would proceed west back to Cascade Avenue, north to Bijou Street, east to Tejon Street, turning north to the Colorado College campus.[17]

With the arrival of automobiles the city believed necessary regulation would be required. The first ordinance passed was in 1901, stating that the police patrol wagon and ambulance were to be given the right-of-way. Failure to yield could find a person fined from $10.00 to $200.00.[18] Also considered was regulations needed due to several main streets having trolleys operating in the middle of the streets. In 1902, the city directed the speed of a street railway car be limited to eight miles-per-hour (mph) within the city fire limits and not to exceed sixteen mph outside these limits.[19]

The first speed limit on autos was introduced in 1903. Vehicles were not to exceed six mph within the fire limits and ten mph outside those limits. Also, at any intersection or stopped streetcar, passing had to be no greater than five mph. Auto owners were required to purchase an annual license for each vehicle at $5.00. The city would assign a license number for the vehicle, but the owner was expected to make a plate—out of something! Vehicles were required to have two lamps at the front of the vehicle, demonstrating white light visible at a reasonable distance and a red light at the rear. These lights had to be used between one hour after sunset till one hour before sunrise. Opening of mufflers within the limits of the city was not allowed.

Fines for violation of this ordinance were considered serious, because the fine for the first offense was $100, but not more than $200. If further violations were to occur, the fines were to escalate beginning at $200, and up to $300, and the driver could be confined to jail for a period not more than 90 days![20] (In 2024 money a $100 fine would be the equivalent of over $3,500!) The city proved they were serious about speeding violations, because during August, Burt Wade was fined $100 and costs, while W. Coleman, was fined $50 and costs. The police department was to enforce the law. Officer Clyde McReynolds on his beat on Washington Avenue[21] saw Mr. Wade driving at an excessive rate. The officer yelled for the driver to stop, but he just sped up. Jumping on his bicycle, he pursued, peddling as fast as he was able. He fired a shot into the ground with no response from the evader. Chasing the car east to Cascade Avenue, the driver turned north. Apparently, the driver believing he had made a clean getaway, turned back south where the officer was able to stop Mr. Wade. The officer estimated the vehicle was traveling in excess of 30 mph. Was this the first police auto chase in Colorado Springs?[22]

One year after the enacting of the city's speed ordinance the membership of the Colorado Springs Automobile Club met to discuss the ordinance as being ill-conceived and was causing wealthy members of the business community to be angry enough to move from the city. Being the largest auto club in the west, it had considerable political sway. There was much desire for the ordinances amendment to be more reasonable.[23]

Two well-to-do businessmen and auto enthusiasts, William Wells Price and Robert Parsell Davie, Jr., met with Chief of Police William S. Reynolds to discuss the problems with the auto speed ordinance. They were encouraged to find the police chief shared some of their concerns and also believed the ordinance should be amended.[24] In June 1905, the auto speed ordinance was amended, increasing the speeds to 12 mph and 18 mph, within the fire limits and outside same, respectively. A new feature was the forming of a board, made up by the chief of police, one member of the City Council and one member of the Colorado Springs Automobile Club, to examine people desiring to operate a motor vehicle in the City of Colorado Springs. If an applicant satisfied the three board members, a certificate would be issued. By presenting the certificate to the city clerk with payment of fifty cents a license would be issued. And the bone of contention—the fine structure—was revised. A first offense of speeding was now between $5 and $50. Violations of a second occasion were then to be $25 and maximum of $100.[25] Quite a drastic modification from the 1903 ordinance.

In September 1905, Chief of Police Alexander Adams was giving thought to the abandonment of the department's horses for an automobile. Then an incident occurred: the chief, a detective, and their driver, were thrown from the patrol wagon and injured. Then Detective Charles E. Shultz, drove the chief from his home to headquarters in an automobile, which the chief found to be a more positive experience.[26] However, the CSPD did not purchase a non-horse powered vehicle until it bought a motorcycle in April 1910.[27]

Until 1908, the city had not codified an ordinance to direct vehicles to be driven on the right-hand side of the street.[28] Also, the streets still being unpaved at this time, there were no such things as lane lines to assist drivers as to their portion of a roadway. Nor, were there stop signs or other traffic directing signage. The mind set was all driving was to be polite.

In 1912, Police Commissioner James A. Himebaugh and Police Chief Stanley Dean Burno contracted to purchase an $1,100 Buick, to be used for answering calls for service.[29] The following month the department sold their three horses and purchased a second vehicle, a four-passenger Ford for $775. This being a new thing for everyone, Officers Carpenter and Berry were to receive driving lessons.[30]

The State of Colorado, awakening to the fact that places like Colorado Springs had been licensing vehicles since 1903, jumped into the fray in April of 1913. Governor Elias Milton Ammons, signed a bill for the collection of from $2.50 to $10.00 per vehicle for a license, the proceeds were to be divided equally between the state and the counties for road improvements.[31]

The summer of 1916 found the city ready to install a "Traffic Semaphore" to control traffic flow at the intersection of Pikes Peak Avenue and Tejon Street. It would be no longer necessary for an officer to direct traffic during "the season" (tourist season.) Each side of the signal would have an arm labeled "GO" and one labeled "STOP." This was to be mounted in the middle of the intersection on a tall iron post. This device was only to be used during "the season," and would be removed at the end of that time.[32]

That same summer, the city purchased cast iron "safety zone" sign posts which were about four feet tall and plainly marked as to where a safe zone for pedestrians existed as they were crossing a street. Thirty standards had been purchased and placed at the major intersections in the downtown area. By end of the summer, drivers seemed to delight in running over the signs and destroying them faster than they could be replaced. One officer said the signs might have to be embedded in the pavement and then maybe it would not be such a sport to destroy the signs.[33]

Believing traffic congestion during the summer was becoming heavy enough, by 1923, the city was entertaining the idea of installing traffic control signals at some major intersections in the downtown business district.[34] Chief of Police Hugh D. Harper wanted a signal that could be controlled from City Hall electronically, and the installation was being considered either at Pikes Peak and Nevada Avenues or Pikes Peak and Tejon Street. The preferable signal had a red lighted globe on top and glass lenses. A red glass lens had "Stop" etched in the lens and a green lens was etched with "Go" on it. The corner by the post office was described as more dangerous than other intersections and many believed this would be the best location for a trial. Part of the reason for the intersection's problem was both streets were nearly 100 feet wide and caused problems for pedestrians trying to cross the streets.[35]

During February of 1924, a traffic signal was ordered from Klug and Smith Manufacturing Company of Milwaukee, Wisconsin, to be installed at Pikes Peak and Nevada Avenues. It was placed in the middle of the intersection where it would not interfere with the street car rails. The street car tracks amounted to two sets of rails on Pikes Peak Avenue and two on Nevada Avenue. The traffic control device would have lights on the four sides. A red lens at top was etched with the word "Stop" on two opposite sides; in the middle a light, yellow in color, was engraved with "Traffic Change" located on all four sides; finally, the bottom light was a green lens etched with "Go" on the other two sides from the red lens. This was to be installed on a concrete base and was a total height of ten feet. The signal would have a motor inside the base of the instrument which would rotate the light head at top.[36]

The city had an article published in the newspaper explaining to the public how to act and react to the new device about to be installed downtown. The light post itself would be painted white and the rotating portion would be black to contrast the large rectangular colored lenses. The police chief reported the light timing would be set for a 25-second interval on Pikes Peak Avenue and 35-seconds on Nevada Avenue. Since the roadway would be wide enough to accommodate three lanes of traffic, it was being considered lines might be painted on the roadway to help the traffic. Realizing this was a new experience for the public it was planned to have officers stationed at the intersection to help people to understand how to navigate through.[37]

When the signal was first installed there was a flange on the upper part of the mechanism wide enough that the street cars could not pass. It was immediately removed, trimmed and reinstalled.[38] Some motorists were totally confused by this contraption, but with the help of the police officers stationed on the corners, people were soon having little difficulty navigating through the intersection—when they were supposed to be moving or not. With the motoring public seemingly approving of this new method of controlling traffic, the city manager planned to install two more signals, but of another style, both on Tejon—one at Pikes Peak Avenue and the other at Colorado Avenue. This location was where traffic conditions seemed to warrant need during the summer months.[39]

The Colorado Springs Automobile Club adopted a resolution, for the CSPD's ability to recover stolen vehicles. In fact, the department was so good the insurance companies were providing a 25% lower rate to automobile owners over many other cities in Colorado.[40]

Colorado Springs began paving roads after a bond election in September 1920.[41]

Not everyone was enthralled with the installation of traffic signals. At the end of the tourist season, the traffic signal at Pikes Peak and Nevada Avenues, was removed and put in storage. It was not believed to be warranted during winter months, due to less traffic.[42] The following March, Chief Harper let the city administration know his frustration over the removal of the traffic signal the previous fall, when he wasn't consulted. Interestingly, after the Automobile Club's original unhappiness with the traffic signal, they were suggesting the city put in signals at four downtown intersections![43]

August found the city had purchased and installed seven traffic lights. These were installed downtown at Cascade & Colorado Avenues; Colorado Avenue & Tejon Street; Colorado & Nevada Avenues; Cascade & Pikes Peak Avenues; Pikes Peak Avenue & Tejon Street; Nevada & Pikes Peak Avenues and Tejon & Kiowa Streets. These were not to be removed in the fall, but be permanent.[44]

With the invasion of mechanical contrivances clogging the streets with autos, trucks, motorcycles, etc., who knew the city would need parking meters, more traffic signals, traffic control signs and now, the dreaded "red-light cameras!" Of course, this all came about because of the popularity of our beloved mountain resort community. The city grew, more vehicles were introduced, until we went from a community covering a few blocks to over 195 square miles and a population of around 500,000 souls.

In 1872 the town was patrolled by a single man. Now, over 750 officers and authorized strength of 818 officers are needed.[45] What was a small community, easy to navigate even if a person had only been here a few days, became streets that meander all over the place.

Notes

1. *Colorado Springs Daily Gazette*, 21 Jul 1899, Page 5.
2. *Denver Rocky Mountain News*, 21 Jul 1899, Page 10.
3. *Cripple Creek Morning Times*, 22 Jul 1899, Page 1.
4. *Cripple Creek Morning Times*, 23 Jul 1899, Page 1.
5. *Denver Rocky Mountain News*, 24 Jul 1899, Page 3.
6. *Denver Rocky Mountain News*, 26 Jul 1899, Page 2.
7. *Denver Rocky Mountain News*, 27 Jul 1899, Page 2.
8. *Denver Rocky Mountain News*, 09 Aug 1899, Page 5.
9. *Leadville Herald Democrat*, 18 Aug 1899, Page 8.
10. *Colorado Springs Gazette*, 18 Oct 1892, Page 4.
11. *Colorado Springs Gazette*, 05 Jan 1900, Page 5.
12. *Colorado Springs Gazette*, 26 Jul 1900, Page 5.
13. *Colorado Springs Evening Telegraph*, 27 Jul 1900, Page 10.
14. *Newport in the Rockies — Life and Good Times of Colorado Springs*, 1961, Sage Books, Chicago, Page 200.
15. *Colorado Springs City Directory*, 1900, Page 74.
16. *Colorado Springs Gazette*, 10 Sep 1900, Page 3.
17. *Colorado Springs Evening Telegraph*, 27 Jul 1903, Page 5.
18. Colorado Springs City Ordinance, 590, 05 Sep 1901.
19. Colorado Springs City Ordinance, 596, 19 Feb 1902.
20. Colorado Springs City Ordinance, 652, 18 Aug 1903.
21. Colorado Springs City Directory, 1903, Page 13. — Describing that it was an extension of Pikes Peak Avenue west to the city limits of Colorado City.
22. *Colorado Springs Evening Telegraph*, 29 Aug 1903.
23. *Colorado Springs Gazette*, 01 Aug 1904, Page 4.
24. *Colorado Springs Gazette*, 02 Aug 1903, Page 3.
25. Colorado Springs City Ordinance, 689, 22 Jun 1905.
26. *Colorado Springs Gazette*, 18 Sep 1905, Page 5.
27. *Colorado Springs Gazette*, 08 Apr 1910, Page 12.
28. Colorado Springs City Ordinance 750, 14 Apr 1908.
29. *Colorado Springs Gazette*, 12 Feb 1912, Page 8.
30. *Colorado Springs Gazette*, 27 Mar 1912, Page ??.
31. *Colorado Springs Evening Telegraph*, 12 Apr 1913, Page 2.
32. *Colorado Springs Gazette*, 13 Jun 1916, Page 1.
33. *Colorado Springs Gazette*, 14 Aug 1916. Page 5.
34. *Colorado Springs Gazette* Telegraph, 21 Oct 1923, Page 1.
35. *Colorado Springs Gazette* Telegraph, 06 Dec 1923, Page 7.
36. *Colorado Springs Evening Telegraph*, 18 Feb 1924.
37. *Colorado Springs Gazette*, 13 Apr 1924.
38. *Colorado Springs Evening Telegraph*, 19 Apr 1924.
39. *Colorado Springs Gazette*, 05 Jun 1924, Page 1.
40. *Colorado Springs Evening Telegraph*, 28 Mar 1925.
41. *Colorado Springs Gazette*, 09 Sep 1920, Page 4.
42. *Colorado Springs Evening Telegraph*, 26 Sep 1924, Page 1.
43. *Colorado Springs Evening Telegraph*, 28 Mar 1925.
44. *Rocky Mountain News*, 24 Jul 1925.
45. Information from Colorado Springs City Human Resources.

Chapter 14

ALBERT W. MARKSHEFFEL

The population motor-vehicle death rate reached its peak in 1937 with 30.8 deaths per 100,000 population. In 1913, 33.38 people died for every 10,000 vehicles on the road. In 2021, the death rate was 1.66 per 10,000 vehicles, a 95% improvement. — injuryfacts.nsc.org

Tuesday, September 17, 1907, was the night a terrifically bad auto accident occurred, causing the death of three men. William H. Ralston, an employee of Standard Electric; John S. Grey, new to Colorado Springs and employed as a chauffeur; and H. Winnall, who came with his employer from New York city to act as a chauffeur were all victims of this collision. There were six more men injured in this event—Britton L. Graves, Frank H. Ward, Philip Ahearne, George Buckley, Addison N. Wheelock, and Albert W. Marksheffel the driver of the ill-fated vehicle.[1]

The coroner, David F. Law, called together a coroner's jury to investigate the deaths from the accident, a new experience for the coroner. This was the first traffic accident with multiple deaths for the community. The coroner's jury was sworn in at the morgue that morning before viewing the body of William H. Ralston. Then at 2:00 o'clock, the jury met in the basement of the courthouse, in the coroner's office.[2] The jury consisted of six men. The investigation was overseen by the coroner, District Attorney Clarence C. Hamlin, and Clyde I. Starrett was the stenographer.[3]

On the day, the coroner's jury began their investigation. Mayor David N. Heizer and Police Chief William S. Reynolds met to discuss the traffic accident. It was decided the driver's license issued to Albert W. Marksheffel was to be rescinded immediately. The police chief announced that Marksheffel was ordered not to drive a vehicle in the city of Colorado Springs as he no longer had driving privileges. It was believed that strong enforcement of the speed ordinances had not been strictly enforced.

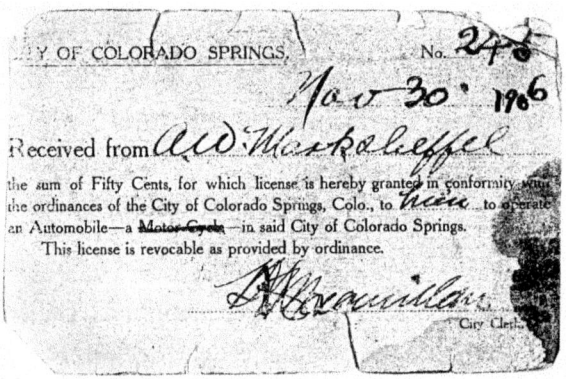

Colorado Springs issued drivers license to A.W. Marksheffel.
Pikes Peak Library District, Special Collections,
Marksheffel Collection.

The coroner jury's verdict found Albert W. Marksheffel was responsible for the death of the victims in the car crash. The accident scene was located about 200 feet west of Chestnut Street on the south edge of Huerfano Street (today's Colorado Avenue) on the morning of September 17th, between 2 and 3 a.m. It was determined the accident occurred at a speed well in excess of the city's speed limit. An arrest was ordered for Marksheffel. The coroner issued a coroner's warrant for the arrest. El Paso County Deputy Sheriff's Harry C. Allward and John E. Scofield went to the Western Automobile and Supply Company, where Marksheffel worked and arrested him. He was taken before Justice of the Peace William N. Ruby where he posted a $500 bond.[4]

The case was filed with the grand jury and on Thursday, September 26, 1907, they returned an indictment charging Albert W.

Marksheffel with involuntary manslaughter. The indictment was filed in the district court clerk's office. District Court Judge Wesley S. Morris placed the defendant under a $1,000 bond. The bond was signed by Charles P. Campbell, president of the Western Automobile and Supply Company, one of Marksheffel's partners and Dr. Walter D. Marlowe. Due to a crowded court docket, the case was not set before the November session.[5]

What happened the day of the accident? Monday evening there was entertainment and a friendly gathering at the Elks Club located at the southeast corner of Bijou Street and Cascade Avenue. As the festivities were ending, Marksheffel walked across Cascade to the automotive shop and picked up his car to give several people rides to their homes. When he later returned to the club, someone suggested they all get in the car and take it out for a ride. The vehicle was a 40-horsepower, three-seat Ford racing car. In this vehicle eight men were "attached" to the vehicle in several manners. Two men were in the right front seat next to the driver, one man was sitting upon the hood of the vehicle, one was in the single back seat, and four others were on the running boards and trunk area.[6]

Marksheffel testified at the coroner's hearing he was not sure when they all left the Elks Club and admitted to having consumed a few drinks, but thought he was unaffected by the alcohol before driving west to Colorado City. They stayed there about an hour. The entire party was sober, he said, and some members of the group had done more drinking in Colorado City, but he did not remember who they were. Colorado City's Night Captain John H. Hill, testified he saw the party gathered in front of the Red-light Sporting house; they were under the influence of liquor, but he did not believe they were intoxicated.[7]

Marksheffel told the coroner's jury that he was not sure what happened or what caused the fatal accident. He was driving east on Colorado Avenue toward Colorado Springs, and as he approached the curve on Huerfano Street east of 8th Street, he was driving no faster than 35 mph when on the curve he lost control of the vehicle.

The car exited the roadway on the south side, flying over the ditch box and striking a utility pole before the car spun around and came to rest. People were thrown off and out of the car, killing three members. Some were thrown as far as 50 feet from the car. The two men seated in the right front seat were killed. Marksheffel said he had passed this way nearly a hundred times and never had a problem before.[8]

At the time of the accident the area was unpaved and the road had two sets of trolley tracks running between Colorado Springs and Manitou as it passed through Colorado City. Also, there were no curbs along the roadway. The rails did not have exposed cross-ties, as the space between the rails was dirt filled making it a continuation of the roadbed.

The driver stated as he crossed the right-hand track, a rear wheel slid against the rail and suddenly they were in the ditch. He believed—regardless of how much he may have had to drink—he was clear headed and the drink did not affect his ability to control the vehicle.[9]

When I was a police officer, it seemed everyone I suspected of driving under the influence always stated they only had two drinks and never drove over 35 miles per hour. As has been learned since 1907, a person does not have to be falling down drunk to be under the influence and have their abilities to control a motor vehicle affected. In this case, the speed limit was 18 miles per hour, because it was in the city of Colorado Springs, but outside the fire limits.

Interestingly a few weeks earlier on Labor Day there were races at the Denver area Overland Race Track. Two men were killed during the race. Marksheffel entered his Ford 3-seat racing car. He was believed to be the one who ran over C.V. Dasey during the race.[10] Obviously, this did not temper his driving on the night of the fatal accident.

The write up of the accident in the *Colorado City Iris* stated before leaving Colorado City the members of the party spent time on West Washington Avenue.[11] Today, that street is Cucharras, and is the first street south of Colorado Avenue. The speed at which Marksheffel was driving after he passed 8th Street and approached the curve may have caused the steering not to respond. The vehicle ran into the ditch box on the south side with its right wheels. Crossing the irrigating ditch and colliding with the utility pole caused the car to turn around before coming to a stop, making it face to the west. Because of the sudden stop of the machine, the occupants were all ejected.[12]

Albert W. Marksheffel's 6-cylinder Ford had nine men in the vehicle, three were killed. Courtesy of Pikes Peak Library District, Special Collections, Margaretta M. Boss Collection.

Colorado Springs horse-mounted officer Henry Cornell was near Limit Street when he saw a car coming from the west towards him from about four blocks. Because he believed the car was speeding, he tried to signal the driver to stop, but the car flew on by. The officer believed the car was traveling 60 miles per hour. The officer then pursued the vehicle and about 1½ blocks away he heard the crash. He was soon on the scene and saw four bodies on the ground. Going to the nearest police call box, he notified the police headquarters that he needed the ambulance and the coroner.

Several times the district attorney tried to pin down what the surviving members of the party believed was a safe speed for attempting the turn, but none would give a definitive answer. One member, Ward, stated he was sure that Marksheffel applied the brakes before entering the turn, lowering the speed by maybe five miles per hour, slowing the car to 30 to 35 miles per hour.[13]

Marksheffel's trial in district court, originally set for November 1907, was reset to February 1908 with the charge of involuntary manslaughter.[14] A Pueblo newspaper wrote in March 1908, they believed that Marksheffel was likely to go free of the charges. "The case has been continued until public sentiment has worn out."[15] On Saturday, October 3, 1908, it was reported that Albert W. Marksheffel was acquitted of the charge of involuntary manslaughter after a directed verdict by District Court Judge John W. Sheafor. Even though the prosecutor put on evidence from the coroner's inquest—a record of the inquest was made by a stenographer—the judge stated that the prosecution failed to make a case, Marksheffel's attorney did not even have to put on a single witness or mount any kind of defense.[16]

By 1911, Marksheffel had bought out his partners in the auto dealership and it was renamed Marksheffel Motor Company.[17] With the operation of a successful business, Marksheffel planned in 1914 to build a new building, to be located at the southwest corner of Cascade Avenue and Kiowa Street. (today's location of the Penrose Library). It was to cost $50,000.[18] The following year an addition was added to the new auto dealership at the cost of $10,000.[19] In May of 1917 while this extremely large dealership was being expanded, Marksheffel married Dr. Zeo Zoe (Wilkins) Cunningham secretly in Pueblo.[20] Mrs. Cunningham was an osteopath. Marksheffel was to be her 5th husband and Zeo, his third wife. Marksheffel met Mrs. Wilkins when she brought her 70-plus year-old previous husband to Colorado Springs. Mrs. Thomas (Wilkins) Cunningham, obtained over $300,000 in a settlement for a divorce from Cunningham.[21] Zeo (Wilkins) Cunningham was described as a very beautiful woman, who was successful at scamming all her previous husbands out of their money before dropping them like a bad penny.[22]

Marksheffel met Mrs. Cunningham while she was living at 21 East Willamette Avenue in Colorado Springs for a short time with her former husband, a multi-millionaire banker from Joplin, Missouri. Marksheffel acted as a driver for the young woman. After her divorce she returned to Colorado Springs where Marksheffel was operating the largest auto dealership in the United States.[23] As she had with her previous husbands, she began her pursuit of Marksheffel.

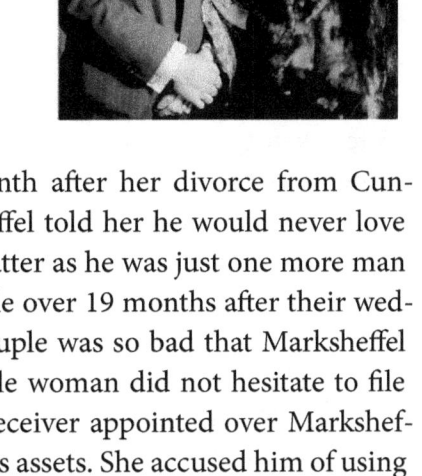

Zeo Zoe and A.W. Marksheffel.
Pikes Peak Library District,
Special Collection,
Margaretta M. Boss
Collection. 001-6126.

Zeo married Albert one month after her divorce from Cunningham in April 1917. Marksheffel told her he would never love her, but that did not appear to matter as he was just one more man to defrock of his fortunes.[24] A little over 19 months after their wedding, the tension between the couple was so bad that Marksheffel "disappeared" from town. The little woman did not hesitate to file suit in district court wanting a receiver appointed over Marksheffel's estate so she could liquidate its assets. She accused him of using her money to make her all but penniless. Judge John S. Little appointed her as the receiver.[25]

A little over two weeks passed before Marksheffel returned to the Springs and answered the suit filed in the court. He denied all of her claims.[26] After being unsuccessful in her suit against Marksheffel, a divorce was filed in Colorado being concluded

July of 1921. After reclaiming her name of Wilkins, she moved to Kansas City, Missouri and rented a house at 2425 Park Avenue. She restarted as an osteopath, working out of the home.[27] Dr. Wilkins had squandered the fortunes she had obtained from her previous husbands, estimated to be over $1,500,000. (2024 value of over $26 million). In fact, a judgment was obtained by a Colorado Springs man which required the sale of her car.[28]

In March the doctor was found in her home with her throat slashed. It was approximately three days after her death when she was found. The murder was thought to have happened Saturday, March 15, 1924. She lived alone at the home. It remains as an unsolved homicide. She was described by newspapers as a "heart pirate and marriage adventuress."[29] After her death, many articles were published across the nation describing her trail of broken romances, and her deceptions to obtain her real love—money. Though intelligent, and a beauty, she was ruthless in her dealings with people, especially husbands. It appeared she may have really cared for Marksheffel, but he was the one man who did not fall completely into her clutches. In a manner of speaking, they both were taken to task for past deeds. Although death was her final sentence. Marksheffel, after three unsuccessful marriages, did not participate in the matrimonial process again. He operated a very successful auto dealership until his passing in 1938. Born in Manhattan, Kansas in 1881, he was 57 when he died in Colorado Springs. He is buried at Evergreen Cemetery. Regretfully, he was never held responsible for the deaths of three men in the traffic accident of 1907. It is interesting to note, on September 10, 1910, New York was the first state to pass drunk driving laws. California soon followed. These laws made it illegal to drive under the influence of alcohol.

Three of nine occupants were instantly killed and a fourth is hovering between life and death…what is wondered is not that some were killed, but any escaped alive.—The Bakersfield Californian, September 1907

Notes

1. *Colorado Springs Evening Telegraph*, 17 Sep 1907, Page 1.
2. *Colorado Springs Gazette*, 18 Sep 1907, Page 1.
3. *Colorado Springs Evening Telegraph*, 18 Sep 1907, Page 1.
4. *Colorado Springs Gazette*, 19 Sep 1907, Page 1.
5. *Colorado Springs Gazette*, 27 Sep 1907, Page 1.
6. *Colorado Springs Evening Telegraph*, 17 Sep 1907, Page 1.
7. *Colorado Springs Gazette*, 19 Sep 1907, Page 1.
8. *Colorado Springs Gazette*, 18 Sep 1907, Page 1.
9. *Colorado Springs Gazette*, 18 Sep 1907, Page 1.
10. *Colorado City Iris*, 20 Sep 1907, Page 1.
11. *Brothels, Bordellos, & Bad Girls — Prostitution in Colorado — 1860-1930* by Jan Mackell, 2004, University of New Mexico Press, Pages 72, 75.
12. *Colorado City Iris*, 20 Sep 1907, Page 1.
13. *Colorado Springs Evening Telegraph*, 18 Sep 1907, Page 1.
14. *Colorado Springs Gazette*, 21 Jan 1908, Page 5.
15. *Pueblo Sun*, 04 Mar 1908, Page 4.
16. *Colorado Springs Gazette*, 03 Oct 1908, Page 5.
17. *Colorado Springs Gazette*, 08 Jan 1911. Page 10.
18. *Colorado Springs Gazette*, 17 Jan 1914, Page 1.
19. *Colorado Springs Gazette*, 27 Jan 1915, Page 5.
20. *Manhattan Mercury*, 12 May 1917, Page 3.
21. *St. Louis Star & Times*, 10 Apr 1917, Page 8.
22. *Ogden Standard-Examiner*, 04 May 1924, Page 2.
23. *Colorado Springs Gazette*, 30 May 1917, Page 5.
24. *Ogden Standard-Examiner*, 04 May 1924, Page 2.
25. *Colorado Springs Gazette*, 29 Jan 1919, Page 1.
26. *Colorado Springs Gazette*, 09 Feb 1919, Page 5.
27. *Colorado Springs Gazette*, 19 Mar 1924, Page 1.
28. *Colorado Springs Evening Telegraph*, 20 Mar 1924, Page 2.
29. *Muskogee Daily Phoenix*, 22 Mar 1924, Page 1.

Chapter 15

ADVENTURES OF THE MOTORCYCLE

The first Harley-Davidson police motorcycle was delivered to the Detroit Police Department in 1908. Right from the start, police departments recognized the tactical advantage provided by a maneuverable vehicle such as a motorcycle along with Harley-Davidson's reputation for reliability. — https://policemotorunits.com

The CSPD did not purchase a non-horse powered vehicle until it bought a motorcycle in April 1910.[1] The motorcycle had a bad experience within its first three months. Speed Officer George Carpenter, while riding on Chestnut Street, was struck by an electric truck of Wandell & Lowe Transfer & Storage Company. Other than suffering torn clothing and bruises, the officer was able to walk away, but not so for the motorcycle. The cost to repair the motorcycle was $96.50.[2]

During January of 1912, the department purchased its second motorcycle, costing $192.50. This was followed in February 1912, when Police Commissioner James A. Himebaugh and Police Chief Stanley D. Burno completed the purchase of an automobile. This would replace the patrol wagon and horses.[3] This vehicle was a four-passenger Buick costing $1,100.[4]

April of the same year two patrolmen were sent out on motorcycles to stop ruffians driving through the streets with open mufflers! Three men were arrested by the motor officers for riding at night without lights and in a reckless regard.[5]

Believing there were too many motorcycle accidents occurring, City Council asked the city attorney to draft an ordinance making it unlawful to carry a passenger on the front of a motorcycle. In the previous month of March 1913, there had been four motorcycle accidents. There were two accidents where young ladies riding on the front of a motorcycle were injured, but the proposed ordinance would not prohibit passengers from riding on the rear of the cycles.[6]

Councilman Johnson in August 1915, traded in one of the old motorcycles to purchase a new one for $285.00.[7] Soon after, Councilman Johnson again traded in an old motorcycle to purchase a new one from Lucas Sporting Goods Company and spent $255.00.[8]

Wednesday night, the 30th of June, 1926, Officer George L. Taylor, a motorcycle officer, was set up on the south end of town after learning that a car had been stolen in Pueblo and was believed to be headed north. About 10:30 p.m., the officer spotted the stolen vehicle entering Colorado Springs at Las Vegas Street and South Nevada Avenue. The officer attempted to get the Cole 8 auto to stop.

1925 Cole 8 motorcar.
Photograph public domain.

He followed it east on Fountain Street to Weber Street where it neared Las Animas Street and headed into an alley. At this time the officer fired three shots at the vehicle. A passenger returned fire at the officer, but he was not struck. The car then crossed the railroad tracks on Fountain Street, and the officer had to slow down because the street's sand surface was soft and made it hard to ride the motorcycle across it. The car was able to escape the officer.

Officer Taylor went to the headquarters and obtained more ammunition and reinforcements. Deputy Chief Fred H. Springer took out a car and helped look for the stolen car. Taylor returned to the area where he lost sight of the car and was able to follow the tire tracks until the car was located on a dead-end road approaching Prospect Lake, but the thieves were already gone.[9]

1926 motocycles in front of City Auditorium. L-R: Officers, Cecil Caldwell, M.L Risc, J.E. Sanders, Larry Kelleher, Hugh Y. Higgins, George Taylor, Olin Burton, and Roy Chapin. Courtesy of Pioneers Museum.

A month had barely passed before Officer George Taylor was involved in another chase and gun-battle while working on his motorcycle. About 8:00 p.m. the officer saw what he believed was a suspicious car. He stopped the car which contained two shabbily dressed men who said they purchased the auto in Chicago for $500. Taylor did not believe that anyone could purchase a Chrysler roadster for $500, so he ordered them to drive to police headquarters. The officer followed the car until they were near the station. The auto driver forced the officer's motorcycle against the curb and made a run for it. The passenger aimed a rifle at the officer and fired. The officer did not return fire as he feared he might hit an innocent person.

The officer immediately took pursuit of the miscreants. The stolen auto headed north, with the intent of getting on the road to Denver thereby escaping the city. Taylor pursued them to a curve in the far north end where he received four more rifle shots and upset the motorcycle. The motorcycle's speedometer was locked at 74 miles per hour, when he laid it down. Somehow, the officer walked away without sustaining any major injuries.

After this incident occurred, Chief Harper announced he was going to have sidecars installed on the motorcycles, so they would have two officers with each machine instead of just one.

Notes

1 *Colorado Springs Gazette*, 08 Apr 1910, Page 12.
2 Colorado Springs City Council Minutes, Book 12, Page 312.
3 *Colorado Springs Gazette*, 10 Feb 1912, Page 6.
4 *Colorado Springs Gazette*, 12 Feb 1912, Page 8.
5 *Colorado Springs Gazette*, 06 Apr 1912, Page 5.
6 *Colorado Springs Evening Telegraph*, 07 Apr 1913, Page 7.
7 Colorado Springs City Council Minutes, 25 Aug 1915, Book 14, Page 434.
8 Colorado Springs City Council Minutes, 03 May 1918, Book 15, Page 318.
9 *Colorado Springs Gazette Telegraph*, 01 Jul 1926, Page 1.

Chapter 16

SERIAL KILLER WITH AN AXE?

A serial killer is defined as a person who commits a series of murders, often with no apparent motive and typically following a characteristic, predictable behavior pattern. — Oxford Language Dictionary

On Sunday, September 17, 1911, an unknown person entered two homes at 321 West Dale Street and 742 Harrison Place. The homes, located next to each other, would be the site where six people were murdered by someone using an axe.

The following Wednesday, Mrs. June Ruth went to the home of her sister Alice Burnham on West Dale Street to do some sewing and was accompanied by Miss Anna Merritt. They found the front door locked. June believed her sister might have walked to Miss Merritt's home so they made a trip there and back but did not find Alice. With a key to the Burnham home, they were able to unlock the rear door and enter the home. After making a gruesome discovery the two women rushed across the street to Collins Grocery and made calls to the police and coroner. They had found Alice Burnham on the bed covered in blood. Blood was sprayed on the walls and on the floor. Beside the woman were two children's bodies with their heads smashed like their mother's.

Upon hearing the women's alarm many neighbors came outside. After officers arrived at the scene, one onlooker, Mrs. Nealie A. Campbell, mentioned no one had seen the Wayne family, who lived next door, in several days. It was found the shades to the

Wayne home were all drawn closed. Acting Chief of Police Fred H. Springer found the front door of the Wayne home locked and got no response, so he forced the door open. The family of three was found with their heads smashed like those of the Burnham family.[1] Other than the families living next door to each other, there was no connection.

Arthur J. Burnham, husband and father of the murdered family, was a cook at the Modern Woodmen sanatorium about nine miles northwest of Colorado Springs. He suffered from consumption (tuberculosis) and was at the sanatorium when the murders occurred. However, the police went straight to the institution and arrested him for the crime. He was described as 41-years-old and not strong physically.

Mrs. Burnham was described as 25, with two children. The children, Alice and John, were six and three years old respectively. In the Wayne's family were Henry F. Wayne, 24, his wife Blanche, 22, and their two-year-old baby daughter, Blanche. Interestingly, the motive did not seem to be robbery as there were valuables, including jewelry, left undisturbed.[2]

Dr. James A. Rutledge, Superintendent of the Woodman Sanatorium, explained that Arthur Burnham was in the third stage of tuberculosis. He would not be able to mount a horse or walk a hundred yards without coughing his head off. The sanatorium had a night watchman and Burnham's tremendous cough would absolutely attract the guard's attention. Burnham's only movement was to sit all day and peel potatoes. When he would eat, he had to use both hands to lift his dinner bowl. Making a trip to Colorado Springs, killing six people by swinging an axe and then riding back to the sanitorium would not be possible.[3]

Mrs. Burnham was last seen alive on Sunday evening about 9:30 p.m. by her sister when she stopped by the Burnham house for tea.[4] Two weeks earlier ladies within a block or two of the crime scene told police they saw a man acting in an insane manner. The women attacked the man with hoes and brooms, running him off.

He had been seen since that time, but avoided the adversarial ladies.

Bertillon fingerprint expert Superintendent L. Seymour from the Thiel Detective Agency[5] traveled from Denver to check the homes for possible fingerprints. The detective put mercury and chalk where he believed there were prints and then transferred these images to paper.[6] The night of the tragedies the moon did not come up until just before morning, so it would have been very dark.[7] In those days there were no street lights.

Twelve investigators from the Denver Police Department, the El Paso County Sheriff's Office, Thiel Detective Agency, and two officers of the Pinkerton Agency had involved themselves in the investigation. The sheriff's office took the lead in the investigation but were not getting anywhere in discovering a culprit or culprits. Then on the 27th of September the investigation was handed over to the Pinkertons.[8] Any agency or officers that could solve this homicide would have quite a feather in their cap.

Ira Weedman, an officer in the Denver Police Department, wrote a letter to the *Gazette* city editor on the 25th. He explained that he had worked on 17 homicides with 13 solved. He bragged that he worked 18 out of 24 hours each day. He made a sales pitch to the Colorado Springs citizens. He wanted to be in complete charge of the murder investigation—with the understanding he would be made chief of police in Colorado Springs when he solved this case.

Seven days after the murders, a carefully concealed axe was discovered under the rear stairway of a vacant home south of Wayne's residence. It was covered with hair and blood. It appeared to be the murder weapon.[9]

Because of friction between the Colorado Springs Police Department and El Paso Sheriff's Office there was not much cooperation. Having the Denver police involved also added to the strain of finding out who had committed the crimes. The Pinkertons opened a local office at the Joyce Hotel, 10 South Weber Street.

"Experts," were putting forth this was a woman's crime, unlikely done by a man.[10]

J. Ward Erb from the Pinkerton agency, announced their investigation would be concluded the next day. He hinted two men and a woman were soon to be arrested for the crime. This was a problem during the early part of 20th century. Often private detective firms would declare that they had solved a case and that would be last heard about the case![11]

A coroner's inquest was held on Saturday, September 30, 1911. Investigators believed not enough evidence was available to hold an inquest and no suspect had been identified. Many of the coroner's jurors were unhappy with the process. The only statement the jury could make was; the deaths occurred on Sunday, September 17, 1911. The killing was felonious, with no suspect.[12] Then the CSPD received some clippings with regard to murders in and near Portland, Oregon. Nine people were killed in a crime that mirrored the case in Colorado Springs.[13] Also, there were similar cases in Rainier, Washington and Monmouth, Illinois.[14] Commissioner of Public Safety J.A. Himebaugh received a letter from Police Chief E.C. Hilyer and the district attorney of Monmouth, Illinois. In the murders in their location, the entry into a home and method of killing were a copy of Colorado Springs.[15] In Monmouth, a flashlight was discovered at the scene which had "Colorado Springs, September 4" etched in the instrument.[16]

The *Gazette* reported a similar crime had occurred October 15, 1911, in Ellsworth, Kansas. Five people were killed: husband, wife and three children.

On Monday, February 6, 1912, Arthur J. Burnham died at St. Francis Hospital at 7:00 a.m.[17] The murder of his family remains unsolved.

My research has led me to believe these people were victims of a serial killer. In each of the above-mentioned cases the victims' residences were located near the railroad. This was the mode of transportation during the early 1900s.

Following is a list of crimes that occurred around the same time pointing to a serial murderer, all with blows to the head by an axe with exception to one done with a hammer:

Ardenwald, Oregon - Friday, 09 Jun 1911
 Four people while asleep in their bed.[18]
Rainier, Washington - Monday, 10 Jul 1911
 A young couple in their beds, less than 90 miles away from the people in Oregon.[19]
Colorado Springs, Colorado - Sunday, 17 Sep 1911
 Six people in two homes next door to each other.[20]
Monmouth, Illinois - Sunday, 01 Oct 1911
 Three people.[21]
Ellsworth, Kansas - Sunday, 15 Oct 1911
 Five people, two adults and three children.[22]
Paola, Kansas - Wednesday, 05 Jun 1912
 A young couple killed with a brick mason's hammer.[23]
Villisca, Iowa - Sunday, 09 Jun 1912
 Two adults and six children.[24]

The idea of a serial killer was not a concept well known when these crimes occurred, although the case of Jack the Ripper (late 1880s) in England would have been known. I believe these axe murders were committed by the same person—a serial killer—riding the railroad, possibly as a hobo. None of the families murdered were well-to-do, but just average folks. It appears this crime spree began in Ardenwald, Oregon, just outside Portland with the murderer moving across the country to the east. In the early 1900s there were many unsolved homicides, but the ones listed here formed a pattern, a modus operandi, if you will. Fingerprints were found at some of the scenes and in others, the information went unreported. Every year police departments in the United States work harder at sharing information. Credit for solving a crime is still desired, but solving the crime itself, I believe, is more important. Regretfully, I will not ever be able to prove my theory that these were all committed by one person. If fingerprints of the scenes could be compared, it would only take one match to back my thinking.

Notes

1	*Colorado Springs Gazette*, 21 Sep 1911, Page 1.
2	Colorado Springs Herald-Telegraph, 20 Sep 1911, Page 1.
3	Colorado Springs Herald-Telegraph, 21 Sep 1911, Page 1.
4	Colorado Springs Herald-Telegraph, 21 Sep 1911, Page 1.
5	*Colorado Springs Gazette*, 23 Sep 1911, Page 1.
6	Colorado Springs Herald-Telegraph, 23 Sep 1911, Page 2.
7	Colorado Springs Herald-Telegraph, 25 Sep 1911, Page 2.
8	Colorado Springs Herald-Telegraph, 27 Sep 1911, Page 1.
9	Colorado Springs Herald-Telegraph, 27 Sep 1911, Page 1.
10	*Colorado Springs Gazette*, 28 Sep 1911, Page 1.
11	*Colorado Springs Gazette*, 29 Sep 1911, Page 1.
12	Colorado Springs Herald-Telegraph, 30 Sep 1911, Page 1.
13	*Colorado Springs Gazette*, 30 Sep 1911, Page 1.
14	*Colorado Springs Gazette*, 03 Oct 1911, Page 6.
15	*Colorado Springs Gazette*, 08 Oct 1911, Page 5.
16	*Colorado Springs Gazette*, 18 Oct 1911, Page 1.
17	*Colorado Springs Gazette*, 06 Feb 1912, Page 1.
18	*Portland Morning Oregonian*, 10 Jun 1911, Page 12.
19	*Rainier Morning Olympian*, 12 Jul 1911, Page 1.
20	*Colorado Springs Herald-Telegraph*, 20 Sep 1911, Page 1.
21	*Moline Dispatch*, 02 Oct 1911, Page 1.
22	*Topeka State Journal*, 18 Oct 1911, Page 1.
23	*Junction City Union*, 07 Jun 1912, Page 1.
24	*Bayard News*, 13 Jun 1912, Page 3.

Chapter 17

WOMEN HAVE ARRIVED, EVER SO SLOWLY

In the United States on December 16, 1891, City Health Department Inspector Marie Owens was appointed to the Chicago Police Department as a police officer assigned to the Detective Bureau, becoming the nation's earliest-known female sworn law enforcement officer. — The Department of Justice

The first mention of women being possibly involved with the CSPD was in 1892. The Humane Society requested of City Council for a matron to take care of women prisoners. The matter was referred to the Police Committee and the marshal, but nothing further was located about this matter.[1] With regard to a matron, Mrs. J. Chezum applied to the Police Committee in 1905 with the hopes to be appointed as police matron. The council read her letter and referred it to the Police Committee, but there did not seem to be any follow-up.[2] In the *Colorado Springs City Directories*, from 1904 through 1908, Mrs. J. Chezum was listed as a widow and had a son in school, but there was no listing of any employment.[3]

By November of 1913, citizen's groups were requesting the hiring of a policewoman. The judge of the juvenile court, William Palmer Kinney, announced he was proposing in the budgeting for 1914 for two positions working out of the court.[4] However, this did not come to pass, as the county commissioners declared they just did not believe such a thing was necessary.[5]

Just days later, a group of sixteen individual businessmen met with the county commissioners to discuss the need for a policewoman. They noted that the "Mother's Compensation Act" provided for two juvenile officers for El Paso County. Commissioners argued that the Act did not provide enough money to pay for this and they did not plan on using any other money, so the request died.[6]

Georgia S. Easley, Colorado College Senior Ppicture, 1923.
Courtesy of Colorado College.

By January 1914, the City Council, being pressured by the Civic League, were giving hiring women lip service, at least, and were writing other communities for information as to how such women were employed and their duties, etc. It was recommended to the City Council that a policewoman should be paid $100 per month.[7] In June of that year, Mrs. Georgia S. Easley was hired as an experiment for the summer months. She was referred to as a policewoman, but would not be a uniformed officer. She was to work with young people at amusement attractions, parks, etc.[8] Mrs. Easley was officially titled as a social investigator and did not have powers of arrest, thus, she was not a policewoman.

By November, Commissioner of Public Safety Daniel G. Johnson, remarked the experiment was successful, but was not up to what they expected. Also, the budget was being downsized for the next year, and he did not believe there would be room for hiring a woman. Maybe if there was more work, employment would be reconsidered.[9]

June of 1915, found Mrs. Easley hired again, with an office in police headquarters. She was responsible for developing her duties. While she would work directly for Commissioner of Public Safety D.G. Johnson, he did not believe a woman's place was with the police department. Mrs. Easley would work with young girls and their parents who felt they could use some advice on how to raise a young girl.[10]

Returning to this position the following summer, Easley was responsible for helping settle quarrels between neighbors, searching woman prisoners, watching over dances and stopping inappropriate behavior of the male variety concerning young women, among other things.[11]

Carrie Louise (Dench) Stetson. Courtesy of CSPD.

Fall of 1917, a second woman, Mrs. Louise D. Stetson, was proposed to work with Mrs. Easley. With the opening of more dance halls, Mrs. Easley was unable to cover all of the duties required. However, Mayor Charles E. Thomas refused to appoint a second woman. He said the woman was being paid $100 per month and it was more than patrolmen were making.[12]

The Federation of Women's Clubs wrote to the City Council urging the hiring of an additional woman.[13] The following day a letter was printed in the editorial section of "Open Parliament" from Lyda M. Touzalin, who took the mayor to task for not hiring a second woman to assist Mrs. Easley.[14] Much consternation was had by several groups appearing at the City Council meetings representing organizations such as the Women's Society of the First Presbyterian Church and the City Federation of Women's Clubs, along with a number of individual women. A motion was made by a councilman to put the $900 for another woman back into the following year's budget, but it failed for a lack of a second.[15]

The mayor found himself being protested for his lack of action, and women picketed around the city hall for three days. Council members overrode the mayor and the money for the second woman was put back into the following year's budget. Following the pressure of the citizens, and the backing of at least three of the council members, the mayor acquiesced and Mrs. Stetson was hired.[16] She was officially hired the fifth of December.[17]

In November of 1918, Mrs. Easley resigned because of a ruling by Mayor Thomas that she would be reporting to the police chief instead of the commissioner of public safety.[18] The next day Mrs. Stetson also resigned for similar reasons.[19]

Mrs. Frankie W. Eagan was hired by the mayor in January 1919. Eagan had worked in El Paso County, Texas for five years as a probation officer, was the mother of two preteen children and was a widow.[20] Things seemed to work well for a year and then in January 1920, Commissioner of Public Safety D.G. Johnson, refused to approve the salaries of two police officers and Mrs. Eagan. He did not believe the three were recorded in the city clerk's office as permanent employees. The real reason for the hoopla was the commissioner had been in France working for the YMCA when the mayor made the three people's appointments and Johnson was upset that he did not have a say in the matter. Since he was upset, he decided to suspend Mrs. Eagan for ten days, not paying her. Johnson said Mrs. Eagan did not properly supervise the dance halls.[21]

A resolution (No. 1110) was presented to the City Council by

Mayor Thomas that said a mayor or council member could be removed from the office because of inability or willful neglect of duties. This was the consequence of the actions of Councilman Daniel G. Johnson, the Commissioner of Public Safety. It was proposed that he had improperly notified the Civil Service Commission about change of employment of members of the police department and refused to approve the payroll of employees in his department without cause. These were just two of the charges presented against the commissioner, and a hearing by the council members was scheduled to see if the commissioner should be removed from office.[22]

The hearing of Commissioner Johnson began on Friday, May 14, and was completed 14 days later with the removal of the commissioner from the City Council.[23] Mrs. Eagan returned to her work and her pay situation was corrected by the council. She continued to work till May of 1921, when she resigned from the city.[24] It was not until the end of November before another woman, Mrs. Elizabeth S. Morse, was hired. Her position was to be in the office of the city manager, working with the police department.[25] She served in this position until September of 1926 after she had remarried, and offered her resignation. Friday, September 17, 1926, Dorothy M. Springer was hired as the replacement.[26]

The city had been receiving pressure from a citizen's group known as "The Taxpayer's Association" who wanted to see reduction in salaries of certain members of the city's employees. It was believed to be a move to anger the citizenry over the pressure of this group, City Manager E.L. Mosley wrote a letter to Mrs. Springer, telling her that her position was discontinued as of July 1, 1932.[27]

The city went until July of 1934 before the hiring of a new social investigator. Then Dorothy J. Kemp was added to the city's payroll, again working from the office of the city manager.[28] The salary of Miss Kemp was $100 per month, the same as was paid in 1917.[29] In May of 1936, Miss Kemp married Lawrence Glenn Heller, and continued her work with the city.[30] Mrs. Heller worked in this position until 1962, when City Manager John M. Biery moved her position from his office to that of the police department.³¹ Mrs. Heller, after completing thirty-one years as the city's social investigator, retired.³²

Dorothy Jean (Kemp) Heller, 1961. Courtesy of CSPD.

Miss Barbara J. Herzberger, age 22, was named the next social investigator, replacing Mrs. Heller, on July 1, 1965. She had just graduated from the University of Colorado the previous month.³³ Miss Herzberger stayed about one year before being replaced by Charlotte Ann Mahan. According to her oath of office, she was sworn in as a probationary "policewoman in the police department" on August 1, 1966, at a starting salary of $422 per month.³⁴

In a newspaper article in December 1972, City Personnel Director Norman Gieseker, was interviewed with regards to the hiring of women police officers. The possibilities were being investigated after a civil rights complaint had been filed by a woman against the City of Colorado Springs.

It was determined that in the city code there were no provisions for hiring women as officers under civil service and the one woman (Charlotte Mahan) wasn't considered a uniformed status officer.³⁵

At a civil service meeting, of August 13, 1973, a discussion was held with regards to the former Charlotte Mahan (now Morris) being classified as a patrolman first class and making her eligible for police pension benefits.[36] The police pension rules required that a police officer had to have 25 years of service and be a minimum age of 55 years to retire. Mahan was born in 1929, so in August of 1973, she was 44-years of age. That would mean for a normal retirement, for a starting date in 1966, the earliest date to retire would be 1991. Mahan would be 62 years old. Although that would not have been an unreachable goal, she had been with the department for seven years and was under the Colorado Public Employees Retirement Fund and not under the police pension. This then required a very large payment into the police pension fund so she could be eligible for a police officer retirement.

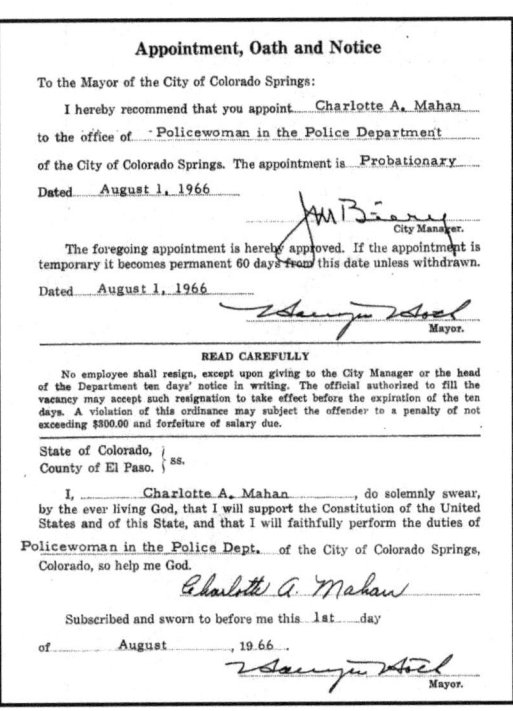

Charlotte A. Mahan's initial hiring Oath of Office. Courtesy of CSPD.

More policewomen were not hired until December of 1973 when Kathleen A. Flynn and Cheryl E. McKinney were hired as police officers. This marked the beginning of regular hiring of women for the department.[37]

On April 1, 1975, Charlotte Ann (Nolan) (Mahan) (Wittges)

(Morris) Buckley, was sworn in as the first female uniformed sergeant of the Colorado Springs Police Department.[38] This was followed by her promotion to the rank of lieutenant on January 5, 1979—the first female lieutenant.[39] Not stopping there, she was promoted to the rank of captain on May 4, 1986,[40] being the first female captain, a rank she retained until her retirement on August 1, 1989, after 23 years of service.[41]

By 2023 of the 821 sworn officers, the department was represented by 130 (16%) female officers.

Notes

1 Colorado Springs City Council Minutes, 16 May 1892, Book 4, Page 301.
2 Colorado Springs City Council Minutes, 04 May 1905, Book 9, Page 463.
3 *Colorado Springs City Directories*, 1904 through 1908.
4 *Colorado Springs Gazette*, 22 Nov 1913, Page 5.
5 *Colorado Springs Gazette*, 30 Nov 1913, Page 5.
6 *Colorado Springs Gazette*, 02 Dec 1913, Page 1.
7 *Colorado Springs Gazette*, 08 Jan 1914, Page 1.
8 *Colorado Springs Gazette*, 07 May 1914, Page 1.
9 *Colorado Springs Gazette*, 14 Nov 1914, Page 5.
10 *Colorado Springs Gazette*, 20 Jun 1915, Page 5.
11 *Colorado Springs Gazette*, 23 Jul 1916, Page 6.
12 *Colorado Springs Evening Telegraph*, 26 Oct 1917, Page 1.
13 Colorado Springs City Council Minutes, 07 Nov 1917, Book 15, Page 256.
14 *Colorado Springs Gazette*, 08 Nov 1917, Page 4.
15 Colorado Springs City Council Minutes, 21 Nov 1917, Book 15, Page 261.
16 *Colorado Springs Evening Telegraph*, 27 Nov 1917, Page 9.
17 Colorado Springs City Council Minutes, 05 Dec 1917, Book 15, Page 269.
18 *Colorado Springs Evening Telegraph*, 11 Nov 1918, Page 5.
19 *Colorado Springs Gazette*, 12 Nov 1918, Page 6.
20 *Colorado Springs Gazette*, 12 Jan 1919, Page 7.
21 *Colorado Springs Gazette*, 17 Jan 1920, Page 1.
22 Colorado Springs City Council Minutes, 05 May 1920, Book 16, Page 144.
23 Colorado Springs City Council Minutes, 28 May 1920, Book 16, Page 180.
24 *Colorado Springs Gazette*, 21 May 1921, Page 1.
25 *Colorado Springs Evening Telegraph*, 09 Jan 1923, Page 1.
26 *Colorado Springs Gazette* and Telegraph, 01 Jul 1928.
27 Common Sense Weekly, 10 Jun 1932, Page 1.
28 Letter to Chief Harper from City Manager E.L. Mosley, 24 Jul 1934.
29 *Colorado Springs Gazette* and Telegraph, 25 Jul 1934, Page 10.
30 Colorado Marriage record, 29 May 1936.
31 City of Colorado Springs, Inter-Office Memorandum, 19 Dec 1961.
32 *Colorado Springs Gazette* and Telegraph, 09 May 1965, Page C2.
33 *Colorado Springs Free Press*, 01 Jul 1965, Page 9.
34 *Colorado Springs Free Press*, 03 Aug 1966, Page 12.
35 *Colorado Springs Gazette* Telegraph, 03 Aug 1966.
36 Colorado Springs Civil Service Minutes, 13 Aug 1973.
37 *Colorado Springs Gazette* Telegraph, 06 Jan 2974, Page D1.
38 Colorado Springs Appointment, Oath and Notice, 01 Apr 1975.
39 Colorado Springs Appointment, Oath and Notice, 01 Apr 1979.
40 Colorado Springs Appointment, Oath and Notice, 04 May 1986.
41 *Colorado Springs Gazette* Telegraph, 04 Aug 1989. Page B6.

Chapter 18

THE DAY THE CHIEF OF DETECTIVES DIED

The first gang incident in the newly formed Colorado Territory of 1861 was the Espinosa gang. In 1863 they went on a rampage from southern Colorado into the middle ranges west of Pikes Peak, killing over 30 people. Colorado's first serial killers moved north through Colorado City before their ultimate demise at the hands of former Army Scout Thomas Tate Tobins. — Denver Tribune-Republican, 28 Feb 1886.

Criminal gangs were well known in the "wild west" during the years following the Civil War. The West was wide open with the law few in numbers. Names like Billy the Kid, the Dalton Gang, Butch Cassidy, and Soapy Smith are familiar today. Soapy and his fellow gang of con men ran the bunco racket in Denver in the late 1800s. Soapy was known to visit Colorado City for gambling, drink and women.

Colorado City, founded in 1859, became the western most portion of Colorado Springs on Saturday, June 9th, 1917.[1] Colorado City had been Colorado Territory's first capitol. The annexation of Colorado City gave Colorado Springs the opportunity to obtain John W. Rowan for the Colorado Springs Police Department. Rowan had served as a police officer in Colorado City and as a special agent for the Denver & Rio Grande railroad for 14 years. He shortly worked his way to the position of chief of detectives of Colorado Springs, a position he held in 1918.[2]

By 1918, the city's population was around 30,000 people. The area was thriving with people arriving for health reasons and also tourism. The residents of El Paso County were the proud owners of over 1,400 automobiles of over 115 different makes.[3] The prosperous town founded with "No Alcohol Allowed" was not a place to expect wild west style gangs.

The city, although growing, was a quiet place to live and raise a family. Crime was very low. Then, 1918 happened. On Friday, the 13th of September, the city's second police officer was killed in a shoot-out downtown at Colorado and Nevada Avenues. This would become a Friday the 13th to remember.

The Frank Lewis-Dale Jones gang had been causing havoc throughout Missouri and Kansas since around 1913, robbing banks and stores. The gang was involved in the deaths of seven police officers in those states. The gang moved west arriving in Denver in September of 1918. On Friday, the 13th, Pinkerton National Detective Agency Agent Joseph F. Miller, hired a car and followed members of the gang to Colorado Springs. Miller followed Dale Jones, his wife Margie and Roscoe "Kansas City Blackie" Lancaster who were in a stolen Marmon auto. Upon arrival in Colorado Springs, Miller stopped at the police headquarters and warned the officers the gang was in town. The Pinkertons had sent information ahead to all the major cities in the West about the gang.[4]

While Miller was speaking to the officers, the headquarters received a telephone call from Frank Henderson of the Pikes Peak Petroleum service station, located on the northeast corner of Colorado and Nevada Avenues. Earlier all the filling stations had received a call from the police to keep a look out for a stolen Marmon. Around 3:00 p.m. the suspected vehicle pulled into the station. Awaiting their turn to use the gas pump, the occupants were parked behind a Hudson vehicle driven by Mrs. Mary B. Harmon, whose car was being filled with fuel. One of the mechanics took his time while awaiting a response by the police.

The Chief of Detectives, John William Rowan and Officer John Dolan Riley were on their way. Also accompanying the chief were Augustus Eden Beery, a former officer of the department, Pinkerton Agent Joseph F. Miller and James B. Taylor, a pharmacist. In one car they drove south down the alley from the police headquarters. Using the alley between Nevada Avenue and Weber Street they reached Colorado Avenue, turned west and pulled in behind the bandit's car, blocking it in.

Dale Jones, the bandit driver, was out of the Marmon, adding oil to the engine and water to the radiator when he saw the plainclothes officers and others approaching. He knew right away the men were police. He reached into the Marmon, grabbed a handgun, and began firing at the officers. Jones' wife had been in the service station, and came running out, jumped into the car, while yelling "Don't shoot my husband." Jones shot Chief Rowan, while the other member of the gang, Lancaster, who was in the back seat of the open vehicle, started firing at Officer Riley. Riley was struck by a piece of debris, taking out his left eye, another bullet struck the officer's trigger finger and a third shot struck the officer's foot. Riley, prior to being injured fired his sawed-off pump 12-gauge shotgun into the sides of the Marmon car until he had emptied it of ammunition.

Marmon 34 Touring Car Advertisement. Photo public domain.

With all this gunfire occurring, mechanic Henderson, fearing for the safety of Mrs. Harmon, got her car started and she exited onto Nevada Avenue, driving one block north to the post office where she parked and tried to gather her wits. This allowed for the bandits to enter their vehicle and escape north on Nevada Avenue. Unfortunately, Rowan had not waited for Chief of Police Harper, Sergeant Reuben Webb and Officer Thomas Shockley. They were going to use the department's Case automobile which was an old car and, in the excitement, Officer Shockley had trouble getting the car to start. Shockley, described as being rattled, killed the motor on their car which quit across from the filling station. Chief Harper exited the car and was about to fire upon the escaping bandits with a high-power rifle, but at that moment a large streetcar loaded with passengers came around the corner and would have been in his line of fire. Quickly kneeling so he would be aiming upward, he fired but missed his mark. Unable to restart the Case, a pursuit was not possible.[5]

Chief Rowan was placed in a vehicle and rushed to Glockner Sanatorium (now Penrose Hospital), on North Cascade Avenue. Rowan's watch, struck by a bullet, had stopped at 3:10. Officer Riley, was placed in another car and driven to Beth El Hospital (now Memorial Central) on East Boulder Street. Rowan died on his way to the hospital, after having been shot one time. Riley, after surgery, would recover from his wounds.

Right after the shooting and the escape of the Marmon from the station, the car proceeded north on Nevada Avenue, passing Mrs. Harmon, who was still parked by the post office. Officers were prevented from shooting at the bandit vehicle because the incident had drawn a large crowd of people.

Fire Chief Patrick "Patty" Daniel McCartin mounted his Stutz Bearcat vehicle and tried to pursue the bandits. He chased them north on Nevada Avenue to where he believed they turned at Cache la Poudre Street. This was necessary to escape north out of town, because the main road to Denver through town was Cascade in those days. McCartin was driving so fast that when he got to Cache la Poudre, he was unable to slow enough to turn the corner. After backing up and turning toward Cascade Avenue, he continued northbound, but never saw the bandit car again.

The Marmon did not continue north to Denver, but turned to the east, arriving in Limon, Colorado, where it stopped at a filling station and refueled. William Samson Pershing, who lived on the south side of Limon, was approached by a man about 25 years of age in a car driving without lights and asked if there was a way to drive east without going through town. Mr. Pershing, went in to get his coat after telling them he would direct them, but upon returning the vehicle was gone.[6]

Before midnight, a car sped south into Sedalia, Colorado, about 40 miles north of Colorado Springs. The Reserved Watch, consisting of a large posse, were watching the road looking for any suspicious people that might have been involved in the shootings at Colorado Springs earlier in the day. Earlier, Frank Lewis hired a cab in Denver driven by William Rose. They entered Sedalia and were stopped by the Reserved Watch. Frank Lewis tried to convince them he was in pursuit of his wife who had run off with another man. Being unsuccessful, he was arrested and taken to Colorado Springs where he was fingerprinted and photographed, before being booked into the city jail.[7]

Near two o'clock the following morning, a Hudson Super-Six approached Sedalia from the north at a high rate of speed. Officers tried to flag the vehicle to a stop, but it wheeled by. The guards opened fire on the vehicle and the car swerved off the road and stopped. A woman exited the car and walked around in front of the car, hands in the air. She was Frank Lewis' youngest sister, Eva. The officers approached the car and found it contained three automatic rifles, revolvers, and a bag containing a lot of ammunition. They then heard a man who sounded to be in pain in the grass near the car. The man who had been driving the vehicle was LeRoy Dale Sherrill. He had been shot twice in his left knee. There had been one more passenger in the car, but the police were unable to locate that person. Both of the bandits were taken to the Denver jail.[8]

Officers waited until daylight and while looking for the third party, saw a match struck. Ray Long tried to light a cigarette which led to his capture. Like the other two occupants of the Hudson, he was taken to Denver and locked up.[9]

After all the encounters of the Denver and the Colorado Springs police with the bandits over Friday and Saturday, the tally of injured and dead amounted to:

    Colo. Springs Chief of Detectives John William Rowan, Dead
    Denver Officer Luther McMahill, Dead
    Colorado Springs Detective John Dolan Riley, Wounded
    Denver Detective Harry Lane. Wounded
    Denver Detective Frank Cole, Wounded
    Denver policeman Carl Wilson, Wounded
    Bandit LeRoy Dale Sherrill, Wounded[10]

Arrested at Sedalia, Colorado by the Reserved Watch:
    LeRoy Dale Sherrill, 22, aka: Charles D. Gillings; aka: Charles A. Rollings; aka: Gabe Price; aka: George Ryan
    Eva Lewis, 20; aka: Eva De Morris; aka: Eva De Orman
    Ray Long; aka: Jesse Morgan; aka: George Eudaley; aka: Snyder
    Frank Lewis, 26; aka: Henry J. Clayton; aka: Fred Rogers; aka: Frank De Morris; aka: James Clayton; aka: Frank DeMorris; aka: Frank Rogers; aka: Grey; aka: De Orman

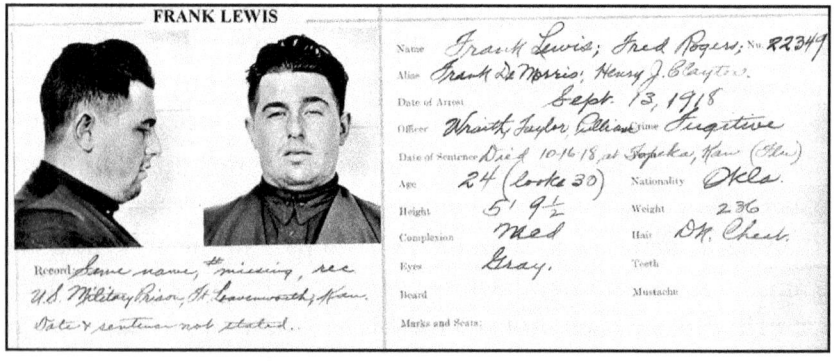

1918 booking record of Frank Lewis.
Courtesy of CSPD.

Arrested in Denver:
    John Bubb: Step-father to the Lewis side of family, husband of Martha
    Martha (Humphrey) (Lewis) Bubb: Mother of the Lewis family
    Bessie (Rogers) (Clayton) Goetz: Wife of Frank Lewis[11]

Dale and Margie Jones, Pinkerton files wanted poster. Courtesy of Library of Congress.

Dale Jones, his wife, and Roscoe Lancaster left Colorado for Kansas City, Missouri. Lancaster was dropped off at his family home at 1904 Montgall Avenue. Police received information regarding Lancaster's location, so it was said that more than 100 police officers surrounded the home. This also drew a very large crowd of onlookers, estimated at around 5,000. Officers demanded Lancaster give himself up, but it erupted into a gun-battle. Before the conclusion, Lancaster was mortally wounded. "Blackie" Lancaster told the officers that he was shot up badly around the lower legs in the shoot-out in Colorado Springs. He died later that same day, and the coroner reported that Lancaster had five bullet wounds in his right leg.[12]

On October 1, 1918, the stolen Marmon car was found dumped in the Missouri River, near Kansas City, Missouri. Forty-two bullet holes were counted in the left side of the car body. The stolen car had been taken from George T. Cook, president of the Kansas City Nut and Bolt Company on September 7th in a carjacking.[13]

1918 Marmon driven by Dale Jones at the time of shoot-out in Colorado Springs. Verne O. Williams Commercial Photography. Courtesy of CSPD.

Frank Lewis was transported from Colorado by U.S. Marshals, arriving in Kansas City on October 2, to be arraigned for a train robbery of the Missouri, Kansas & Texas (MK&T) train near Paola, Kansas, on July 10th that same year.[14] While awaiting trial, Frank Lewis was held in the Shawnee County jail, at Topeka, Kansas. A jailer while doing his rounds found Lewis had died in his cell, Wednesday, October 16, at age of 25. Because the Spanish flu was responsible for many deaths nationwide during this time, it was just incorrectly assumed the reason for his death.[15]

Only his cause of death was more interesting than the flu epidemic. During May of 1914, Frank Lewis and a brother, Ora Lewis, were stopped by a city marshal at Pierce City, Missouri, for passing counterfeit money. A gunfight ensued and the marshal and Frank were both shot up. Frank was hit in the upper body five times. Ora was able to get Frank into a freight car and went to Tulsa, Oklahoma, where he was nursed back to health. However, the bullets were not removed from his body as Frank did not trust doctors.[16] After an autopsy, it was found that one of the bullets had entered his heart, causing his death from pneumonia. (Can you say lead poisoning !?)

Dale Jones and his wife Margie escaped to Los Angeles after leaving Roscoe Lancaster in Kansas City. They rented a house in a community northeast of Los Angeles, called Arcadia, and were trying to keep under the police radar. However, fliers had been put out to the gas stations in the area and one day the operator of the White Oaks Filling Station in the town of Arcadia recognized the vehicle and the couple that had been stopping there for fuel somewhat regularly. The L.A. County sheriff's office was notified and placed two deputies at the station to see if the people would return. Tuesday, November 19, 1918, about 5:00 p.m., a Cadillac roadster with Missouri license plates driven by Margie slowly passed the filling station, stopping about 150 feet past. The passenger, Dale Jones, exited the car and watched the station from behind a tree to see if there was any danger. Not seeing any problem, they drove the car into the filling station to obtain fuel.

Two deputies, William J. Anderson and George Van Vliet, were hidden behind the station, while two Pinkerton National Detective Agency agents were concealed in a shed. Dale Jones entered the station, purchased some oil, and walked to the car. The attendant signaled the deputies who stepped out and ordered the two bandits to give themselves up. Jones pulled out two pistols and started shooting. Margie then grabbed a weapon from inside the car and began firing at the deputies. It was concluded that one of Margie's shots struck Deputy Van Vliet—a fatal strike. Deputy Anderson, armed with a shotgun, shot Jones in the head and then turned his attention to Jones' wife and killed her in a like manner. Including this confrontation, the gang members were known to have killed nine police officers since 1913.[17]

As with the capture of bank robber Henry Starr, criminals did not fare well after visiting Colorado Springs. Maybe the Frank Lewis-Dale Jones gang escaped from Colorado Springs, however, they all came to a fatal end within two months of their outrage here. Criminals beware! Go somewhere else!

Notes

1 *Colorado Springs Gazette*, 03 Jun 1917, Page 5.
2 *Colorado Springs Gazette*, 14 Sep 1918, Page 1.
3 *Newport in the Rockies, Life and Good Times of Colorado Springs*, By Marshall Sprague, 1961.
4 *Colorado Springs Gazette*, 14 Sep 1918, Page 1.
5 Unpublished Manuscript of Hugh D. Harper, 1933, Pages 12, 13, from the Colorado Springs Pioneers' Museum
6 Numerous Colorado Springs & Denver Newspapers, 14 Sep 1918.
7 *Colorado Springs Gazette*, 14 Sep 1918, Page 1.
8 *Colorado Springs Gazette*, 14 Sep 1918, Page 1.
9 *Colorado Springs Evening Telegraph*, 14 Sep 1918, Page 1.
10 *Kansas City Star*, 14 Sep 1918, Page 1.
11 *Rocky Mountain News*, 14 Sep 1918, Page 1.
12 *Colorado Springs Evening Telegraph*, 25 Sep 1918, Page 1.
13 *Kansas City Star*, 01 Oct 1918, Page 7.
14 *Kansas City Star*, 02 Oct 1918, Page 1.
15 *Topeka Daily Capital*, 17 Oct 1918, Page 4.
16 *St. Louis Post-Dispatch*, 25 Sep 1916, Page 1.
17 *Los Angeles Times*, 20 Nov 1918, Part II, Page 1.

Chapter 19

PEYTON BANK ROBRERY

Based solely on longevity, Jessie James was one of America's most successful bank robbers; He eluded authorities for nearly fifteen years. — pbs.org

Known as "the war to end all wars," World War I came to a close November, 1918, and the surviving men began to be returned to the United States. People were ready to let their hair down and forget the horrors of war. Celebrating often involved the partaking of alcoholic beverages, but by January of 1919, the 18th Amendment to the United States Constitution was signed into law. Known as the Volstead Act, (prohibition) it became the law of the land. This law seemed to encourage criminal gangs to gain control over beer and liquor supplies.

Soon several gangs throughout the United States were robbing banks and other businesses. There was no federal law covering such activities. The Bureau of Investigation (forerunner of the Federal Bureau of Investigation), whose jurisdiction was extremely limited, seldom got involved in the investigation of bank robberies.

The Colorado Springs area was one that enjoyed low crime for several years. Starting with the gang shooting that killed Chief of Detectives John William Rowan in 1918,[1] the 1920s marked an increase in bank robberies and similar crimes across Colorado.

Mid-summer of 1920 in the small unincorporated community of Peyton, Colorado, located about 30 miles northeast of Colorado

Springs, the Farmer's State Bank was held up.[2] Thursday, July 29, 1920, two men wearing goggles parked in front of the bank. They exited a green car around 2:00 p.m., entered the bank, locked an employee and a customer in the vault which had been unlocked, and took over $15,000 in cash and bonds. A posse searched the area well into the night but were unsuccessful in tracing the bandits, believing by that time they were probably in Denver. The men locked in the bank vault were yelling for assistance when a woman passing the bank heard the cries and notified authorities. The men were released from the vault.[3]

The following day the bandit's car was located in Englewood, Colorado. It had been stolen in Colorado Springs from the 2100 block of North Cascade Avenue.[4] This was not the end of the crime spree. By October, banks in Colorado had been robbed in Fountain, Parker, Peyton, Sedalia and Simla. Over $30,000 was taken. Because the descriptions of the bandits were similar at each bank, it was believed that the same parties were involved in all the robberies. The only time a robbery was unsuccessful was in Elbert, Colorado, when the Elbert County State Bank was broken into, the safe combination was blown off the vault, but entry to the vault was unsuccessful.[5]

After the failed attempt to rob the Elbert County State Bank, the robbers returned the following week to give it a second try. This time citizens of the town were on the lookout for such an attempt. The bandits were met with fierce gunfire from the citizens. The robbers' Buick used in the attempt was found abandoned. The car had been stolen in Colorado Springs several days earlier.[6]

When Colorado Springs Police Chief Hugh Harper received information regarding the bank robbers, he was able to direct the posse to possible locations to search for them. When the Buick was found it contained 34 bullet holes from shots fired in Elbert. Believing that the bandits were secreting themselves in the Black Forest area, searches were focused there.[7]

Colorado Springs Police Officer Sergeant Jesse Schisler, and

Motorcycle Officer Robert Wraith, were stationed south of Husted (today, an area encompassed by the United States Air Force Academy) on the road to Denver, about 18 miles north of Colorado Springs. There the officers encountered a Chevrolet car containing three men. After being stopped by the officers, the men refused to allow a search. When ordered to exit the car, the men pulled handguns and started a battle. With the clearing of the smoke, two of the men from the car were dead and the third wounded. Remarkably, the officers were unscathed. The third injured man was taken

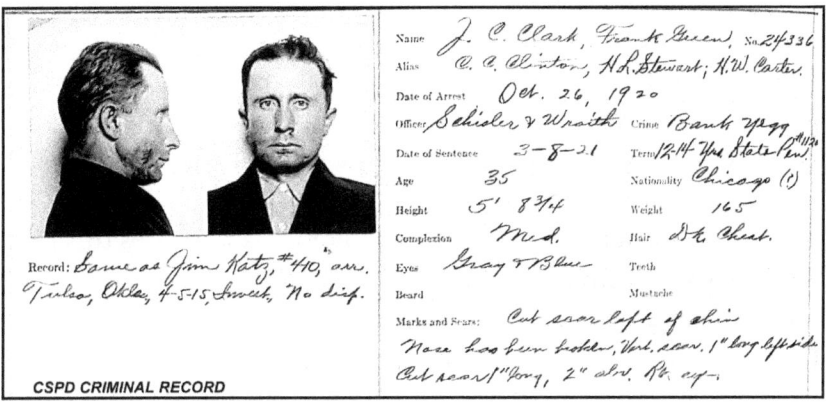

Charles Chester Clinton criminal booking record.
Courtesy of CSPD.

to Colorado Springs.

At the time, one of the deceased was identified by a driver's license with the name of Charles Seitz. The second deceased man was said to be George H. Brown, both of Pueblo. Interestingly, Brown's name had been registered in a rooming house 2305½ West Colorado Avenue, although the bed did not appear to have been slept in after renting it for just one night. The third member, said to be Frank Green, was seriously wounded and was undergoing treatment at St. Francis hospital. Upon an inspection of their clothing, it was found that high carbon steel saws were hidden inside the belts of both Brown and Green.[8]

Palmer Lake Deputy Sheriff William Holloway arrested a man

believed to be the fourth member of the bank robbers whose name was said to be William W. Sterling. CSPD officers, knowing that the names provided by the bandits were sure to be aliases, continued to go over any and all evidence in an attempt to find their true names. A handkerchief found at the scene had a laundry mark, an indelible mark placed in an inconspicuous area of a garment to identify the owner. Laundry marks were used in the mid-20th century by businesses that did laundry when most people did not have their own washing machines. When followed up, it proved the owner of the cloth was J.C. Clark, living at 812 West Colorado Avenue, the person calling himself Frank Green. Clark and Green were both aliases for Charles Chester Clinton, the survivor of the gun battle. Brown was identified as Cyrus Maddox, who had been arrested in Colorado Springs in 1914 after robbing a tea company. He was convicted and sent to Cañon City.[9]

Oklahoma authorities notified Colorado authorities this gang had their way with banks in Oklahoma. It was believed they had taken as much as one-half million dollars. They also identified George H. Brown as Archie Kitterman, who had just been released from an Oklahoma prison the previous May. These robbers were using many identifications to keep the police working hard.

The Bandits

Charles Chester Clinton: aka: J.C. Clark, Frank Green, H.L. Stewart, H.W. Carter, Jim Katz, Frank Allen, George Dixon, William Green, J.B. Williams, Charles Morris, or Charles Seitz.

Archie Kitterman: aka: George H. Brown or Cyrus Maddox.

William W. Sterling: aka: Bill Starling, Joseph Yale, Will Verdue, Will Sterling, or J.W. Sterling.

Josie May Clinton: aka: Josie May Morris, Mrs. J.C. Clark, or Josie May Clark.

Clinton's wife Josie had been arrested in Oklahoma for being involved in a robbery of a bank in Evans, Colorado, in which she and her husband took $11,000. The bandit's identities were able to be verified because of the Bertillon measurements taken by CSPD's Chief of Detectives, Irvin Bruce.[10]

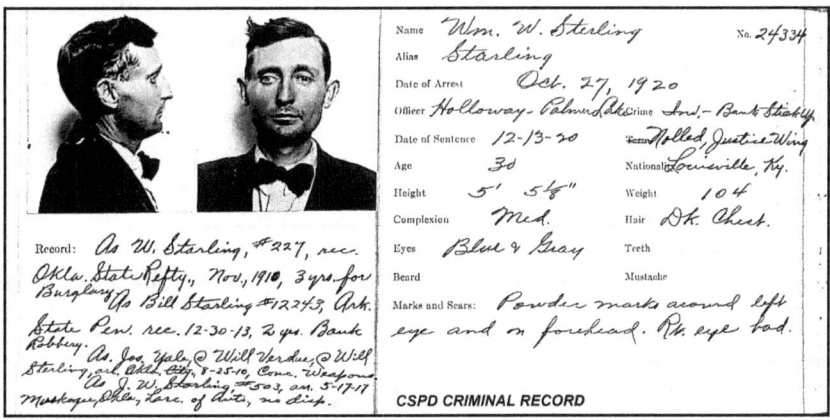

William Sterling criminal booking record.
Courtesy of CSPD.

Working with officials from Oklahoma City, Chief Harper, while in Oklahoma, was able to locate an earthen jar buried in an isolated place outside Tulsa, Oklahoma. It contained some loot taken from robberies committed by Clinton and Sterling, then in jail in Colorado Springs. William W. Sterling guided the officers to the area where the jar was buried.

Further investigation into the miscreants found they had been working from a summer resort near Larkspur, Colorado just 30 miles north of Colorado Springs. When scouting future "hauls," the gang represented themselves as rich ranch men from Texas.[11] As the investigation continued, Sedan, Kansas, authorities sent information that Clinton was wanted there for the murder of a bank cashier. Recovered bonds were found to have been stolen in the Jacksonville, Florida, area.[12]

Late in the month of November, 1920, two men were arrested as the ones Clinton sent stolen bonds to for fencing. It was recorded the gang sent as much as $300,000 worth of Liberty Bonds to James Steff and Bruce Emery.[13]

Clinton went on trial in the beginning of February 1921 and the case finally went to the jury on the 15th of February. The jury returned a verdict of guilty of attempting to commit murder when shooting at the police officers north of Colorado Springs the previous October 26th.[14] The following 8th of March, Judge John Weller Sheafor announced that Clinton was to spend twelve to fourteen years at hard labor in the Colorado State Prison at Cañon City. After sentence was pronounced, he proffered a five-minute statement. When finished, the judge went over the case point-by-point. The judge remarked, if Clinton was released, Clinton would possibly kill someone or be killed.[15]

Just two months following Clinton's conviction, his former wife, Josie Mae, died in an Oklahoma City hospital after an operation. She was just 18 years old.[16]

Charles Chester Clinton studied to become a preacher while serving his time at the Cañon City prison. He was reading about the Mormon religion and said when he was released, he would go to Salt Lake City and work in the Mormon Church.[17] After serving time in Colorado, he was transferred to a Texas penitentiary. Then on December 19, 1927 a Nebraska newspaper reported the Nebraska City National Bank was held up and one of the robbers was identified as Charles C. Clinton.[18] Well, so much for becoming a Mormon!

Charles C. Clinton was later a suspect in a bank robbery in Lamar, Colorado where the bank president and his son were killed. He was subsequently transported to Nebraska City to be tried for their bank robbery.[19] Trial was held and the jury could not decide on the guilt or innocence of Clinton.[20]

Later, another trial was convened in March 1930, to charge Clinton for bank robbery. After being positively identified by three different witnesses as being one of the robbers, the jury agreed and found him guilty of stealing $6,500 in cash and $109,000 in bonds. Interestingly, $65,000 in bonds that were non-negotiable were mailed back to the bank just a few days after the robbery.[21] This robbery resulted in a sentence of twenty years.[22]

Clinton was not destined to leave prison before his demise, October 21, 1934. He died in the prison and was buried in the prison cemetery.[23]

Notes

1   *Colorado Springs Evening Telegraph*, 13 Sep 1918, Page 1.
2   *Calhan News*, 29 July 1920, Page 1.
3   *Colorado Springs Gazette*, 29 Jul 1920, Page 1.
4   *Colorado Springs Evening Telegraph*, 30 Jul 1920, Page 1.
5   *Colorado Springs Evening Telegraph*, 20 Oct 1920, Page 5.
6   *Colorado Springs Gazette*, 26 Oct 1920, Page 1.
7   *Colorado Springs Evening Telegraph*, 26 Oct 1920, Page 1.
8   *Colorado Springs Gazette*, 27 Oct 1920, Page 1.
9   *Colorado Springs Evening Telegraph*, 29 Oct 1920, Page 1.
10 *Colorado Springs Evening Telegraph*, 13 Nov 1920, Page 1.
11 *Colorado Springs Gazette*, 14 Nov 1920, Page 1.
12 *Colorado Springs Evening Telegraph*, 15 Nov 1920, Page 1.
13 *Colorado Springs Gazette*, 28 Nov 1920, Page 1.
14 *Colorado Springs Gazette*, 17 Feb 1921, Page 1.
15 *Colorado Springs Gazette*, 09 Mar 1921, Page 1.
16 *Oklahoma City Times*, 11 May 1921, Page 1.
17 *Daily Oklahoman*, 18 Dec 1921, Page D10.
18 *Wichita Beacon*, 22 Dec 1927, Page 1.
19 *Lincoln Evening Journal*, 29 Aug 1929, Page 1.
20 *Lincoln Evening Journal*, 24 Sep 1929, Page 1.
21 *Lincoln Star*, 04 Mar 1930, Page 1.
22 *Lincoln Evening Journal*, 24 Mar 1930, Page 1.
23 *Lincoln Star Journal*, 22 Oct 1934, Page 11.

**1928 Souvenir copy of International Association of
Chiefs of Police convention program.**
Courtesy of CSPD.

Chapter 20

INTERNATIONAL ASSOCIATION OF CHIEFS OF POLICE (I.A.C.P.) CONVENTIONS

The first successful use of fingerprints in a murder case in the United States was in 1910 in Illinois. Thomas Jennings was accused of murdering Clarence Hiller after his fingerprints were found at Hiller's house. In 1911 Jennings appealed his conviction, but the Supreme Court of Illinois upheld the evidence thus established fingerprint evidence as a reliable standard, formalizing its admissibility. — Francine Uenuma, Smithsonian Magazine 12/05/2018

The earliest record found indicating the Colorado Springs Police Department had participated in a national or international police organization was during 1898. Marshal John Walter Garthright, attended an annual session of the National Association of Chiefs of Police of the United States and Canada held at Milwaukee, Wisconsin.[1] In 1904, Chief of Police William Sullivan Reynolds was sent to St. Louis.[2] The next time anything was found to be written about the subject was in 1906. Police Chief Alex Adams traveled to Hot Springs, Arkansas, to attend a conference. Even though two-hundred delegates attended, only three cities were represented from the western United States.[3]

Chief Hugh D. Harper attended the convention in New Orleans, April 1919,[4] and again during 1921 in St. Louis, Missouri.[5] The following year, Chief Harper spoke to the San Francisco-sponsored convention about youth growing up in cities tending to developing criminal traits. This included the downside of pool halls and the automobile.[6]

September of 1928, Colorado Springs hosted the 35th annual convention for the International Association of Chiefs of Police. Attendance to the four-day conference was high, bringing in chiefs from across the country and Canada.[7] On the last day of the convention, the group urged the adoption of a federal law, making possession of a firearm illegal unless properly registered and the owner fingerprinted. Chief Harper was elected to the position of fifth vice-president.[8]

At the conference in St. Petersburg, Florida, October of 1931, Chief Harper was elected as president of the organization to serve for a period of one year.[9] While attending the 1932 conference in Portland, Oregon, the chief was "knighted" by the Rose Bowl Association. When this occurred, it was tradition to be named after a rose. The chief decided on "Souvenir."[10]

For the time that "Dad" Bruce was chief of police, he was a continuous member of various committees of the I.A.C.P. By 1947, Bruce was on the executive and memorial committees and added to the education and training committees that same year. At the 1949 convention, Colorado Springs was determined to be host of the 1950 site.

New Fords loaned for the use of IACP members to be chauffeured in during the 1950 convention.
Courtesy of CSPD.

By April, Bruce was already deep into the planning stages of the 1950 Annual Convention. He worked with Ford Motor Company to provide 70 new Fords to ferry the delegates around the town during the October convention. Roy Best, warden of the Colorado State Prison, had prisoners make custom license plates for each delegate's vehicle. Chief Carrel of the Colorado State Patrol was to provide officers as drivers for the delegates.[11]

Ending the day prior to the convention's start, Colorado Springs was the center for a movie world premiere. Warner Brothers' production *Rocky Mountain* was shown at the Chief Theater and the 8th Street Drive-In. This was the first movie premiered in Colorado Springs.[12]

September 1952, Chief Bruce was installed as the second vice-president of the I.A.C.P.[13] The following year he advanced to being the first vice-president.[14] He reached the pinnacle of the association with his installation as its president in 1954 when the convention was held in New Orleans.[15] Bruce attended every conference from the time he was chief until his death in 1960.

Notes

1 *Rocky Mountain Daily News,* 04 May 1898, Page 10.
2 Colorado Springs City Council Minutes, 23 May 1904, Book 9, Page 282.
3 *Colorado Springs Gazette,* 16 Apr 1906, Page 5.
4 *Colorado Springs Gazette,* 12 Apr 1919, Page 12.
5 *Colorado Springs Gazette,* 15 Jun 1921, Page 7.
6 *Colorado Springs Gazette,* 20 Feb 1922, Page 3.
7 *Colorado Springs Gazette,* 04 Oct 1927, Page 6.
8 *Reno Nevada Gazette-Journal,* 29 Jun 1928, Page 7.
9 *Greeley Colorado Daily Tribune,* 15 Oct 1931, Page 10.
10 *Colorado Springs Gazette,* 24 Jun 1932, Page 2.
11 *Colorado Springs Gazette* Telegraph, 06 Apr 1950, Page A1.
12 *Colorado Springs Gazette* Telegraph, 07 Oct 1950, Page ??.
13 *Colorado Springs Gazette* Telegraph, 26 Sep 1952, Page A1.
14 *Colorado Springs Gazette* Telegraph, 18 Sep 1953. Page A10.
15 *Denver Rocky Mountain News,* 15 Aug 1954, Page ??

Chapter 21

WIZARDS & DRAGONS

On July 4, 1923, a 30-foot-tall cross was set ablaze on Pikes Peak, announcing the formation of a KKK chapter. Members of Pikes Peak Klan No. 11 secretly approached residents to join the terrorist organization. In response local officials, police, and business owners formed an anti-Klan alliance known as the Citizens Committee — "Ku Klux Klan" CSPM Curator of History, Dr. John Harner, Professor, University of Colorado, Colorado Springs,

Following the four-year Civil War which ended in April, 1865, to which the country had sacrificed over 600,000 young men, the country was still not at peace. Unscrupulous opportunists and carpetbaggers moved from the North into the South,[1] ready to make money off the South that had been devastated and was in economic and political ruin. Property taxes became exorbitant, forcing landowners to abandon much of their property. The assassination of President Lincoln at the end of the war sent any healing with the South into a tailspin.

The vindictiveness and bad character of people moving to the South to take advantage was one thing that brought about a group which began in Tennessee, called the Ku Klux Klan, founded by six ex-Confederate soldiers. Another reason for the groups formation was its dislike of free Negros. The groups name was derived from the combination of the Greek word "kuklos" (circle) with the Scottish word "clan."[2] The organization was founded as a white supremest secret society. New members had to take the following oath:

> I, before the immaculate Judge of Heaven and Earth, and upon the Holy Evangelists of Almighty God, do, of my own

free will and accord, subscribe to the following sacredly binding obligation:
1. We are on the side of justice, humanity, and constitutional liberty, as bequeathed to us in its purity by our forefathers.
2. We oppose and reject the principles of the radical party (the Republican party, then rulers of the U.S. Congress).
3. We pledge mutual aid to each other in sickness, distress, and pecuniary embarrassment.
4. Any member divulging, or causing to be divulged, any of the foregoing obligations shall meet the fearful penalty and traitor's doom, which is Death! Death! Death![3]

The groups often were operated under many names: White Camelia, Order of the White Rose, The White Caps, White League, Palefaces, the White Brotherhood. Blacks were dragged from their beds, whipped, lynched and mutilated. As Southerners began to wrest back control of the South, "Black Codes" were introduced to keep blacks from voting and anything else the Klan members did not like. By 1868 it was believed that membership in the Klan had reached as many as one-half million. By 1877, the Klan had fallen out of favor and all but disappeared.[4]

During the 1900s, the Klan was restarted, this time by a country preacher named "Colonel" William Joseph Simmons. He had found a book of anecdotes about the secret society and while dreaming one night said he dreamed of men on horseback in white robes. When he awoke, he "got down on my knees and swore that I would found a fraternal organization which would be a memorial to the Ku Klux Klan." He traveled the South as a Methodist preacher spreading his word.[5] This did not at first make much of an impact, then in 1915, the movie *Birth of a Nation* was shown in Atlanta, Georgia. The movie was based on a Thomas Dixon novel entitled *The Clansman*. The movie inflamed many white people, who were now listening to preacher Simmons. Simmons was preaching not only against blacks, but against Catholics and any non-native born people coming to the United States after WWI and taking jobs away from white, native-born Americans. Rocky Mountain PBS pointed out in its show *Colorado Experience-KKK*, the Klan got a foothold in Colorado and the K.K.K. were stating that lawless foreigners were drinking during prohibition and causing unrest in the workforce. The K.K.K. also stated that foreigners, mostly Catholics, were taking Colorado jobs.

Simmons began paying for advertising. The organization was estimated to have reached a membership of over seven million by its heyday in the 1920s.[6] A book of rules was produced and copyrighted which used the letters "kl" to preface many terms the organization used, such as:

The rule book was called:	Kloran
A local lodge:	Klavern
Klavern administrator:	Kligrapp
A recruiter:	Kleagle
Administrator assistant:	King Kleagle
Initiation ceremony:	klonversation
Initiation fee:	klecktoken[7]

By 1921, the National Association for the Advancement of Colored People (NAACP) demanded a federal investigation be conducted into the workings of the K.K.K. It was even asked that the postmaster general refuse privileges to the Klan in the use of the mails.[8]

Midyear reports were coming out that the Klan was organizing in the middle of the country, to include Missouri, Kansas, Nebraska, Iowa, Minnesota and North and South Dakota.[9] The K.K.K.'s Imperial Wizard, William Joseph Simmons, from his headquarters in Atlanta, Georgia, had sent flyers out stating a new branch would be opened in Ordway, Colorado.[10] Ordway was 50 miles east of Pueblo, Colorado. In July the Klan claimed a membership of 175 in Denver after the Grand Goblin had been there only four weeks. This

Goblin was the organizer for Colorado, Wyoming, Idaho, Montana and Utah. The Goblin said, "The membership is not known even to members. The roster of officers is never published. It never meets in the same place twice." It was also reported that a branch had been formed in Colorado Springs and consisted of 100 local residents.[11] Local law enforcement stated that if laws were not broken by the K.K.K., they would not molest the Klan.[12]

A highly respected and well-known doctor, Charles E. Locke, died in Denver and was to be laid to rest in the Denver area, Tuesday, February 21, 1922. The doctor had served in the Civil War, the Spanish American War, and fighting in the Philippines. In 1895 he served as a Colorado state senator.[13] During the services at Fairmount Cemetery, five white-robed and hooded K.K.K. Knights suddenly appeared and placed a "beautiful floral tribute" shaped as a white cross, with blue lettering: "Knights of the Ku Klux Klan." Just as quickly, the members of the invisible empire were gone. The sudden appearance and departure stunned many of the attendees. A letter was mailed to the local papers "declaring" that the doctor was not a Klan member; the Klan just wanted to honor the doctor as "a real American."[14]

Wednesday, July 4, 1923, the Klan, consisting of about 50 people, met at a secluded place on the west side of Pikes Peak's summit to perform an installation and initiation ceremony of new members which also included the burning of a 30-foot-high cross.[15] Over the next couple nights several more burning crosses were reported across the city.[16]

The K.K.K. made themselves known in the city at the end of November 1923, by burning a 25-foot-tall cross on 700 West Monument Street, which is a high hill just west of downtown. It was also reported there were other crosses burned, but locations were not identified. This location was ideal for a large portion of the city to have a view of the cross burning. No one was located that was involved in the incident.[17] During the end of the following January, a 100-foot cross with 25-foot arms was placed on the north slope of Mount Washington and set afire.[18]

Mount Washington, which was the original name for Evergreen Cemetery, had a hill located on the southwest edge, only about 100 feet in height. I remember a motorcycle club would race Cushman motorcycles up the face of the hill. The hill was leveled—possibly in the 1960s—and is now gone.

It was 1924 before it was publicly reported the Grand Dragon of the realm of Colorado, Dr. John Galen Locke, son of Dr. Charles Locke, was the head of the K.K.K. in Colorado. Of course, they would honor the father of their leader. Up until that time John Locke denied involvement with the K.K.K.[19] John Locke knew how to manipulate people. To gain power himself, he would financially help people get elected to government. The Republican party was taken over by the Klan in Colorado.

Colonel Philip Sidney Van Cise, Denver's district attorney, took on the Klan at a Republican assembly at the Denver City Auditorium the first week of January 1924. Van Cise wanted to thwart the Klan's goal to take over the government of Colorado during the upcoming election.[20] Van Cise had earlier successfully taken on the Denver City/County government corruption.

Regretfully, the election went badly for the citizens of Colorado. Judge Clarence J. Morley was elected as the new governor of Colorado.[21] Morley was the Klan's candidate and was controlled by Dr. John Galen Locke, Grand Dragon of the Realm of Colorado. Often it was said that Morley was not allowed to make a decision without first getting permission from Locke.[22]

The Klan's agenda was to get rid of as many commissions and boards as possible, so they could obtain control. For example, the Klan wanted the state's Civil Service Commission removed, because it was protecting state employees who "must be eliminated since '70%' of the office holders ... were Catholics."[23]

The Klan-controlled sector of the Republican party was in the majority in the house and were willing to rubber stamp anything the governor sent them. However, a group including six Republican senators and fourteen Democrat senators banded together to thwart the agenda of Locke and the Klan. This group was large enough to stop most anything. The house tried many tactics to put pressure on the anti-Klan coalition, but were unsuccessful. With the end of the Twenty-fifth Geneal Assembly, the Klan had been defeated and were unable to wield their previous power. Internal corruption and dissension soon brought down Grand Dragon Dr. John Galen Locke. He resigned as the head of Colorado's Klan.[24]

Prior to the annual city election of 1925, "several hundred leading professionals and other Colorado Springs businessmen formed an organization to prevent Klan dictation." They pledged to "not only resist the Klan, but to exert every influence to counteract the Klan influence."[25]

Efforts to tamper with members of the police department in Colorado Springs were made by the K.K.K. Headlines in the *Gazette* in October stated "Police are Warned not to Join Klan." Chief Harper declared it was inconsistent with the police oath to join such an organization. Chief Harper said the Klan was dangerous for everybody.

In a letter to the Colorado Springs City Council, Mr. V. Eleverton Rowton requested that the Ku Klux Klan, Realm of Colorado, be permitted to use the Auditorium on Sunday, November 22, 1925. Moved by Councilman Drake, seconded by Councilman Birdsall, the request was granted upon payment of the regular charge. Motion carried, Councilmen Birdsall, Drake, Jones, Kirkwood voting aye. Councilmen Mowry, Taylor, President Harris voting no. Councilmen Dern and Hungerford absent.[26] Mr. Rowton was the owner of Mountain State Tire & Gas Company.[27]

Colorado Springs had been put on notice to expect 5,000 Colorado Klansmen for their convention. Two trains were especially run to carry 1,000 delegates each from Denver and Pueblo, respectively. Dr. John Galen Locke had resigned the position of Grand Dragon of Colorado and a new one was to be chosen at this convention. Another 1,000 were to motor to Colorado Springs from northern Colorado and 700 from Cañon City.[28]

Eighty Colorado Klan organizations were represented at the convention where Reverend Frederick G. Arnold, 39, of Cañon City was to be the new Grand Dragon. The state was reorganized and divided into three provinces, which would each be governed by a grand titan. Arnold formerly had been chaplain at the state penitentiary and was involved in executive positions in several other organizations. In celebration of the new grand dragon, crosses were burned in Colorado Springs, Pueblo, Cañon City, and other locations.[29]

In another underhanded move on the part of Governor Morley, he removed two men from the board of control for the Colorado Deaf and Blind Home and replaced them with Reverend Arnold and William Althouse. Since the group in the state senate had been so successful in the stopping the Klan agenda in the legislature, the governor tried to put the two men in as recess appointments. However, Attorney General Boatright wrote a letter to the governor and told him the appointments were not legal because the legislature was still in session. The removed board members were reinstated.[30]

The Klan having been unsuccessful in getting control of the municipality of Colorado Springs, published in a Klan paper, the *Colorado Springs Independent*, support for four candidates in the upcoming city election in April, 1927. Support was pledged to:

J.R. Rose	4-year term
Mathew J. Decker	
Douglas C. Jardine	6-year term
Reverend Duncan Lamont	6-year term[31]

The 1927 *Polk City Directory* listed the above men as:

Mathew J. Decker & Son, funeral directors and embalmers, 225 North Weber Street.[32]

Douglas C. Jardine, Jardine & Knight Plumbing & Heating, 312 Custer Avenue.[33]

Rev. Duncan Lamont, 212 North 23rd Street, no church listed.[34] J.R. Rose, was unlisted.

Jardine strongly denied that he had sought Klan backing and was not a member of the Klan.[35] Wednesday the papers reported in Colorado Springs, not one backed Klan contestant won a seat. Also, it appeared the Klan was not very successful in many of the other elections throughout the state.[36]

The City Council minutes recorded on July 1, 1927, the Ku Klux Klan applied for a permit to parade on certain streets in the City of Colorado Springs. After consideration it was moved by Councilman Bennett, seconded by Councilman Crissey, that it was the sense of the council that the city manager should not issue a permit for this parade. The motion carried.[37]

On Memorial Day former Denver District Attorney Philip Sidney Van Cise spoke to honor military veterans at Crown Hill Cemetery. Van Cise spoke of two parades that day, one for the Grand Army of the Republic and Spanish-American War veterans and one for the Ku Klux Klan. The veterans did not need to boast of their deeds. The other parade boasted to produce a crowd of 60,000 and only produced around 500. Van Cise skewered the Klan from the pulpit, for being a secret society afraid of the light, parading behind masks and disguises. Klan attendees were upset at how they were portrayed and had to even the score. Six nights later, the Klan erected a burning cross on the lawn of Van Cise's home. The Van Cise family weren't home and being out of town, missed the event. Neighbors called the fire department and the cross was extinguished. From that time on, the Klan became more fractured and lost a majority of its membership and all of its political power. So ended the reign of the Klan of the 1920s, especially in Colorado.[38]

Notes

1 This was a description of people that to exploit the chance to take advantage of opportunities during what was known as Reconstruction.
2 *Encyclopedia of World Crime,* Volume III - K-R, By Jay Robert Nash, CrimeBooks, Inc., Wilmette, IL 1990, Pages 1854, 1855.
3 *Encyclopedia of World Crime,* Volume III - K-R, By Jay Robert Nash, CrimeBooks, Inc., Wilmette, IL 1990, Page 1855.

4   *Encyclopedia of World Crime,* Volume III - K-R, By Jay Robert Nash, CrimeBooks, Inc., Wilmette, IL 1990, Page 1855.
5   *Encyclopedia of World Crime,* Volume III - K-R, By Jay Robert Nash, CrimeBooks, Inc., Wilmette, IL 1990, Page 1856.
6   *Encyclopedia of World Crime,* Volume III - K-R, By Jay Robert Nash, CrimeBooks, Inc., Wilmette, IL 1990, Page 1856.
7   Gangbuster: One Man's Battle Against Crime, Corruption, and the Klan, By Alan Prendergast, Citadel Press, New York, 2023, Pages 135, 136.
8   Denver Colorado Statesman, 01 Jan 1921, Page 1.
9   *Westcliffe Colorado Wet Mountain Tribune,* 20 May 1921, Page 3.
10 *Ordway Colorado New Era,* 10 Jun 1921, Page 3.
11 *Denver Rocky Mountain News,* 03 Jul 1921, Page 5.
12 *Colorado Springs Gazette* and Telegraph, 28 Jul 1921, Page 6.
13 *Denver Rocky Mountain News,* 20 Feb 1922, Page 2.
14 *Denver Rocky Mountain News,* 22 Feb 1922, Page 14.
15 *Colorado Springs Gazette,* 05 Jul 1923, Page 1.
16 *Colorado Springs Gazette,* 05 Jul 1923, Page 2.
17 *Colorado Springs Gazette,* 30 Nov 1923, Page 1.
18 *Colorado Springs Gazette,* 23 Jan 1924, Page ??.
19 *Denver Rocky Mountain News,* 05 Jan 1924, Page 1.
20 *Denver Rocky Mountain News,* 05 Jan 1924, Page 1.
21 *Denver Rocky Mountain News,* 06 Nov 1924, Page 1.
22 Colorado Under the Klan, By James H. Davis, The Colorado Magazine, Vol XLII, No. 2, Colorado State Historical Society, Spring 1965, Page 94.
23 Colorado Under the Klan, By James H. Davis, The Colorado Magazine, Vol XLII, No. 2, Colorado State Historical Society, Spring 1965, Page 96.
24 Colorado Under the Klan, by James H. Davis, The Colorado Magazine, Vol XLII, No. 2, Colorado State Historical Society, Spring 1965, Pages 93-108.
25 *Denver Rocky Mountain News,* 16 Apr 1925, Page 18.
26 Colorado Springs City Council Minutes, 10 Nov 1925, Book 17, Page 416.
27 *Colorado Springs R.L. Polk City Directory,* Vol. XXII, Page 316.
28 *Denver Rocky Mountain News,* 22 Nov 1925, Page 9.
29 *Denver Rocky Mountain News,* 23 Nov 1925, Page 1.
30 *Denver Rocky Mountain News,* 17 Dec 1925, Page 4.
31 *Denver Rocky Mountain News,* 02 Apr 1927, Page 5.
32 *Colorado Springs R.L. Polk City Directory,* Vol. XXII, Page 55 & 144.
33 *Colorado Springs R.L. Polk City Directory,* Vol. XXII, Page 232 & 637.
34 *Colorado Springs R.L. Polk City Directory,* Vol. XXII, Page 252.
35 *Denver Rocky Mountain News,* 02 Apr 1927, Page 5.
36 *Denver Rocky Mountain News,* 06 Apr 1927, Page 4.
37 Colorado Springs City Council Minutes, 01 Jul 1927, Book 18, Page 70.
38 Gangbuster: One Man's Battle Against Crime, Corruption, and The Klan, By Alan Prendergast, Citadel Press, 2023, Pages 271-273.

The Bank of Manitou vault door
Photograph by D. Kallaus, courtesy of THE VAULT,
Manitou Springs, CO.

Chapter 22

MANITOU BANK ROBBERY
THE CUSP OF THE GREAT DEPRESSION

During the Great Depression, with much of the United States mired in grinding poverty and unemployment, some Americans found increased opportunities in criminal activities like bootlegging, robbing banks, loan sharking, even murder. — history.com

The Great Depression was the longest financial downturn in United States history. By the late 1920s the lack of jobs brought desperate people to crime. The depression would last from the crash of the stock market in 1929 until the ending of WWII.

On Thursday, March 10, 1927 the Bank of Manitou was robbed by four people. Ten minutes before noon, three men who appeared to have been drinking moonshine, entered the bank. Pointing guns at the employees, they took cash and locked the employees in the bank vault. Later, when a customer entered the bank and heard the calls from inside the vault, the trapped people were rescued and the robbery was reported to authorities. Locking the people in the vault gave the bandits the needed time to escape without pursuit.

By 12:30 p.m., it was believed the Buick automobile used in the getaway by the yeggs was seen traveling east on Colorado Avenue. About $14,000 in cash and close to $20,000 in traveler's checks had been taken. Some of the robbers wore fleece-lined coats and were stocky built, but a fourth man was described as a youth, thought to be about 15 years old. A quick call went to the CSPD for assistance after the robbery. Police Inspector Irvin B. Bruce and six officers and detectives rushed to Manitou to assist. The streets of the city were mostly empty at the time of the robbery, so there were no witnesses outside the bank.[1]

Of the three men who had robbed the bank, one was described as a "young giant." The information was shared with the local newspapers. Gene Cerva, who worked at Colorado College taking care of the school's furnaces, remembered overhearing a conversation days earlier that a "young giant" had rented one of a string of garages in the rear of an apartment house to store a car. Cerva went in search of the garages and was successful in locating and entering the garage where he found a car that contained masks and pieces of clothing possibly used in the Manitou Bank robbery. He contacted the CSPD with the information.[2]

208 East Uintah Street above and garages below where Manitou bank robbers stored automobiles.

The Buick used by the culprits was located in a garage at the rear of 208 East Uintah Street in Colorado Springs. The light blue Buick Master Six, contained overalls and sheepskin coats. David D. Raley, owner of the garage where the car was found, called the police to report the vehicle found in the garage. Chief of Police Hugh Harper, Inspector Irvin B. Bruce, and Detective Robert Wraith along with Sheriff R.M. Jackson responded and began an investigation of the discovery. It was learned the Buick had been stolen in Hutchinson, Kansas, in February. The car had stolen license plates from another Colorado Springs car. Neighbors told police about 1:00 p.m. the Buick arrived at the garage and was quickly put in and the door locked. The occupants ran south in the alley.[3]

After the information about the bank robbers was printed in the local newspapers, people living in the 500 block of East Fontanero Street became suspicious of a group renting a house at 513 East Fontanero Street. The renters included three men and a woman. One man was described as a "young giant."[4] The police were called with a tip regarding these people. The woman renter drove a 1926 Nash four-door sedan to the house a little over an hour after the Manitou robbery. The woman was not wearing a coat, and considering it was cold and had just stormed, this seemed suspicious. The house was searched and a pile of papers burnt in the furnace of the house was believed to be the traveler's checks taken during the robbery of the bank. The officers did not have a proper camera to photograph what they saw. It was not possible to collect the ashes or preserve what the officers believed were remnants of traveler's checks.[5]

A description of the woman was given. She was said to be of slight build, good looking with auburn hair, wore a very short skirt and was smartly dressed. It was said the house had been rented by a young couple and then later two other men joined the couple at the house.[6]

Sunday, following the bank robbery, the 1926 Nash was spotted in Garden City, Kansas, and there was an exchange of gunfire between the vehicle's occupants and the police of Garden City. The officers, after riddling the vehicle with rifle shots, were of the opinion that one or maybe two of the passengers were wounded in the exchange. The car stopped near Dighton, Kansas, and asked for directions to Dodge City. Residents of the farmhouse in Dighton, said the vehicle had been struck numerous times by gunfire.[7]

Colorado was having a storm at the time the bandits were escaping the area. They had driven south to Pueblo, then east toward Lamar, then on east into Kansas and Garden City, somehow maneuvering through the storm. Reports came in from several locations between Pueblo and Garden City providing the trail of the bandits.[8]

Chief Harper had contacted Garden City Chief of Police Lee Richardson to be on the lookout for the Manitou bank robbers' car going east toward their location. Sheriff Ben Strawn and Chief Richardson along with Officer R.S. Terwilliger took two autos to the west side of Garden City and set up a road block they believed would stop any car. A car approached from the west, slowed as if it was going to stop, then suddenly drove onto the side of the road grazing the chief's car, and slipped by. Realizing the car was the wanted bandits, the police opened fire on the vehicle as it passed. A rear tire was damaged, but it did not make the car stop.[9]

Garden City officers followed a trail made by a flat tire, assumed to be the bandit's car, about 14 miles north of the town. They located a mound of dirt that had been recently dug up and found a bag containing gold and silver amounting to nearly $4,000, proceeds from the bank robbery.[10]

Chief Harper traveled to Wichita to follow up on a clue and met with Wichita's Chief of Police, Ike Walston. He assigned Detective Red Dickerson to assist Harper. After telling Dickerson he had information that a liquor runner, known as Alton, was possibly one of the men who had robbed the Bank of Manitou. The detective suddenly said he knew of a "young giant" named Alton Crapo who lived in Wichita. He was aware that Crapo had recently purchased a new car that matched the description of the car used to get away from Colorado Springs. He continued to say that Alton had a sister, Opal Crapo, who was a "tall, well-built Amazon and would go any route." They were sure that she was the person who drove the car used in the bank robbery.[11]

Police, working on clues that were undisclosed to the public, were able to locate Alton Crapo in Wichita, Kansas. One of the bandits was described as being very tall and slender, and Crapo was six-foot-four and skinny. He and his sister, Opal, had spent several visits to the Colorado Springs region over the past few years and were therefore familiar with the town. Chief Hugh Harper, the Pinkerton agents, and Wichita Police Chief I.B. Walston had been following clues that led them to Alton Crapo. He was arrested April 26 at his home on 2010 East Douglas in Wichita, but his sister and another suspect, Walter W. Snyder had left the home earlier.[12]

Alton F. Crapo
Killed in gun battle, Howells, Neb. 6-11-49

Henry E. Clopp
Robbed five banks, A lifetime criminal

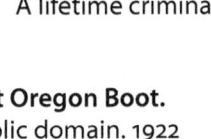

Advertisement Oregon Boot.
Photograph public domain. 1922 Popular Science.

Prisoner Wearing Metal Boot Can't Escape

DANGEROUS criminals, shackled with a metal "Oregon" boot, have little chance to escape during long railway journeys. The boot, a modern adaptation of the old-fashioned ball and chain, consists of a steel framework fitting over the shoe, with a 50-pound collar above the ankle.

The prisoner who wears it can walk slowly with a fair degree of comfort, but should he attempt to run, or move quickly, the heavy weight will break his leg.

The police were convinced enough that they had the leader of the robbery team, they requested a pair of "Oregon Boots" sent to Wichita to assist during the transportation of Crapo back to Colorado Springs.[13] April 30th the extradition order arrived in Wichita, and the prisoner, with his "Oregon Boot" and six escorts left for Colorado Springs.[14] After almost a month, Kansas City police found Opal Crapo, Alton's sister, living with her father. She was arrested and held for Colorado Springs authorities.[15]

In September, the brother and sister, Alton and Opal Crapo, were taken before the federal district court in Denver where they pled not guilty to the transportation of a stolen vehicle across state lines in violation of the Dyer Act. However, that did not affect the upcoming trial of the two for the bank robbery in Manitou.[16] After more than two weeks of trial, the jury was unable to reach a verdict regarding the stolen car.[17]

The following February, Walter Snyder, one of the remaining bandits to be arrested, surrendered to police in San Diego, California. It was unknown what caused this turn of events.[18] Chief Harper went to California to return Snyder to Colorado.

When Chief Harper arrived at the San Diego Police Department, he met with the assistant chief of police. The officer said he did not believe Walter Snyder could possibly be a bank robber. "Why," he said, "he looks like a college boy and has no earmarks whatever of being a thief." Chief Harper when interviewing Snyder, told him robbery of a bank while armed carried a life sentence in Colorado. Snyder could be charged if he was not willing to cooperate with him. If he would cooperate, Chief Harper had already obtained authority to offer Snyder a charge of simple robbery, which would limit time in the penitentiary to a maximum of ten years. Snyder confessed to everything and gave an account of the robbery. Following the confession, Harper wired Inspector Bruce to have William Clopp, who was at Pawhuska, Oklahoma, arrested as the third man involved in the bank robbery.[19] Clopp was then arrested for his connection with the bank robbery.[20]

In April of 1928, the second trial of Alton Crapo was held. Without any warning, Alton, suddenly changed his plea from not guilty to *nolle contendere*.[21] This change of plea came as Walter William Snyder was about to confess his involvement in the robbery of the Manitou bank and Crapo's connection.²²

Henry E. Clopp, alias William Clopp, 35, having pled guilty to the robbery, and Alton Crapo were both sentenced to nine to fourteen years at Cañon City.²³ Walter Snyder, having already pled guilty to his part in the robbery and the transporting of a stolen car across state lines, was sentenced to four years at Leavenworth Federal Prison, in the federal court at Denver.²⁴ With the change in plea by Alton Crapo, his sister's prosecution was dropped.²⁵ While serving his time at the prison, Crapo, except for an 8-month period, served as the warden's driver. Not only was he seemingly privileged while in prison, but also after only serving three years and four months of his sentence, he was released September 11, 1931.²⁶ When taking a closer look at Alton Crapo's criminal career, it was found that Manitou was not his first bank robbery nor his last.

Less than two years after his release, he and four other men robbed the Emporia, Kansas, Citizens National Bank on March 1, 1933. During the escape attempt two members of the gang were shot by authorities. One, Charles Fargo, was shot in the back and was paralyzed. The other was identified as Sam Herman Craig who confessed and named three other members of the gang. Two other members were Carl Anderson and Allen Woolworth.²⁷

Again, authorities arrested Crapo and Louis Conley in 1934 after they had been identified as being involved in the bank robbery of the State Bank of Winfield, Kansas, a small community about 35 miles south of Wichita in May of 1926. However, he was not prosecuted because by the time of their arrest, the statute of limitations had run out.²⁸

In September 1937, the FBI arrested Albert C. Gladson, Hurbert Munger, Glenn Van Hook, John W. Davidson and Alton Crapo after a secret federal grand jury indicted the above persons for the robbery of the Sedalia, Missouri, Bank and Trust Company on March 19, 1935.²⁹ Unlike earlier robberies where the bandits entered the bank with guns, locked everyone in the vault and took the valuables, this time it was much more involved.

The bandits took the family of the bank's assistant cashier hostage at the employee's home the night before the robbery. James E. Norlin had been at National Guard training, and upon arriving home, was confronted by two armed men. After spending the night and binding the family members, the criminals drove the cashier to the bank about 8:15 a.m. After they entered, the cashier was told to open the safe, which was just after the time lock would allow. Everyone in the bank was locked in the vault. With no witnesses, they took the cash and walked out the front door to a waiting Ford V-8 auto and drove south out of town. After all this elaborate execution, they were only able to take $16,000, but left no trail.[30]

The FBI reported upon the arrest of the four men, they believed they had stopped one of the largest bank gangs in the midwest. It was found Crapo and Van Hook were responsible for the robbery of State Exchange Bank at Yates Center, Kansas and a wholesale grocery company in Colby, Kansas.[31] While in custody, Munger confessed to robbing the Kearney, Nebraska State Bank in February 1934. His companions were Allen Woolworth, Earnest Clopp, Albert C. Gladson, Eddie Van Hook, and Alton Crapo.[32]

When Crapo was arrested, he was found to be in possession of a stolen car and an unregistered sawed-off shotgun. Because of this the Feds charged him with violating the Dyer Act (taking a stolen car across state lines) and violating the National Firearms Act, for possession of the sawed-off shotgun.[33] The following June, Federal Judge Richard J. Hopkins sentenced Crapo to five years at Leavenworth Federal Prison for the possession of the sawed-off shotgun and five years' probation for a second violation.[34] However, again, authorities decided that Crapo's prison term should be reduced from 5 to 3 years![35] So, June of 1941, Crapo was let out to prey on the citizens of the midwest.[36]

By July of 1942, the FBI were again after Crapo and his life-long friend and co-conspirator, Albert Gladson. When Gladson was arrested, he was found to possess several bullet proof vests and was sleeping with a pistol under his pillow. Crapo, arrested at a different location the same night also had a weapon under his pillow. Neither of the suspects offered any resistance to the officers.[37] Both men were being pursued for the theft of tires and similar items and selling $5,000 worth on the black market.[38] With rubber so necessary with the war effort during World War II, selling stolen tires was highly frowned upon.

Alton Crapo's parole was revoked and he was sent back to Leavenworth to complete his five-year sentence.[39] May of 1943, Crapo was transferred to Alcatraz Penitentiary, "The Rock," near San Francisco Bay, to complete his incarceration.[40] Completing his time, he was released April 13, 1946, and was returned to Kansas City, Missouri, to answer to the violation of the Dyer Act, from 1942, which had not been previously pursued. He willingly pleaded guilty to the charge and was sentenced to 90-days confinement.[41]

No major problems involving Crapo were reported until June of 1949. Crapo and his pal, Gladson, on the 17th, robbed Elton L. Goldberg, a jewelry salesman, and Willard Davidson, a clothing salesman, who were driving on a detour near Lyons, Nebraska. A car containing Crapo and Gladson pulled alongside, pointed a shotgun at the two victims and made them stop their car and get out. The robbers took around $75,000 in jewels. Alton Crapo, now 47 and Albert C. Gladson, 48 were still committing crimes. After over twenty plus years of committing robberies, they had not reformed.

While in the process of the robbery, a witness stopped, thinking someone needed help and was told to get the blankety-blank out of there. The man immediately upon reaching a place where he could contact police notified them of the robbery. About two hours later, Colfax County Sheriff Edward J. Patach and Nebraska Safety Patrol Officer John Meistrell spotted the bandits' car about 12 miles south of Howells, Nebraska. Patrolmen James Everett Kruger and Robert Kline, hearing the call from officers, also converged on the area. After a heated gun battle, the bandits both lay dead.[42] It just seemed a fitting outcome for the 6-foot-4 Alton Frank Crapo and his longtime companion and crime partner, Albert Charles Gladson.

As for Henry Clopp, the other Bank of Manitou robber, he and two other men robbed the First National Bank of Holdrege, Nebraska, of over $5,000 on September 22, 1934. Included in his charges was violation of the "Dillinger Law." Originally enacted in the spring of 1934 and now cited in 18 U.S. Code § 2113(e):

> Whoever, in committing an offense defined in this section, or in avoiding or attempting to avoid apprehension for the commission of such offense, or in freeing himself or attempting to free himself from arrest or confinement for such offense, kills any person, or forces any person to accompany him without the consent of such person, shall be imprisoned not less than ten years, or if death results shall be punished by death or life imprisonment.

A summary of Clopp's criminal career is as follows:

Henry Estine Clopp, alias: William Clopp, John Clott and John Clopp[43]

DOB: 12 Mar 1891[44]
DOD: 27 Dec 1981 — Age 90[45]

Charged with the robbery of the:

09 May 1926	State Bank of Winfield, Kansas[46]
10 Mar 1927	Bank of Manitou, Colorado[47]
20 Feb 1934	State Bank of Fort Kearney, Nebraska[48]
11 Apr 1934	Security State Bank of Sterling, Colorado[49]
22 Sep 1934	First National Bank of Holdrege, Nebraska[50]

Convicted:

07 May 1928	Sentenced from 9 to 14 years at Cañon City, Colorado for Manitou robbery.[51]
11 Sep 1931	Paroled from Cañon City.[52]
06 Jan 1935	Arrested for Winfield, Kansas robbery.[53]

28 Jun 1935	Charged with bonds possession from Sterling, Colorado bank.[54]
11 Dec 1935	Sentenced to 4 years at McAlester, OK penitentiary for bonds.[55]
30 Apr 1938	Completed McAlester term, then arrested for Holdrege, Nebraska robbery.[56]
20 Apr 1939	Sentenced to 45 years at Leavenworth Federal Penitentiary for Holdrege robbery.[57]

During the Nebraska robbery five hostages were taken from the bank. L.B. Titus the bank cashier along with Nora Hueftle and Eva Crissman, both school teachers, were freed after a few blocks. The other two hostages, William Lindstrom and Belle Manley, were let go miles in the country. Because the hostages were taken, the above law violation was charged, but was later dropped during trial.[58]

Clopp's last sentence of 45 years means if he served the entire term, he may have died in prison. This information was not definitive. He did live to be 90 years of age.[59]

Notes

1. *Denver Post*, 10 Mar 1927, Page 2.
2. Unpublished manuscript, Hugh Harper, 1933, Page 54, from the Colorado Springs Pioneers' Museum.
3. *Colorado Springs Evening Telegraph*, 11 Mar 1927, Page 1.
4. Unpublished manuscript, Hugh Harper, 1933, Page 55, from the Colorado Springs Pioneers' Museum.
5. Unpublished manuscript, Hugh Harper, 1933, Page 56, from the Colorado Springs Pioneers' Museum.
6. *Colorado Springs Gazette* & Telegraph, 13 Mar 1927, Page 1.
7. *Colorado Springs Gazette*, 14 Mar 1927, Page 1.
8. *Colorado Springs Evening Telegraph*, 14 Mar 1927, Page 1.
9. Unpublished manuscript, Hugh Harper, 1933, Page 59, from the Colorado Springs Pioneers' Museum.
10. *Colorado Springs Evening Telegraph*, 16 Mar 1927, Page 1.
11. Unpublished manuscript, Hugh Harper, 1933, Pages 64 & 65, from the Colorado Springs Pioneers' Museum.
12. *Wichita Evening Eagle*, 28 Apr 1927, Page 1.
13. *Colorado Springs Evening Telegraph*, 29 Apr 1927, Page 1.
14. *Wichita Eagle*, 01 May 1927, Page 11.
15. *Wichita Evening Eagle*, 30 May 1927, Page 1.
16. *Colorado Springs Gazette*, 20 Sep 1927, Page 1.

17 *Wichita Evening Eagle*, 16 Jun 1928, Page 1.
18 *Colorado Springs Evening Telegraph*, 08 Oct 1927, Page 1
19 Unpublished manuscript, Hugh Harper, 1933, Pages 71 72, from the Colorado Springs Pioneers' Museum.
20 *Burbank Daily Review*, 20 Feb 1928, Page 6.
21 Nolle Contendere — a plea by which a defendant in a criminal prosecution accepts conviction as though a guilty plea had been entered but does not admit guilt.
22 *Denver Post*, 27 Apr 1928, Page 8.
23 *Denver Post*, 08 May 1928, Page 14.
24 *Wichita Evening Eagle*, 16 Jun 1928, Page 1.
25 *Colorado Springs Evening Telegraph*, 08 Oct 1927, Page 1.
26 *Denver Post*, 11 Sep 1931, Page 43.
27 *Emporia Gazette*, 03 Mar 1933, Page 1.
28 *Wichita Eagle*, 21 May 1935, Page 2.
29 *St. Louis Post-Dispatch*, 14 Sep 1937, Page 7.
30 *Sedalia Democrat*, 19 Mar 1935, Page 1.
31 *Sedalia Democrat*, 17 Sep 1937, Page 7.
32 *Lincoln Journal Star*, 26 Oct 1937, Page 5.
33 *Sedalia Democrat*, 12 Dec 1937, Page 1.
34 *Emporia Gazette*, 09 Jun 1938, Page 7.
35 *Herndon Nonpareil*, 02 Mar 1939, Page 1.
36 *Iola Kansas Register*, 05 Aug 1942, Page 1.
37 *Sedalia Democrat*, 30 Jul 1942, Page 4.
38 *Hutchinson News-Herald*, 28 Jan 1943, Page 1.
39 *Iola Register*, 05 Aug 1942, Page 1.
40 United States Penitentiary Prisoner Index.
41 *Kansas City Star*, 10 Jun 1946, Page 3.
42 *Lincoln Star*, 13 Dec 1949, Page 6.
43 *Muskogee Oklahoma Daily Phoenix & Times-Democrat*, 01 May 1938, Page 13.
44 Find-a-Grave Index
45 Find-a-Grave Index
45 *Newkirk Oklahoma Herald Journal*, 10 Jan 1935, Page 1.
47 *Colorado Springs Gazette*, 29 Sep 1928, Page 9.
48 *Lincoln Nebraska Journal Star*, 26 Oct 1937, Page 5.
49 *Tulsa Oklahoma World*, 29 Jun 1935, Page 7.
50 *Lincoln Nebraska Evening Journal*, 03 Aug 1937, Page 7.
51 *Denver Post*, 08 May 1928, Page 14.
52 *Denver Post*, 11 Sep 1931, Page 43.
53 *Ponca City Oklahoma News*, 07 Jan 1935, Page 5.
54 *Tulsa Oklahoma World*, 29 Jun 1935, Page 7.
55 *Ponca City Oklahoma News*, 11 Dec 1935, Page 6.
56 *Muskogee Oklahoma Daily Phoenix & Times-Democrat*, 13 May 1938, Page 7.
57 *Lincoln Nebraska Star Journal*, 20 Apr 1939, Page 9.
58 *Lincoln Nebraska Evening Journal*, 03 Aug 1937, Page 7.
59 Find-a-Grave Index

Chapter 23

GIDDINGS & KIRKWOOD DEPARTMENT STORE BURGLARY

The Black Sox Trial of 1921 was a result of players on the Chicago White Sox purposefully losing the 1919 World Series against the Cincinnati Reds for money. Eight members of the White Sox were tried for throwing the game but were found not guilty after records and the confessions disappeared during the trial. — elawtalk.com

The Roaring 20s would be a decade of many famous crimes: the St. Valentine's Day massacre, the bombing of Wallstreet killing 30 and injuring 200, the Black Sox trial and a bank in Texas was robbed by Santa Claus in December of 1927. One crime committed in Colorado Springs showed the downfall of a teenage boy who loved the finer things of life.

Sunday, November 27, 1921, should have been a typical quiet day of rest in Colorado Springs, but someone did not get the memo. During the early morning hours, the Giddings & Kirkwood store located on the northeast corner of Kiowa and Tejon Streets was entered and between thirty and forty thousand dollars worth of goods were taken. Fur coats, silk goods and undergarments, hosiery, petticoats and bolts of cloth were all removed.

By getting on the roof of the neighboring building, a window was pried open, allowing the perpetrator(s) to enter the building. Everything removed went out the back door of the store, where an alley was located. The burglar(s) were very discerning, only taking those things of the highest quality and value.

The store had a night watchman, but he did not work Saturday nights. Part of the items taken were four sheep-lined overcoats, three raccoon coats, one opossum coat, one blended rat coat (Really!?), one seal coat and one pony fur coat. The owners said these items retailed for up to $1,250 each. Complete cases of fountain pens, gold cuff links and stickpins were also taken.[1]

Thursday, December 1st, two employees of the YMCA contacted Chief Hugh Harper regarding a man who had been staying at the YMCA since mid-November, reporting he had given the matron an envelope containing $1,400 in cash. His activities also caused uneasiness, because at times he refused to leave his room so it could be cleaned. It was discovered the man, Gene Logan, had rented a house at 528½ West Pikes Peak Avenue, but continued to stay in his room at the YMCA. A detective was sent to check out the house where he found a trunk completely filled with silk stockings. Nothing else was found at that time. Detectives Robert Wraith and Michael Grant stayed in the house Thursday night hoping to catch the thief. Early the next morning Detective Grant found a trap door that entered into the garret above. He climbed into the garret and found close to two dozen fur coats hanging.

Chief of Police Hugh Harper believed the police should have a good relationship with the media. He learned through interviews with criminals that after they had committed a crime, they would read the newspaper to find out what the police knew. After the police had located the rental Logan was using, he called the newspapers. He showed them the recovered trunks and asked them for help. The reporters asked if they had apprehended the thief, and the chief replied, "No, but we will get him if your papers will cooperate with us."

The papers were happy to help and asked what they could do. Harper instructed the morning news to run a story stating the police were certain the silks and furs had been removed from the city, passed through Billings, Montana, and were on their way to Canada. He also instructed the editor of the evening paper to do the same, but said the goods were traced through Salt Lake City on their way to the Pacific coast. He did not want the misleading story to die in hopes the information would make Logan think he had gotten away with his crime.²

The following Tuesday Logan was arrested around 1:00 a.m. as he drove a Paige auto into the Birdsall garage on Nevada Avenue. Santa Fe Special Agent San Frabizio and CSPD Officer George Kaltenberger made the arrest. When questioned, Logan said the trunk full of silk stockings belonged to him. Most everything taken in the burglary of the store was recovered. The Hiltbrand Music Company at 125½ North Tejon Street, half a block north of Gidding's building, had also been robbed the same night as the other burglary. Numerous musical instruments had been taken. The instruments were also recovered.³

After several hours of questioning, Logan admitted to the burglary. The car he was driving at the time of his arrest was found to be stolen. He told officers the burglary took him four and one-half hours to complete, hauling all the goods in a Buick he had recently purchased in Colorado Springs. He would not give any information about his past or anything about his family.⁴ After police put out a request for information about the stolen car, they received information from the sheriff of Lyon County, Kansas. The car had been stolen from Emporia, Kansas, after someone broke into a garage, drained gas from two other cars and left with the vehicle.⁵

Logan was said to have committed robberies in Washington, Iowa and Miami, Florida and his real name was Gene Mason. He was accused of escaping from the Ohio State Reformatory at the end of October.⁶ Police received a complete criminal record from a Department of Justice agent at Leavenworth, Kansas. The record showed his name was Gene Mason, age 19. His specialty was taking silks and furs. His criminal history began in Miami, Florida, where he was arrested February, 1920, for grand larceny. He was sentenced to a state farm at Rayford, Florida in March to serve one year. By November of that year, he was arrested in Kansas City, Missouri and turned over to Ohio, where he was wanted by Wayne County for stealing an auto. He was then sent to a reformatory at Mansfield,

Ohio, for a short term.⁷ Sheriff Charles Gibson of Emporia, Kansas, in his investigation, found that Mason (aka: Logan) had stolen a Paige auto from Washington, Iowa, where he robbed two stores, and then one in Centerville, Iowa. The Washington, Iowa, sheriff spotted the car and gave chase but lost track in Kansas City. Emporia's Sheriff Gibson found the Paige abandoned in Emporia, with a ruined engine. The next night Mason took another Paige auto belonging to Omar Kirkendall of Emporia. This was the vehicle recovered in Colorado Springs.⁸

El Paso District Court Judge John Sheafor, sentenced him to a term at Cañon City of seven to ten years after the defendant's plea of guilty.⁹ Born in Butte, Montana, in 1902, Mason was only 19 years old.¹⁰ The day before Mason/Logan was to be taken to the Colorado State Penitentiary, he escaped from the county jail.

Somehow Mason/Logan obtained a saw while being closely watched, and sawed through a bar. With a piece of metal conduit, he pushed out a screen in his cell and dropped eight feet to the ground. Guards were instructed to check on the prisoner often. When they went by his cell they could see the shape of his body under the blankets, only he was gone and had formed a body-like shape from blankets and other clothing. He made it three blocks north on Cascade to the Holleman Company, 122 North Cascade Avenue, where he broke into the garage, obtained a Paige auto, relocked the business and drove south from town.

Around midnight, an auto going east by Stratton Home toward the Harrison school, known as the Bates Ranch Road, tried to drive through a sharp turn. The car was traveling too fast and skidded off the road, rolling over several times. The driver was trapped under the car.¹¹ A car was following the car when it wrecked. The two men, Merle Clow and William O. Kelly, managed to lift the car and pull the driver from underneath. The one man thought the youthful driver looked like Gene Logan. A call was quickly made for an ambulance. The ambulance arrived around midnight, but the driver was dead, his head having been crushed. Coroner Russell

Law was the driver of the ambulance. He also believed the deceased was Gene Logan. He called the county jail and inquired whether Logan was still in jail and was told the jailer had checked on Logan a few minutes earlier.

Police officers not being satisfied with the answer of the jailer, went to the jail and had the cell of Logan checked. It appeared that he was in the bed asleep, but when they entered the cell, they found Logan was missing.[12]

An effort to locate Logan's family by Coroner Law was attempted. After several days with no reply, Logan was buried at Evergreen Cemetery in Colorado Springs, lot 107.[13]

Notes

1. *Colorado Springs Gazette*, 28 Nov 1921, Page 11.
2. Unpublished manuscript, Hugh D. Harper, 1933, Pages 5, 6, at Colorado Springs Pioneers' Museum.
3. *Colorado Springs Gazette*, 06 Dec 1921, Page 1.
4. *Colorado Springs Gazette*, 07 Dec 1921, Page 1.
5. *Emporia Gazette*, 09 Nov 1921, Page 1.
6. *Denver Post*, 14 Dec 1921, Page 27.
7. *Colorado Springs Gazette*, 14 Dec 1921, Page 1.
8. *Emporia Gazette*, 09 Dec 1921, Page 5.
9. *Colorado Springs Gazette*, 05 Jan 1922, Page 3.
10. *Colorado Springs Gazette*, 24 Dec 1921, Page 1.
11. *Colorado Springs Gazette*, 07 Jan 1922, Page 1.
12. *Colorado Springs Gazette*, 07 Jan 1922, Page 2.
13. *Colorado Springs Gazette*, 13 Jan 1922, Page 12

Chapter 24

Albert A. "Danny" Daniels

Tear gas was first used in World War I in chemical warfare, but since its effects are short-lasting and rarely disabling, it came into use by law-enforcement agencies as a means of dispersing mobs, disabling rioters, and flushing out armed suspects without the use of deadly force. — www.britannica.com

Albert A. Daniels, a native of Mississippi, was born August 1, 1891.[1] At twenty he was trying to become a boxer. Christmas, 1911, Daniels was tried out for two rounds by a promoter at Coffeyville, Kansas, in the lightweight division, because his weight was below 152 pounds.[2] He continued to compete in several minor matches. In January 1912 he was arrested for stealing clothing from a man's room in Coffeyville.[3]

During March, Daniels was receiving billing for a fight in Independence, Kansas against a ranked fighter.[4] He was a popular boxer, but that did not help him win the match. He continued to be promoted in small matches till 1915. Then in July, he was arrested again in Tulsa, Oklahoma, for a burglary.[5] The day following his arrest, he was arraigned in court, only to find that a second charge was to be levied for stealing an electric fan from another person.[6]

Daniels does not pop up in the news again until 1924, when he was sent to Oklahoma State Prison at McAlester in February to serve a term of one year after being found guilty of a larceny.[7] The next year, Daniels was arrested and convicted of larceny and assault with intent to kill, but was booked under the name of T.F. Dailey.[8]

Not being able to stay out of trouble, he was again arrested

October of 1926. This time for burglary. He was sentenced to serve seven years at Bartlesville, Oklahoma.[9] He also burglarized a grocery store at Miami, Oklahoma.[10] He was charged with robbing a bank at Billings, Missouri, along with Charley Stalcup.[11] Daniels was not in prison yet, as his convictions were being reviewed by the Oklahoma State Supreme Court.[12] This is just some background on Mr. Albert A. "Danny" Daniels prior to his arrival in Colorado Springs.

Daniels, still out on bail and awaiting decisions on his appeals, was in Colorado Springs in September of 1927. Several places in town had been broken into, safes entered at two cafeterias, a theater and stores robbed during the Memorial Day holiday weekend. Daniels and his gang members were known to be safe crackers and these crimes were later believed to be done by his gang.[13] The gang was based out of Pueblo.

Wednesday night, September 28, 1927, Officer George Kaltenberger was walking his beat downtown on East Colorado Avenue, when near the entrance to Buckwald Jewelry Company, 13 East Colorado Avenue, someone started shooting at him. The officer saw a man on the roof of the building and engaged him in gunfire. Other officers hearing the gunfire, converged on the area, but the man on the roof had escaped.

Looking inside the jewelry store, a heavy amount of smoke was seen and the fire department was called. Right after the fire department arrived, Detective Greenhoe saw a crouching figure in the National Café, 13½ East Colorado Avenue, next door to the jewelry store. The figure was able to get to a coal storage area. Officers, trying to get to the man, rushed the back door and Officer Olin Burton was shot in the right arm, severing an artery. The officer was rushed to Glockner Sanatorium (now Penrose Hospital) for treatment. Chief Harper sent for tear gas bombs to be brought to their location.

Officer John Campbell heard the bandit shout, "If you guys think you are so tough, why in Hell don't you come in after me?" After the arrival of the tear gas, it was thrown into the building, but seemed to be ineffective. After a second siege was made by officers, Officer

Benjamin H. McMahon was shot in his right arm, which shattered the radius bone. He was taken to Beth El Hospital (now Memorial Central) for treatment.

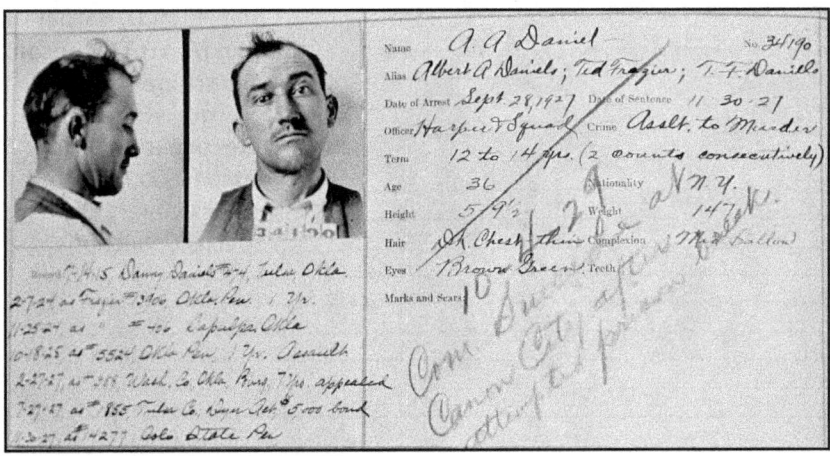

1927 Booking record of Albert A. Daniels. Courtesy of the CSPD.

Since nothing was working, Chief Harper sent Officer Kaltenberger for a Thompson .45-caliber machine gun to be brought to the scene. Officers got on the roof, surrounded a skylight and gave Officer Kaltenberger cover. Inspector I.B. Bruce, Officers George Taylor, Hugh Higgins and Robert Martin, gave cover fire, so Kaltenberger could fire the Thompson down through the coal chute into the building. After emptying the 50-round canister of .45-caliber bullets from the machine gun, the bandit had a change of heart and exited the building and surrendered.

At police headquarters, the bandit, identified as Albert A. "Danny" Daniels, told of gaining entrance into the café at about 2:00 a.m. and then ripping a hole into the wall between the café and the jewelry store. He and some cohorts were using three acetylene torches in an attempt to enter through the back of the safe in the jewelry/pawn store. After the initial shooting at the beat officer, a total of fifteen officers arrived at the scene.[14]

CSPD Chief Hugh D. Harper holding M1921 Thompson submachine "Tommy" gun while Detective Irvin Bruce watches. Courtesy of Pikes Peak Library District, Special Collections.

Information was received the next day from the Pueblo Police Department; they had arrested Foster Paul Kasiah and Ralph Scott, and recovered a pile of loot. Chief Harper traveled to Pueblo to assist in questioning the two arrestees. A bill of sale from a Pueblo garage was found for the purchase of acetylene outfits, which were believed to be the ones used in the attempted safe robbery in Colorado Springs.[15] The police had found Danny Daniels' gang members.

1927 Booking record of Foster Paul Kosiah. Courtesy of the CSPD.

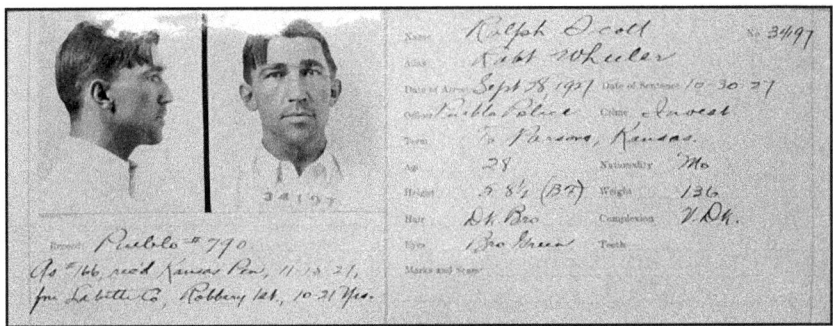

1927 Booking record of Ralph Scott.
Courtesy of the CSPD.

The burglars gained entrance to the National Café, by going through the skylight on the roof using a rope ladder. An awning was placed behind the café counter to block light of the cutting torch from being seen through the windows. Then they began tearing through the wall. A problem occurred when the wallpaper near the safe caught fire and smoked the interior of the building. It forced them to get on the roof and open the skylight to vent the smoke. Then they spotted the officer on his rounds. Thinking they had been discovered, the bandits took pistol shots at the officer. The two on the roof climbed down to a car and escaped, leaving Daniels in the building.[16]

A third gang member being pursued, was identified as George R. Dyer, who was later identified as Ray Terrill, a leader of a gang which included many other members.[17] An unexpected result from the attempted robbery was the 60-year-old owner of the National Café, Charles R. Pittock, in delicate health, died from the stress of the incident. Knowing the business would have to be closed for some time while it was repaired was just too much for him to handle.[18]

Daniels trial was held on Tuesday, November 22, 1927, in El Paso County District Court. The case went to the jury at 3:15 p.m. and the jury returned a guilty verdict on the charge of attempting to kill police officers at Buckwald Jewelry. A second trial was held right after the end of the first trial and this time the jury was out

20 minutes and another guilty verdict was given for the attempted burglary of the jewelry store.[19]

A week later, while in the El Paso County jail, the county jailer, Frank H. Botts was giving Daniels his 4:00 p.m. meal. Daniels reached through the bars and tried to kill the jailer with a safety razor blade he had in his hand. The jailer, seeing movement from the corner of his eye, jerked back just fast enough to receive only a minor laceration.[20] Daniels was taken to the Cañon City Penitentiary that same day, to begin his sentence.[21]

Two years after his incarceration at Cañon City, Daniels was responsible for the worst riot in the history of the institution. In a show of contempt for society norms and proof that Daniels was a sociopath, he started a riot at the Colorado State Prison in Cañon City in 1929. Thursday morning, October 3rd, prison guard Elmer George Erwin entered the crow's nest gun cage. The cage extended over the dining area to oversee the prisoner's noon meal. Danny Daniels and James Pardue left their jobs in the laundry and had donned civilian clothing under their prison garb. Somehow, they had obtained handguns which were previously hidden. Normally prisoners were to return to their cells for a prisoner count before the lunch was served, but instead of returning to line up for lunch, they took stairs to the trustee's dormitory located over the Deputy Warden's office.

Since the trustees ate before the rest of the prison population, the dormitory was empty. Officer Marvin Duncan noticed Pardue was missing from the line of prisoners exiting Cell House No. 1, but failed to report it. Daniels was also missing from his lineup at Cell House No. 2 and was noted by Officer John Pease, who reported the problem, but it was not checked on until after the lunch time.

Daniels and Pardue waited in the dormitory until the end of lunch at 12:20 p.m. After all the prisoners had left the dining hall and returned to the front of their cells, Officer Ferguson unlocked the door by the Deputy Warden's office, which now allowed Daniels and Pardue to come down the stairs. Since the guards were unaware of what was transpiring, guard Erwin unlocked the crow's nest, and stored his Winchester rifle and relocked the door. Halfway down the ladder from the crow's nest, the guard heard a voice tell him to be quiet and give him his keys. Erwin tried to grab Pardue's pistol, and was shot twice for his attempt. A guard on the west gate had been bribed in advance so Daniels and Pardue could escape, but the shooting of the guard warned others of something being amiss and they were unable to get to the gate.

Using the guard's keys, Daniels entered the crow's nest and grabbed the Winchester rifle. The prisoners then made their way to where the telephone equipment was and quickly destroyed it so there would be no outside communications. Daniels ran back to the trustee's dormitory room and with the rifle, shot and killed the tower guard, Walter Rinker. Daniels then proceeded to a window in the chapel where he shot and killed Guard Ray Brown stationed on tower nine.

Pardue, attempted to eliminate Tower 1 Guard Myron H. Goodwin by making his way between the bakery and cell house No. 3. However, Goodwin saw Pardue and fired first, striking the prisoner, breaking Pardue's pelvis. Meanwhile Daniels along with prisoners Alfred Davis and Leo McGenty helped round up the unarmed guards. Weapons had been previously smuggled into Cell House No. 1 and the prisoners took the guards there to recover the weapons. In cell 18, where Pardue was housed, the prisoners dug into the wall and recovered the weapons.

After getting the weapons, guards were lined up by the windows so the tower guards could not shoot into the cell block. Other prisoners went to the kitchen to get kerosene which they took to the chapel, broke up the chairs and set them afire. The fire soon spread to other facilities.

Prisoner Alfred Davis, after breaking into the tailor shop, was in a position that put him above guard tower No. 1. From there Davis shot Guard Goodwin in a lung. Guards began using bullhorns and ordered prisoners to leave cell houses and go to the bullpen and wait. About 400 prisoners did as directed. The bullpen was located on the south side of the complex. It was cold outside and darkness was coming. With Cell Houses 1 and 2 on fire, everyone was forced to go into Cell House No. 3.

Now late in the afternoon, an alarm of a fashion was sounded when the whistle on the prison boiler house and siren of the Colorado Power Company sounded. This drew off-duty guards to the prison, along with hundreds of local citizens. Warden Francis E. Crawford was in Colorado Springs at the CSPD headquarters. A call was made to the CSPD and the warden headed back toward the prison.

By 3:00 p.m., the Colorado National Guard had responded to the prison. Three guards had been killed and 10 more taken hostage. They were locked in cells in Cell House No. 3. At 4:15 p.m., prisoner Joe Schillo was sent to the front gate to give the warden Danny Daniels' demands. Three cars were to be waiting at the West Gate by dark, gassed up, and free passage guaranteed for the prisoners. The guards were to be held hostage during the planned escape. The guards would then be turned loose. If the warden tried to rescue or take the prisoners, the guards would be killed.

After delivering Daniels' message, the prisoner, Schillo, told the warden he was not going back into the prison. The Warden said there would be no deal. Upon hearing the reply of the warden, Schillo told him if the demands were not met, Daniels would kill Guard John Pease. By then police officers had arrived from Denver, Colorado Springs, and Pueblo.

By 7:45 p.m., no answer had come from the warden, so Daniels took Guard John J. Eeles from a cell and shot him in the head, but he did not die. Another prisoner, Red Reilley, shot the guard two more times in the body. Five prisoners carried the wounded guard to the West Gate, and did not return to the prison. Daniels said that if demands were not met, he would kill another guard every 30 minutes. The warden did not capitulate.

Daniels, angered by the warden's refusal, had guard Robert A.

Wiggins shot in the head, killing him. He called out to another guard, Jack Shea, and told him to go with the body of Wiggins and again tell the warden to comply.

Before the siege ended, eight guards had been killed along with four convicts. Daniels shot each of his compatriots, killing each before he turned the gun on himself. Ten other men were wounded during the melee, including Colorado Springs Detective Robert Wraith, who suffered a leg wound.[22] A little before dawn the riot was over. All the rioting prisoners were dead.

Before his crime in Colorado, Daniels was part of much larger gang that terrorized Oklahoma and parts of Kansas for years. Daniels showed his contempt for law and order for over seventeen years.

Notes

1 World War I draft registration, 05 Jun 1917.
2 *Coffeyville Daily Journal*, 26 Dec 1911, Page 2.
3 *Coffeyville Daily Journal*, 06 Jan 1912, Page 5.
4 *Independence Daily Reporter*, 01 Mar 1912, Page 7.
5 *Miami Oklahoma, News-Record*, 29 Dec 1927, Page 5.
6 *Tulsa Daily World*, 16 Jul 1915, Page 4.
7 *Miami Oklahoma, News-Record*, 29 Dec 1927, Page 5.
8 *Miami Oklahoma, News-Record*, 04 Oct 1929, Page 5.
9 *Miami Oklahoma, News-Record*, 29 Dec 1927, Page 5.
10 *Miami Oklahoma, News-Record*, 04 Oct 1929, Page 5.
11 *Neosho Missouri Daily News*, 07 Apr 1927, Page 4.
12 *Springfield Missouri Leader & Press*, 08 Apr 1927, Page 1.
13 *Longmont Daily Times*, 06 Sep 1927, Page 1.
14 *Colorado Springs Gazette*, 28 Sep 1927, Page 1,
15 *Colorado Springs Gazette*, 29 Sep 1927, Page 1.
16 *Colorado Springs Gazette*, 29 Sep 1927, Page 2.
17 *Colorado Springs Gazette*, 01 Oct 1927, Page 1.
18 *Colorado Springs Gazette*, 10 Oct 1927, Page A1.
19 *Colorado Springs Gazette*, 23 Nov 1927, Page A1.
20 *Colorado Springs Gazette*, 30 Nov 1927, Page A1.
21 *Miami Daily News-Record*, 04 Oct 1929, Page 1.
22 *Slaughter in Cell House 3—The Anatomy of a Riot*, By Wayne K. Patterson & Betty L. Alt, 2010, Dog Ear Publishing, Indianapolis.

Chapter 25

LAMAR BANK ROBBERY

Law enforcement aviation was born in 1929 when the New York City Police Department assigned fixed wing airplanes to combat the growing aviation menace of the day; barnstormers! — A Primer on Police Aviation by Kenneth Solosky

Lamar, Colorado, a farm community located 160 miles southeast of Colorado Springs, is about 30 miles west of the Kansas border. Located in Prowers County, the town was only 42 years old in 1928 when it suffered a tragic bank robbery. The First National Bank of Lamar was robbed on Wednesday, May 23, 1928, just after 1:00 p.m. by four men who killed the bank president and his son, leaving with over $219,000, before they escaped in a car.[1]

The bank was located in the center of the town, on the northwest corner of Olive and Main Streets, the two major roads (today, US Highways 385 and 50). Bank president, Amos Newton Parrish, 77, and his son, John Festus Parrish, 40, cashier, were both in the bank at the time of the robbery.[2] When they realized the bank was being

President of Lamar First National Bank, Amos N. Parrish.
Courtesy of Big Timbers Museum, Lamar, CO.

robbed, A.N. Parrish grabbed a single-action Colt .44-caliber revolver, called "Old Betsy" and fired at one of the robbers, wounding him in the face; in response the banker was fatally shot.[3]

Cashier of Lamar First National Bank, John F. Parrish. Courtesy of Big Timbers Museum, Lamar, CO.

John Parrish attempted to get to a weapon located in a closet, but was killed for his effort. The bandit killed John Parrish with a .38-caliber revolver. A total of eleven shots were fired before the robbery was completed. The leader yelled, "Show us the money, the gold and Liberty bonds!"[4]

William H. Hill, a customer, was standing at a teller's window when the robbery began. Those in the bank were told to lie down, face the floor and no one would be hurt. The teller, Eskel A. Lundgren, saw that Hill was frozen and unmoving. Lundgren tried to get Hill's attention and told him to lie down, "They will kill you." At that same time one of the bandits heading toward the rear entrance to the bank suddenly lay on the floor, believing the lead robber had ordered him to lie down.[5] Witnesses in the bank believe his name was Bill.

Of the seven employees in the building at the time of the robbery, no one else was injured. The robbers drove a blue Buick 4-door parked outside to make their escape.[6] Two of the employees, Everett A. Kesinger, 26, and Eskel A. Lundgren (a one-armed WWI veteran), were taken hostage and forced to lie on the floor of the bandit's vehicle. Lundgren was tossed out of the car by the bandits a few miles from Lamar uninjured.[7]

A Denver man, who was in Lamar, heard the shooting and saw the robbers exit the bank. He recorded the license number of their car; however, no one knew in his haste he had transposed a couple of the license numbers.[8]

Prowers County Sheriff Lloyd Earl Alderman, 36, arrived minutes after the robbery and accompanied by one of the bank customers, Harry Anderson, gave chase in the sheriff's Studebaker Commander.[9] At one point the sheriff caught up with the bandits who were armed with rifles and the sheriff's car was hit at least nine times with bullets, partially disabling the Studebaker.[10] After the bandits escaped to the east, Alderman was able to coax his vehicle east to Bristol, Colorado, approximately 15 miles.[11]

Sheriff Alderman called Chief Harper of Colorado Springs and asked for him to go to Lamar and help with the investigation of the robbery and murders. Harper instead sent Detective Sergeant Robert Wraith, who had tracking abilities. Detective Wraith, in company of the sheriff, was able to follow the robber's vehicle tracks about fifty miles into Lakin, Kansas, which is approximately 25 miles west of Garden City, Kansas. The robbers had zig-zagged all over in an apparent attempt to make it hard to track them. Most roads were still dirt in the 1920s making it easier to track a car. Sheriff Alderman had given much assistance to Chief Harper, 51, when the Bank of Manitou was robbed and Harper did feel an obligation to the sheriff. After conferring with the mayor and city manager, they directed Harper to go to Lamar and help with the investigation.[12] The Banker's Association of Colorado, because of Chief Harper's work on solving previous bank robberies in Colorado, retained the chief to assist in solving this crime.[13]

Chief Harper, upon arriving in Lamar, went directly to the bank to view the crime scene, then tried to personally interview as many witnesses in the area at the time of the robbery. Descriptions of the bandits were all over the map. The robbers were described as "all young men, probably less than thirty years of age . . . all about the same height." Actually, the robbers, when apprehended ranged in age from twenty-seven to forty-nine, the shortest 5'8" and tallest 6'6"! The robber driving the getaway car was described as "a young golden-haired kid, bareheaded, with his golden locks blowing in the breeze." After the robbers were arrested, the driver turned out to be a short, white-haired forty-nine-year-old. Due to the poor eyewitness descriptions, several groups of men and many other gangs were arrested and paraded in front of the witnesses. Each time the witnesses were sure the people brought before them were the robbers—BUT—each time they were mistaken. So much for eyewitness identification! [14]

1927 Buick owned by the Fleagle Gang.
Courtesy of Big Timbers Museum, Lamar, Colorado.

Airplanes, for the first time, were used in searching for the bank robbers. Two planes from Lowry field in Denver were dispatched to assist and also a plane from Pueblo.

Late that same night, Dr. William Wesley Wineinger, age 39, of Dighton, Kansas, was awakened and told his help was needed for a person injured on a nearby farm.[15] The doctor followed the men to a ranch north of Garden City, Kansas in his 1925 blue Buick 2-door sedan. He was accompanied by one of the men that had summoned the doctor.

Doctor Wineinger upon seeing the injured man, knew he had suffered a massive gunshot wound to the face. The jaw of the robber was all but cut in two at the chin and the bullet had exited from the side of his neck. All the doctor was able to do was stem the blood flow. The doctor was blindfolded and driven from the bandit's hideout in his car. He was told he would be released, however, after driving several miles the doctor was forced from the vehicle and shot to death.[16]

Dr. William Wineinger's car.
Courtesy of Big Timbers Museum, Lamar, Colorado.

On Friday, May 25th, a Colorado National Guard plane flown by Lieutenant Carlos Reavis and Sergeant John Douglas Hissong, spotted the doctor's car in a ravine.[17] Wineinger's body was found near the car, which was about 22 miles north of Scott City and west of Dighton, Kansas. Upon Alderman being notified, he contacted Garden City Police Chief Lee Clement Richardson, who dispatched his fingerprint expert, Roland S. Terwilliger, 33. The robbers had taken time to clean the doctor's car of evidence. Terwilliger found the right-side window of the car was slightly damaged, the window was rolled down inside the door and resisted being raised. After he removed the frame, he was able to access the window. The window was removed and taken to Garden City, where a single fingerprint was found and recorded. When the suspects were found, a finger print comparison would be invaluable.[18] Photographed copies of the unidentified fingerprint were made and sent to all major law enforcement agencies across the country, including the Bureau of Identification in Washington, D.C.[19]

June 12, 1928, twenty days after the robbery, the body of the kidnapped cashier of the Lamar bank was discovered when a ten-year-old boy was exploring while with a group having a picnic. About ten miles northeast of Liberal, Kansas, the decomposed body of Everett Asa Kesinger was found. He had been shot in the chest and had sustained a major injury to his head from some blunt instrument.[20] Marienthal, Kansas, about 75 miles northeast of Lamar, was where Kesinger was killed. Kesinger's body was then transported to the Liberal, Kansas area.[21]

Over the next fifteen months, over one hundred people were arrested for questioning and possible involvement in the robbery. Even though these arrested individuals were not involved, most turned out to be wanted in other areas of the country and were subsequently turned over to those agencies holding charges and/or warrants.

Saturday morning, March 9th, 1929, a man who stated his name was William Harrison Holden was arrested in Stockton, California, fingerprinted and the prints sent to the Bureau of Identification in Washington, D.C.[22] Albert Bradford Ground, a fingerprint clerk, while classifying the print card, thought one of the prints looked like something for which he had been looking. Pulling out the print sent by Terwilliger in the fingerprint office of Garden City, Kansas, a check found the print belonged to the man arrested in Stockton. Shortly, Holden was identified as Jake Fleagle, who had served a term in the Oklahoma penitentiary, where he had been fingerprinted.[23]

Armed with information about Jacob "Jake" Harrison Fleagle, Chief Harper and Sheriff Alderman found a Fleagle family owned a farm north of Garden City, Kansas. The family's father, Jacob Booth Fleagle, and two of his sons, Walter Howard Fleagle and Frederick Earl Fleagle were arrested and placed in the Garden City jail for investigation.[24] "Little Jake's" aliases included: "James Reed; Joseph Reed; Joe Baker; Clarence Warren; and Henry Warren."[25]

The family was transferred to Colorado Springs, where they were interrogated by Chief Hugh Harper.[26] It was found the family had large deposits in banks at Dodge City, Garden City, Scott City and other Kansas banks; many under assumed names. When asked to explain where the money was derived, they said it was profits from their cattle business. The deposits totaled nearly $100,000.[27]

Another Fleagle, Ralph Emmerson Fleagle, was arrested near Kankakee, Illinois, where a group of bonds and securities were recovered. He was using the name of Arthur Kunz. Also arrested at the same area was George Washington DeMoss, who represented himself as a physician and had been living with "Little" Jacob H. Fleagle presenting as a real estate dealer. Jacob had managed to avoid arrest at that time.[28]

During August, George Johnson Abshier, 32, aka: William C. Messick, had been arrested and confessed to being one of the robbers of the Lamar First National Bank. Howard Lester Royston, 36, arrested in San Andreas, California, at his home, by Chief Harper, admitted that he was the bandit that had been shot in the face during the robbery. Royston identified Ralph and Jake Fleagle as two of the members involved in the robbery. Abshier's confession came about because he was shown the information that Royston had told police, and Abshier saw there was no further reason to hold out telling what happened.[29]

After obtaining confessions from the three arrestees. it was determined that Ralph Fleagle killed the bank cashier and Everett A.

Kesinger, who had been kidnapped by the gang. "Little" Jake Fleagle was the member who killed Dr. William W. Wineinger of Dighton, Kansas, after he had treated Royston. In the confessions, it was told to authorities that many of the bonds stolen during the robbery were burned, but the stories differed as to where that occurred.[30]

September 1929, the three arrested members of the gang were put on trial in Lamar, Colorado. On the first day of the preliminary hearing, the three gang members all pled guilty to murder and robbery. Jury selection began on the last day of September, which happened to coincide with the crash of the country's stock market. With the assumption that Abshier did not commit any of the murders during this crime spree, he was tried first.[31]

Before the trial could really get started, Colorado experienced the worst incident at the Colorado State Penitentiary involving the attempted escape of prisoners. Eight guards and seven prisoners died.

Early in October, Colorado Attorney General Robert Emmett Winbourn issued a statement: "the State of Colorado is a party to the agreement that Ralph Fleagle shall not be hanged, through the district attorney's promise to the bandit and should the jury in his case inflict the death penalty, undoubtedly the state supreme court would reverse it and enforce life imprisonment."[32] This promise was issued because Ralph had made a total confession to the crime and about everyone involved, which allowed the solving of the crime.

On the first day of October, the *Colorado Springs Gazette*, published a statement written by George J. Abshier with regards to the Lamar bank robbery of May 23, 1928. Ralph and Jake Fleagle had met with Abshier and Royston in California shortly after Christmas of 1927 and talked about robbing a bank. Abshier had gone to Kansas in February and made several trips to Lamar to look the bank over. It was decided that they needed another man. Royston was included in the plans. He said that Royston, who lived in San Andreas, California, received a letter from "Little" Jake Fleagle, saying they wanted Royston and Abshier to appear at Fred Fleagle's ranch, at Marienthal, Kansas as soon as he could. After arriving at the ranch at the beginning of May, the four men made several trips to Lamar to scope out the bank.

Ralph Fleagle provided a Buick for the robbery and both Royston and Abshier were to receive 10 percent of the loot. The day of the robbery, they arrived in Lamar about 9:00 a.m. Abshier and Royston stopped at a restaurant to eat breakfast and await the opening of the bank. Their car was parked on Olive Street around the side of the bank and near the back door. Ralph led the men from across Main Street to the front door of the bank, which faced the corner at an angle. Jake followed Ralph, then Abshier and last Royston. Jake had a .38-caliber revolver, Ralph was carrying a .38-short caliber, Royston a .44-caliber revolver, and Abshier was carrying an unknown caliber.

Once inside they found three customers waiting their turn. When they announced it was a holdup, the president, A.N. Parrish, reached his desk where he had an old .45-caliber revolver, and fired a shot, which struck Royston in the front of the jaw, the bullet exiting out the back of the neck, but it did not seem to faze Royston. Jake then shot the president killing him. John Parrish, tried to get to a gun near the safe, and was killed by another shot. The bandits, had pillowcases for carrying the loot, filled the bags and grabbed two of the employees, Everett A. Kesinger and Eskel A. Lundgren. The original plan was to kidnap the president's son, believing the president would hesitate to give pursuit to the bandits. But since both were dead, they grabbed two other men and forced them into their blue Buick and escaped to the east. Several miles out of town, they put Lundgren out and held Kesinger.[33]

On October 11th, George Abshier was found guilty of first-degree murder—the jury recommended the death penalty. The jury deliberated for just over three hours. Abshier's attorney stated the conviction would be appealed to the state supreme court.[34] A few days later Royston's trial began with a trip to the bank, which included Royston, handcuffed to Roy Best. Best would later be a

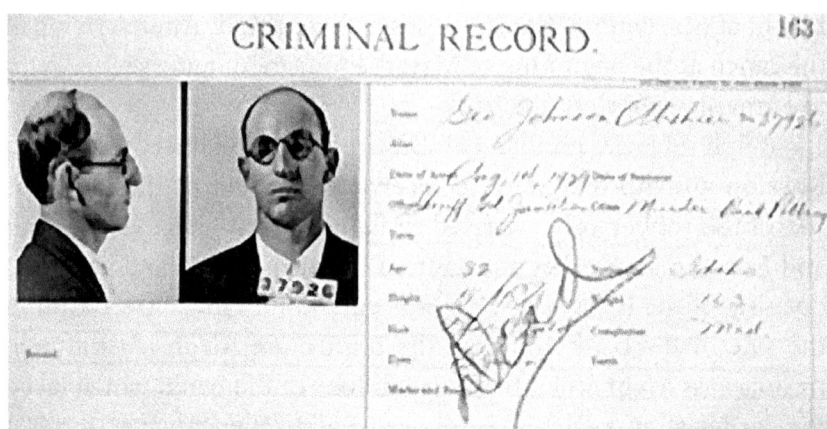

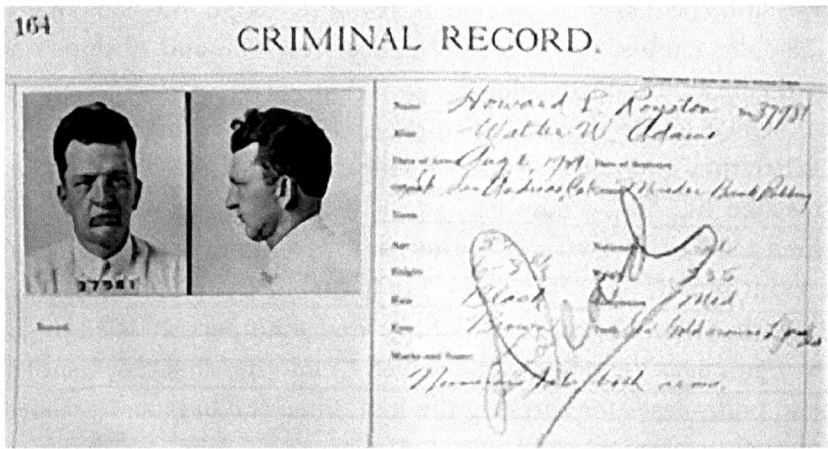

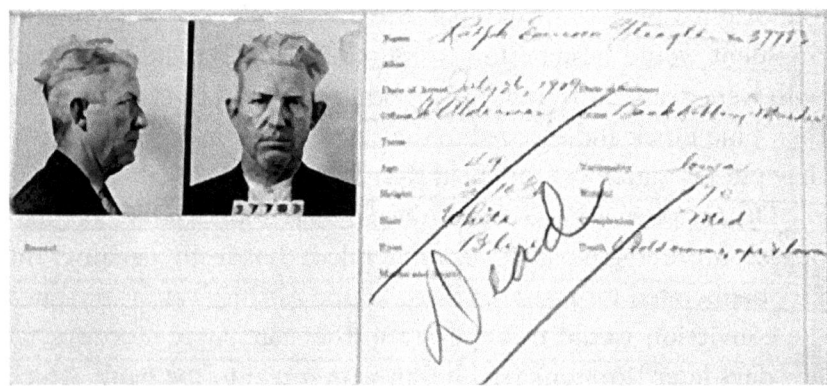

1929 Booking records of George J. Abshier, Howard L. Royston and Ralph Emmerson Fleagle. Courtesy of CSPD.

long-time warden of the Colorado State Penitentiary. Royston explained where he was when the robbery occurred. He said after he was shot, he had hardly any memory of what happened.[35] Like Abshier, Royston was found guilty of first-degree murder and ordered to hang.[36]

Finally, the last trial was for Ralph Fleagle, the mastermind of the robbery. Chief Harper was called to testify regarding his deal with Ralph: ". . . Fleagle would not be hanged for his part in the robbery if he would make a confession."[37] After much arguing among the attorneys about the promise, the judge told the jury they were not held to the promise and were to decide the fate of the prisoner. Trial was begun on October 22nd, 1929[38] and was put to the jury on Saturday, October 26th. After four hours of deliberation the jury came back with a decision of guilty and sentenced to death.[39]

After the three defendants appealed to the Colorado Supreme Court and had their sentences confirmed, Ralph Fleagle was hung July 10, 1930, at the state penitentiary at Cañon City. Ralph's body was taken to Garden City, Kansas, and buried in the Valley View Cemetery; he was 49.[40] July 18th, George Abshier was hung followed by Howard Royston the same evening.[41] Abshier was buried in the prison cemetery, known as Woodpecker Hill.[42] Royston's body was sent to Richmond, California.[43]

All that was left was to find Jake Fleagle. In July of 1930, Jake wrote a letter to Colorado Governor William Herbert Adams. The letter gave a clue as to his whereabouts. Jake pleaded to the Governor to give his brother Ralph the clemency promised.[44] Ralph Fleagle on the night of his execution, during a confession to the prison priest, told Father Regis Barrett, he believed his brother would be captured in a gun battle.[45]

During long interrogations of Abshier and Royston, by postal authorities, it was believed that Fleagle was making contact with cronies of his through newspaper advertisements. Police then placed "blind" ads in newspapers in Kansas City and Wichita. The ads urged that Fleagle meet October 14th at Branson, Missouri.

Since Chief Hugh Harper knew Fleagle by sight, he was asked to be at the meeting location to help identify the gangster.[46]

Tuesday, October 14, 1930, eight officers were on a train from Kansas City to Branson, Missouri. The officers were:

Joe Parham, Missouri Pacific special agent.
Lieutenant Harry Norman Wilde of the Los Angeles police department.
Detective Chester Alvin Lloyd of Los Angeles.
Harry Hall Goodwin, a St. Louis postal inspector.
E.H. Kline, a Los Angeles postal inspector.
Lieutenant Nelson, Kansas City police department.
Detective Alfred Lavan King, Kansas City police department;
Hugh Davis Harper, Colorado Springs Police Chief.

Besides these officers there were three more waiting in an automobile. Law enforcement was very serious about the capture of Jake Fleagle. The officers had received a tip that Fleagle had driven into Branson on Monday night. As the officers were preparing to exit the train, they found Fleagle standing on the platform waiting to board the train. Officers waited for other passengers to leave the train before making any move. Fleagle entered the train and was walking down the aisle when confronted by the officers. He was advised to surrender, but instead tried to draw a weapon from his holster. He was shot by an officer in the abdomen before he could fire his gun. Fleagle did not attempt any further resistance to his arrest.[47]

Jake Fleagle died in the hospital at Springfield, Missouri, on Wednesday, October 15, 1930. His body was taken to Garden City, Kansas, and was buried next to Ralph's grave. The man who shot Jake Fleagle was Los Angeles Police Lieutenant Harry Wilde.[48]

Colorado Springs Police Chief Hugh Davis Harper, after a seventeen-month chase, had finally completed his assigned task. He had overseen the capture of the bandits who robbed the First National Bank of Lamar, Colorado. Rewards of $14,000 had been posted for the capture and conviction of the bandits. This would be spread across twenty different people. Chief Harper was eligible for a reward, but he did not accept any of the money.[49]

The bandits that conspired to rob the Lamar bank were identified at the time of their death, they were:

Ralph Emmerson Fleagle, the eldest of the brothers
　　DOB: 29 Oct 1880
　　Hung at Cañon City Penitentiary
　　DOD: 10 Jul 1930 — Age 49

Jacob Harrison Fleagle, 10 years younger than Ralph
　　DOB: 01 Jan 1890
　　aka: William Harrison Holden
　　aka: William Fleagle
　　aka: Little Jake
　　DOD: 15 Oct 1930 — Age 40
　　Fatally wounded in gun-battle with officers at Branson, MO.

George Johnson Abshier,
　　DOB: 1897
　　aka: W.C. (Bill) Messick
　　DOD: 18 Jul 1930 — Age 33
　　Hung at Cañon City Penitentiary

Howard Lester Royston,
　　DOB: 20 Aug 1896
　　aka: Walter W. Adams
　　DOD: 18 Jul 1930 — Age 33
　　aka: "Heavy" DOD: 18 Jul 1930 — Age 33
　　Hung at Cañon City Penitentiary

In recognition of Chief Harper's work in solving this crime, banks and citizens from around the state contributed several thousand dollars, and without Harper's knowledge, paid off the mortgage of his home.[50]

Notes

1 *The Fleagle Gang, Betrayed by a Fingerprint*, by N.T. Beltz, 2005, AuthorHouse, Indiana, Page 5.
2 *Ibid*, Pages 7-8.
3 *Ibid*, Page 9.
4 *Ibid*, Page 10.
5 Unpublished manuscript, Hugh Harper, 1933, Pages 77 & 78, from the Colorado Springs Pioneers' Museum.
6 "*The Fleagle Gang*," Page 11.
7 *Colorado Springs Gazette*, 24 May 1928, Page 1.
8 Unpublished manuscript, Hugh Harper, 1933, Page 78, from the Colorado Springs Pioneers' Museum.
9 *The Fleagle Gang*, Page 13.
10 *Ibid*, Page 15.
11 *Ibid*, Page 16.
12 Unpublished manuscript, Hugh Harper, 1933, Page 81, from the Colorado Springs Pioneers' Museum.
13 *The Fleagle Gang*, Page 62.
14 Unpublished manuscript, Hugh Harper, 1933, Page 83, from the Colorado Springs Pioneers' Museum.
15 *Colorado Springs Gazette*, 25 May 1928, Page 1.
16 Unpublished manuscript, Hugh Harper, 1933, Page 88, from the Colorado Springs Pioneers' Museum.
17 *The Fleagle Gang*, Pages 30, 31.
18 *The Fleagle Gang*, Page 34.
19 *Denver Post*, 14 Oct 1930, Page 4.
20 *Wichita Eagle*, 13 Jun 1928, Page 1.
21 Unpublished manuscript, Hugh Harper, 1933, Page 92, from the Colorado Springs Pioneers' Museum.
22 *The Fleagle Gang*, Pages 81-84.
23 *Denver Post*, 14 Oct 1930, Page 4.
24 *Kansas City Times*, 23 Jul 1929, Page 2 & *Denver Post*, 24 Jul 1929, Page 10.
25 *The Fleagle Gang*, Page 89.
26 Unpublished manuscript, Hugh Harper, 1933, Page 113, from the Colorado Springs Pioneers' Museum.
27 *Denver Post*, 26 Jul 1929, Page 23.
28 *Denver Post*, 27 Jul 1929, Page 1.
29 *Denver Post*, 17 Aug 1929, Page 1.
30 *Denver Post*, 18 Aug 1929, Page 1.
31 *The Fleagle Gang*, Pages 173, 178.
32 *The Fleagle Gang*, Page 183.
33 *Colorado Springs Gazette*, 01 Oct 1929, Page 10.
34 *Colorado Springs Gazette*, 12 Oct 1929, Page 1.
35 *The Fleagle Gang*, Pages 211-213.
36 *The Fleagle Gang*, Pages 218, 219.
37 *Daily Sentinel*, 25 Oct 1929, Page 8.
38 *The Fleagle Gang*, Page 230.
39 *The Fleagle Gang*, Page 250.
40 *Garden City Telegram*, 16 Jul 1930, Page 1.
41 *The Fleagle Gang*, Page 332.
42 *The Fleagle Gang*, Page 333.
43 *The Fleagle Gang*, Page 335.
44 *Denver Post*, 14 Oct 1930, Page 3.
45 *Denver Post*, 14 Oct 1930, Page 5.
46 *Jefferson City Post-Tribune*, 14 Oct 1930, Page 1.
47 *Denver Post*, 14 Oct 1930, Page 1.
48 *Denver Post*, 16 Oct 1930, Page 1.
49 *Marshall County News*, 29 Jan 1932, Page B6.
50 *Colorado Springs Gazette* & Telegraph, 17 May 1936, Section 2, Page 4.

Chapter 26

PIKES PEAK OR BUSTED

Homicide in itself is typically covered by life insurance, but the circumstances surrounding the death may dictate who receives the life insurance payout. If the primary beneficiary murders the insured or is involved in their murder, they are no longer eligible for the death benefit due to the Slayer Rule. — www.moneygeek.com

If it is true that Satan sometimes walks the earth in the deceptive guise of man, then maybe we know where he has been keeping himself lately, and what he has been up to. If the subject of our story today wasn't the archfiend himself, then surely, he was a most willing acolyte, thoroughly steeped in things of evil, a dreadful monster who spread havoc wherever he set his foot. It is hard to believe that a human being could have done what he has done." This was the opening sentence written by Peter Levins of the *Daily News* on August 2, 1936, in New York, New York, reporting on a criminal that started his spree on Pikes Peak.

On Thursday, September 21, 1932, Robert James, a barber age 38, and his bride of two months, Winona, age 28, were on their honeymoon from California and took a drive to the top of Pikes Peak. Mr. James had driven their Studebaker coupe to the top of the mountain. He told authorities that his wife was an expert driver and had traversed the mountain road a few times before, and he reported that she was the one who drove down the road.

Around 6:00 p.m., at Mile Post 13, approximately six miles from the top of the mountain, Robert James explained, his wife lost control and drove off a switchback. The car flipped end over end. He explained that he was tossed out and she stayed in the car almost 150 feet down an embankment. After he hurried down the slope and extricated her from the vehicle, he laid her on the ground in her unconscious condition. He was slightly injured and managed to walk the two and one-half miles to Glen Cove and get help. The Ambulance Service Company, located in downtown Colorado Springs,[1] had been called about 7:30 p.m. requesting their services. The 28-mile trip to the accident scene[2] would have taken around an hour, as did the trip back to Beth-El Hospital (now Memorial Hospital Central). Mrs. James had managed to survive four hours before she received any treatment at a hospital. Winona James suffered a fractured skull, shock and numerous bruises. It was reported as the first accident where a tourist was seriously injured on the Pikes Peak Highway.[3]

Even though Winona had serious injuries, she was released from the hospital about October 8th, just a little over two weeks after the crash.[4] Her husband rented a cottage in Manitou Springs, referred to as El Cajon House, where he took his wife to recover.[5] Unfortunately, Mrs. James, succumbed to a cerebral hemorrhage while alone at the cottage, and drowned in the bathtub.[6] Apparently, she had fainted while leaning over the tub washing her hair. A letter she had been writing to her sister was found in the cabin. In it she said that her "daddy" was treating her well, reported the *Daily News*.

Her body was taken back to Glendale, California and buried in the Forest Law Memorial Park.[7]

A few years later in 1935, Robert James, then 41, married 28-year-old Mary Emma Busch at Santa Ana, California on the 19th of July.[8] Mr. James was apparently unlucky with wives, because of his five (or six) wives, two died by drowning. After only 18 days of marriage Mary Emma accidentally drowned in a fishpond behind their home in La Crescenta, a suburb of Los Angeles.[9]

Shortly after the death of Mary Emma, James told a reporter for the *Los Angeles Herald and Express* that his second wife, Winona, died in a bathtub in Manitou Springs. The investigation into Mary

Emma's death produced an unfinished letter written by the deceased to her sister.[10] The letter appeared in the *Daily Mail*:

> Dear Sis: Just a line this morning to let you know I am pretty sick; my leg is all swollen; something bit me while watering my flowers this morning. Having lots of bad luck. This is my old blue Monday but my daddy will be home early tonight and takes good care of me. Be sure and write me soon. I will let you know how I get along….

When looking at the two letters by the drowning victims it could be suggested the letters were written by James to mislead investigators. The unfinished letters seem similar. Since Mrs. James carried a $5,000 life insurance policy at the time, her husband took great care of her as was learned later—he killed her![11]

Upon hearing this was his second wife to drown, the newspaper reporter started digging into the background of Mr. James. Reporters found that James had married Vera May Vermillion some years earlier, but divorced her.[12] More inquiries by the press found that Los Angeles County Deputies, Vernon Gray and Willard Killion heard Robert James state his wife, Mary Emma, carried insurance which would pay $21,400 in case of accidental death.[13] It was found during the autopsy that Mrs. James was pregnant.[14] August 16th a coroner's jury agreed her death was by drowning. Two jurors said it was accidental, but the remaining five were unable to make a decision if it was suicide, accidental or homicide.[15]

Robert's claim to the insurance money in the death of his wife, went through the courts and in April of 1936, was denied by a jury. It turned out that the policy was in effect only a few weeks prior to Mrs. James' death.[16]

Then a complaint with regard to Robert James was received. He was believed to be involved with young women. The Los Angeles District Attorney's office started watching the movements of the man. A niece, Lois Wright, age 21, a manicurist in his barbershop, was thought to be involved in an intimate relationship with her uncle. This might have been part of the circumstances that led to the death of James's last wife. He had rented a bungalow where he was taking his niece. District attorney's investigators, rented the bungalow next door and placed two microphones in the suspects rooms for a period of two weeks. This bungalow was about four and one-half miles from where the two worked.

According to the *Daily News*, James brought Lois, his niece, from Alabama with the promise of getting her into movies in Hollywood. She was only 17 when she became his mistress.

After two weeks of recordings, James and his niece were arrested and charged with morals crimes; adultery was not acceptable. Signing a confession, his niece, Lois Wright said their affair went back for years. During the questioning James admitted to being married five times.[17] His first marriage was to Maud Duncan, in 1914, in Birmingham, Alabama, only his name was Major Raymond Lisenba at the time.[18]

Lisenba's (aka: Robert S. James) next marriage was to Vera May Vermillion, 18, in May 1921 in Emporia, Kansas.[19] The marriage to Winona P. Wallace followed in Los Angeles in July of 1932.[20] She was the wife who drowned in Manitou. Then it was thought he married a Ruth Thomas in New Orleans in 1934, but the marriage was supposedly annulled the following day.[21] Finally, Robert James married Mary Emma Busch.

Wives three and five both supposedly drowned accidentally. Because of these two deaths a much more in-depth investigation was begun by Los Angeles District Attorney Buron Fitts. His first successful conviction of James was for three morals violations (mistreatment of his niece), whereupon he was sentenced from 3 to 150 years.[22]

With James safely locked away, District Attorney Fitts had time for a more comprehensive investigation into the deaths of the barber's two wives. Los Angeles Police Investigator Captain John "Jack" Clair Southard was put on the case. During June of 1936, Southard was in Colorado Springs where he told the news media details of the investigation. His investigation determined that James had taken his wife, Winona, up Pikes Peak and she was never in charge of driving their car. James had plied his wife with alcohol while at altitude, causing her to be under the influence. A partially filled bottle containing whiskey was found in a side pocket of the car. Mr. James then drove the Studebaker down to mile post 13, which was about a mile below timber line. Here he stopped the car, struck his wife in the head with a hammer, and pushed the car over the edge, allowing it to tumble down the steep slope.

When James made it to the crashed car, he was disappointed to find that his wife had not been cooperative by dying! Deciding he had to report the accident he trudged the 2½ miles to Glen Cove. Again, being stubborn, his wife did not die in the hospital. So, after a period of time he took her back to a cottage he had rented in Manitou Springs for her to complete her recovery. October 14th around noon time, he half-filled the cottage bathtub full of hot water. How he got the woman to the tub to drown her is unknown. But by drowning her in hot water, it skewed the time for rigor mortis to set in.

To set up an alibi, James went to purchase groceries. Returning to the cottage with a grocery deliver boy, Gerald D. Rogers of Manitou, they both were present when the nude body of Winona James was found drowned in the bathtub. When the coroner, Dr. George Benjamin Gilmore arrived, he was suspicious of the situation, however, the sheriff at that time, Robert M. Jackson, did not wish to pursue anything further, which meant the death certificate was filled out as an accidental drowning. Colorado Springs Police Chief Hugh D. Harper told Captain Southard that his staff had quietly looked at this death, however, there wasn't much cooperation between the departments at that time.[23]

When the death of James' final wife, Mary Emma, was investigated more thoroughly, it was found that James had an accomplice, Charles Hope, 37. Hope was an employee of James and was badly in debt. When police confronted the pair in May 1936, Hope and James took turns blaming the death of Mary Emma on each other. District Attorney Buron Fitts accused Hope of being involved because he had been promised a half-share of a $10,000 life insurance policy. James accused Hope of taking a boxful of black widow spiders to James' home and putting them in the bed with Mary Emma. The coroner had noted there had been a possible insect bite on the leg of the victim. Other plots thought up that came to light in the interview included burning the house down and blaming her death on smoking in bed; shooting the victim during a fake robbery; or, using dried rattlesnake venom powder rubbed on an open wound as it would kill a person in minutes. These were all put to the side as bad ideas.

What the district attorney found to be most repugnant was the fact James took his wife to the Ocean Park reptile den and showed her rattlesnakes prior to killing her. His plan was to get rattlesnakes to do the killing for him.[24] Charles Hope was sent out to purchase rattlesnakes and on the night of August 4th, he took a cage of three snakes to the La Crescenta home and found Mrs. James was tied to a table, immobilized and gagged. The cage was placed in such a fashion to allow her foot to be put into the cage. The big toe of her left foot was bitten, injecting poisonous venom into her body.

After waiting for about an hour, the venom did not seem to be working, so Hope drowned the woman in the bathtub. James arrived a short time later and explained to Hope that this would not do, because he had drowned his last wife in a bathtub and this could be considered suspicious. That led them to take the body of the woman and place her face-down in the fishpond at the back of the home.[25]

James was said to have worked the whole day when the murder occurred, inviting two friends to come home with him for supper after work. When they arrived, they could not find his wife and a search ended when they all found her in the fish pond. Once again, just like Winona's death, he brought people home with him to find the body.

Nine months after the burial of Mrs. James, her body was exhumed and reexamined by Dr. Gustav Boehme, a toxicologist and Dr. Andrew F. Wagner, the county autopsy surgeon. It brought to light that there was a snake bite on the left foot's big toe. The leg was also swollen. These conditions were noted at the time of the original autopsy, but were discounted. The most likely reason that she did not die from the snake bites were because of its location and the lack of large blood vessels for the poison to travel through.[26] The doctors said she most likely would have died, because the wound was not treated, but it would have taken a much longer time than the murderers were willing to wait.[27]

Following the grand jury's indictment, both Hope and James were charged with the poisoning and drowning murder of Mary Busch James, and held without bail. May 11, 1936, James appeared in court for arraignment and offered to plead guilty and serve a life sentence if the district attorney would agree to not ask for the death penalty. District Attorney Fitts said "James must hang. He wants to plead guilty on a promise of life imprisonment, rather face the gallows. That is what criminals call copping a plea. We won't consider it. Our case is complete. We need no more evidence."[28]

Because of the evidence discovered during the investigation of the death of Mary James in California, new interest arose in the case of Winona's death three years earlier in Manitou Springs. El Paso County authorities searched for the Studebaker that was involved in the crash on the Pikes Peak Highway and found it in Pueblo. The car was examined to see if the car had been sabotaged prior to the accident.[29] Because Mr. James reported to James A. Rogers, superintendent at Glen Cove, after the accident that "something went wrong with the steering gear and the car swerved off the road . . ."[30] Results of this examination were not located.

An interview with Mr. Rogers also brought out that when he arrived at the accident scene, he found there was a mechanic's hammer with blood on the hammer's head, and the front seat cushions on the passenger side of the car were wet with blood. He found the victim was outside the vehicle on the passenger side lying on the ground. James had said he placed blankets around his wife. Rogers said that the blankets were still in the car when he observed the accident, still neatly rolled up in the back of the car. Most of what James related to people about the accident were apparently fabrications.[31]

District Attorney Fitts subpoenaed six Colorado Springs residents to Los Angeles to testify in the trial of James for the murder of his wife in California. The purpose was to show the planning done by James in the killing of his wife in Manitou Springs would go a long way to countering any plea of insanity.[32]

In late June, co-defendant Charles Hope, testified that he purchased rattlesnakes at the behest of James. He confessed the victim's left leg was placed in the snake's carrier, to be bitten, with the intention of killing the woman. Hope also admitted to helping James move the victim's body after the drowning to the fishpond outside after Mrs. James was dead. The state also brought out James had purchased a $20,000 life insurance policy on his wife shortly after their marriage.[33]

Grace Yarnell, a cousin of Winona James, told the jury that she was at the hospital in Colorado Springs after her cousin was admitted for treatment, and while there, Robert James kissed Yarnell, twice that day. Once, on the way to the hospital and once again shortly after leaving. Miss Yarnell told James to stop.[34] Another incident which showed the character of James was brought by the testimony of Mrs. Midge Reed of Los Angeles. She said that after the collection of the insurance money and burial of Mary James, Robert asked her to marry him and go north. She further told the jury that if James was indicted, he wanted to use Mrs. Reed as a surprise witness and was willing to pay her $2,000 if she would testify that she saw Mrs. James lying on a swing and saying she did not feel well, but not to mention that she had a sore on her leg. Mrs. Reed said that she did accompany James to a hotel in Hermosa where they stayed one night and registered as Mr. and Mrs. Joseph Wright of San Francisco.[35]

July 24, 1936, the jury of 10 men and 2 women, returned a verdict of guilty against Major Raymond Lisenba, aka: Robert S. James for the first-degree murder of his wife Mary James.[36] A few days later, James was glib in his remarks to newspaper reporters; he said if he was hung, it would cheat the state of the morals charges he was convicted of and sentenced for 150 years.[37]

Superior Court Judge Charles William Fricke sentenced James to be hung for the murder of Mary James, during a session September 10, 1936.[38] This decision was appealed to the California Supreme Court, and it was affirmed by that court in March of 1939.[39] On April 10, 1940, James was taken to San Quentin State Prison to await his execution.[40] A final appeal to the United States Supreme Court was made—the sentence was again reaffirmed.[41]

This crime spree was finally brought to an end on Friday, May 1, 1942, when Major Raymond Lisenba, aka: Robert Sherman James, was hung at San Quentin State Prison.[42] James had the privilege of being the last person to be hanged in California.[43]

Notes

1 *Colorado Springs City Directory*, 1932, Page 59.
2 Google Maps
3 *Colorado Springs Gazette*, 22 Sep 1932, Page 1.
4 *Colorado Springs Gazette*, 15 Oct 1932, Page 1.
5 *Los Angeles Times*, 18 Jun 1936, Part 1, Page 1.
6 *Colorado Springs Gazette*, 07 Aug 1935, Page 1.
7 *Los Angeles Times*, 21 Oct 1932, Page 32.
8 *Rock Island Illinois Argus*, 07 Aug 1935, Page 14.
9 *Colorado Springs Gazette*, 07 Aug 1935, Page 1.
10 *Colorado Springs Gazette*, 07 Aug 1935, Page 1.
11 *Colorado Springs Evening Telegraph*, 07 Aug 1935, Page 1.
12 *Phoenix Republic*, 07 Aug 1935, Page 1.
13 *Colorado Springs Gazette*, 09 Aug 1935, Page 1.
14 *Phoenix Republic*, 07 Aug 1935, Page 1.
15 *Oakland Tribune*, 16 Aug 1935, Page 7.
16 *Los Angeles Times*, 03 Apr 1936, Part II, Page 5.
17 *Los Angeles Times*, 20 Apr 1936, Page 3.
18 Alabama Marriage Record, Jefferson County, 08 Oct 1914, Page 101.
19 *Emporia Weekly Gazette*, 26 May 1921, Page 3.
20 California Marriage License/Certificate of Marriage, 17 Jul 1932, Book 1097, Page 40.
21 *Los Angeles Times*, 20 Apr 1936, Page 3.
22 *Los Angeles Times*, 01 Jun 1936, Part II, Page 1.
23 *Colorado Springs Gazette*, 18 Jun 1936, Page 1.
24 *Los Angeles Times*, 04 May 1936, Page 1.
25 *Los Angeles Times*, 07 May 1936, Page 3.
26 *Los Angeles Times*, 06 May 1936, Page 1.
27 *Los Angeles Times*, 06 May 1936, Page 1.

28 *Los Angeles Times*, 11 May 1936, Part II, Page 1.
29 *Colorado Springs Gazette*, 11 May 1936, Page 1.
30 *Los Angeles Times*, 18 Jun 1936, Page 1.
31 *Los Angeles Times*, 18 Jun 1936, Page 1.
32 *Colorado Springs Gazette*, 26 Jun 1936, Page 9.
33 *Colorado Springs Gazette*, 27 Jun 1936, Page 9.
34 *Colorado Springs Gazette*, 03 Jul 1936, Page 7.
35 *Colorado Springs Gazette*, 04 Jul 1936, Page 2.
36 *Colorado Springs Gazette*, 25 Jun 1936, Page 10.
37 *Colorado Springs Gazette*, 28 Jul 1936. Page 6.
38 *Colorado Springs Gazette*, 10 Sep 1936, Page 7.
39 *San Bernardino County Sun*, 22 Mar 1939, Page 2.
40 *Los Angeles Times*, 11 Apr 1940, Page 8.
41 *Los Angeles Times*, 08 Apr 1941, Page 1.
42 *Los Angeles Times*, 02 May 1942, Page 6.
43 *Corpus Christi Caller-Times*, 16 Aug 1953, Page 2.

Chapter 27

FEMALE SERIAL KILLER IN TOWN

Jane Toppan, nicknamed Jolly Jane, was an American serial killer who is known to have committed twelve murders in Massachusetts between 1895 and 1901; she confessed to a total of thirty-one murders. The killings were carried out in Toppan's capacity as a nurse, targeting patients and their family members. — Wikipedia

What's a nice town like ours doing with a serial killer like this? In 1937, Colorado Springs was unknowingly hosting a female serial killer who not only made her last kill in Colorado Springs, but brought her own victim with her. Anna Marie Filser Hahn, born in Fussen, Bavaria, Germany, on June 7, 1906, was the 12th child of her family. Her father was a cabinetmaker and furniture manufacturer. On May 31, 1925, at the age of nineteen, Anna had a son, Oscar, born out of wedlock. The family quickly saw that Anna was scurried off to the United States while her child stayed with Anna's mother. All to minimize tongue wagging. Anna was sent to Uncle Max Doeschel, her mother's step-brother. Anna arrived in New York from Bremen, Germany, February, 1929, aboard the SS Munchen.

Doeschel, though not a close member of the Filser family, was just a way to get Anna out of her hometown, far away from prying eyes. Anna left New York and took a train to Cincinnati to meet Uncle Doeschel. Living with her "uncle," she soon found work as a housemaid. She did not endear herself to her relatives, as they began to notice she was spending more than her meager income. Their scrutiny caused her to move out suddenly to be near Uncle Charles

"Karl" Osswald, a retired baker, who was even more distantly related. Osswald's wife died in April, 1929, leaving him all alone. Osswald was 71 and Anna was 23. She claimed to have been a nurse in Germany and said she would give companionship and care to the elderly gentleman. November of that year she promised to marry him if he would transfer ninety-nine shares of a utility stock to her which would provide cash to her when she needed extra money.[1]

Anna offered her "services" of care to several elderly German widowers. Many she offered to marry if they would supply her with money. The only catch was she poisoned a total of thirteen people in the Cincinnati area from 1933 into 1937 as listed below:

VICTIM:	DEATH/SURVIVED:
Ernst Kohler	Death – May 6, 1933[2]
Charles "Karl" Osswald	Death – August 14, 1935[3]
Mary Arnold	Survived poison July 1936[4]
Stina Cable	Survived poison July 1936[5]
Philip J. Hahn—(Her husband)	Survived poison 1936[6]
Margaret (Maggie) Hahn —(Her mother-in-law)	Survived poison 1936[7]
George E. Heis	Survived poison 1936[8]
Julia Kresckay	Death – Unknown[9]
Albert J. Palmer	Death – March 26, 1937[10]
Jacob Wagner	Death – June 3, 1937[11]
George G. Gsellman	Death – July 6, 1937[12]
Johan Georg Obendoerfer	Death – August 1, 1937[13]
Olive Louella Koehler	Death – August 16, 1937[14]

Anna Marie Filser met and married Philip J. Hahn on May 5, 1930, in Buffalo, New York. She needed a home and a place to raise her son. On July of 1930, Anna sailed to Germany, picked up her five-year-old son, and brought him back to America.[15] They purchased a bakery where Anna ran an illegal bookmaking operation.[16] She had a problem with gambling and spent more money than she had.

But it was never enough, so she kept scamming old lonely German men. Her favorite method of killing was with Croton Oil. Croton Oil, derived from the Croton plant, is very poisonous. In fact, every part of the plant is poisonous. Symptoms include nausea, vomiting and diarrhea. If taken in large quantities it can cause liver and kidney damage.

Anna would add small amounts of the oil to the victim's food over a period of time, causing the person to lose control of their bowels, and vomit. Eventually, the person would die from the treatments. If this was not fast enough arsenic might also be introduced into her treatments.

June 1937, Anna broke the heel off one of her shoes and was directed to a small shoe repair shop run by a retired shoemaker out of his home. Johan Georg Obendoerfer was 67-years-old and widowed. While fixing her shoe, he invited her to sit and talk, which they did for some time. Becoming enamored with the young German beauty, Johan shaved his large mustache off and tried to make himself look younger. Neighbors told Johan's daughter they had heard him speak of things like honeymoons. Anna told Johan she had planned a trip with her son to the mountains of Colorado and invited him along. If Johan found the country to his liking, they could spend the rest of their lives there.[17]

On July 16, Johan took out $350 for the trip and asked Anna to get his train ticket. She took the money and deposited $250 into her bank. Four days later, Johan went to Anna's home where she prepared a special meal. A healthy elder man entered the home, but after consuming the dinner, the next morning, he required help to enter a taxi to get to the train depot. That afternoon, the trio arrived in Chicago. Anna booked Johan into a 25 cent a night "flophouse" and herself and son into an $8 per night room at what was then the world's largest hotel.[18]

A week later, Johan and his traveling companions arrived in Denver, Colorado, during which time Johan was complaining of feeling less and less well. They checked into the Oxford Hotel. The next morning a porter seeing Johan's room door ajar, peeked into the room and noted that the elderly man "appeared awfully sick and in agony."[19]

Anna was not happy someone was butting into her business, so on the 25th, she checked the trio out of the hotel and moved to a smaller hotel. Here the staff noticed the old man's condition and mentioned it to Anna. She told them, "He'll be all right in a few days. I just gave him a good dose of croton oil." She also was feeding him watermelon, which was a way to disguise arsenic when trying to kill rats. After eating the watermelon, Obendoerfer would repeatedly vomit. All this time Anna's 12-year-old son would watch the old man who was in much pain.[20]

Anna, using a letterhead of the Oxford hotel wrote a letter to the Clifton Heights Savings and Loan in Cincinnati. She sent Obendoerfer's savings pass book, asking they send a check for $1,000 to a Denver bank.[21] Anna then visited the Denver bank and asked for the $1,000 so she and her husband could buy a farm in Colorado. Without proper paperwork and the absence of Mr. Obendoerfer, the bank would not give the money to Anna. By Tuesday, July 27, Johan was in miserable condition and had totally lost control of his bodily functions. Two days later, the room of Johan's was of such a stench that housekeeping refused to enter the room. When Anna was confronted by the management, she said that she had just met the man on the train and said if the hotel would provide clean linens, she would clean the room. The room had been fouled with bodily fluids. Now the management demanded that she get a doctor. This was too much for Anna, so she had a taxi transport the trio to the train depot and headed to Colorado Springs.[22]

Obendoerfer, Hahn, and her son Oscar, arrived in Colorado Springs Friday, July 30, 1937. Checking into the Park Hotel, located next to the train depot, the ill cobbler and his companions had moved away from the scrutiny of the people in Denver. While at the hotel, Anna saw the door to the proprietor's rooms open one afternoon. No one was around, so she went in and found some diamond rings worth $350, which she stole. Mrs. Turner, the owner, saw Anna exit the apartment and was told Anna just was looking around. When the theft was found and the crime reported, CSPD Detective Robert Hope Wraith was assigned to the case.[23]

Saturday, Mr. Obendoerfer's condition continued to be very worrisome. Finally, Mrs. Hahn had the old man transported to Beth-El Hospital (now Memorial Central Hospital). His condition had so deteriorated that he died the following day. The hospital notified Anna as to the death, and she wanted to know why they were contacting her as she only met him on the train. She only spoke with him because they were both Swiss and from Cincinnati.

Detective Wraith went in pursuit of Mrs. Anna Marie Hahn, but found she and her son were gone from Colorado Springs.[24] Mrs. Turner's stolen rings were located in a pawn shop in Denver and had been pawned under the name Marie Fisher, whose description matched that of Anna Hahn. Because the information was now in the hands of the authorities, a fugitive warrant was sent to Cincinnati with regard to the theft of the jewelry and the suspicious death of Mr. Obendoerfer.[25]

Inspector Irvin B. "Dad" Bruce, sent a photo and fingerprints to Cincinnati, in hopes of identifying the deceased man. A telegram was sent back saying that Anna was well-known in Cincinnati as she was suspected of poisoning some people in their city. An autopsy was performed on the old man, but due to the body having been embalmed, no poison was found.[26]

With the information about Anna Hahn's past behavior, Dr. J. Thomas Coghlan, the El Paso County coroner, decided it was necessary to perform a chemical analysis of the victim's organs. Cincinnati reported that three elderly men had died in their city and all with an illness found to be induced by poison while they were in the care of Anna Marie Hahn.[27]

Arrested by Cincinnati police a couple of days later, the 31-year-old German woman denied she had given anything to the men she was suspected of poisoning. A grand jury was then pressed into the investigation. It was found Anna had purchased a bottle of poisonous oil like that found in the body of George G. Gsellman. Police in Germany were contacted and they began looking into the death of Dr. Matscheki, the father of her child. During the eight years that Anna was in the United States, she was said to have obtained between $50,000 and $70,000 from elderly Germans. When pressed about the people she was close to, all dying under similar circumstances, she said she didn't do anything and she was innocent.[28]

A search of Anna's home in Cincinnati turned up bottles of arsenic and croton oil. Six drops of croton oil would be fatal. During the investigation of Anna, the Midland Hotel clerk in Denver reported to police that Anna told him that she had administered croton oil to Obendoerfer.[29]

August 16, a Cincinnati grand jury indicted Anna Marie Hahn for the slayings of two elderly German men—George Gsellman, 67, and Jacob Wagner, 68. Cincinnati Police Captain Hayes reported there were nineteen prescriptions for poisons and narcotics traced to Anna. These were obtained by using forged prescription blanks taken from the home office of Dr. Arthur Vos. Hahn admitted giving narcotics to Ernst Kohler, who died in 1933, but said it was at the direction of Dr. Vos. Vos said he never ordered such treatment and she had given enough narcotics to Kohler to kill a dozen people.[30]

Organs of Johan Obendoerfer had been sent to Dr. Frances McConnell, a Denver pathologist. She reported arsenic was found in the man's liver and one kidney. More organs were still to be tested. Charges of homicide were not filed in Colorado Springs since Anna was indicted by a grand jury in Cincinnati for murder. Johan Georg Obendoerfer was put to rest in Colorado Springs Evergreen Cemetery.[31]

Carson Hoy, assistant county attorney from Cincinnati, traveled to Colorado Springs to confer with local law enforcement. He said because Chief Hugh Harper and Inspector I.B. Bruce had started an investigation into Anna Hahn, they were able to hand down indictments in Cincinnati. Hoy said if their prosecution was unsuccessful, Anna would be turned over to Colorado authorities, who had a very strong case against the woman.[32]

Mrs. Hahn's trial began on Monday, October 11, 1937, in Cincinnati. This was such an event that the news media were present from major cities.[33] It took four days to select and impanel a jury. The jury consisted of eleven woman and one man. Six Colorado Springs witnesses attended the trial, including CSPD Inspector I.B. Bruce and El Paso County Coroner Dr. J. Thomas Coghlan.[34]

The prosecution presented evidence showing when Obendoerfer, Anna and Oscar Hahn arrived in Colorado Springs, Anna checked Obendoerfer's bag at the train depot, figuring it would not be claimed. When police found the bag, they located two salt shakers. One was almost empty and the other full. The full shaker contained 82% arsenic trioxide, a highly toxic chemical. More evidence was shown where Anna was accused of poisoning numerous people; luckily not all had died.

Anna Marie Hahn maintained her innocence throughout the trial, dressing nicely for the court and seemingly happy that the trial would show that she was innocent of all charges. More than 1,000 people wanted to attend the trial, but the judge ordered only people that could be seated would be allowed in the courtroom.[35]

Dr. Otto Behrer, a Cincinnati City chemist, testified that Jacob Wagner died of arsenic poisoning. He stated 7.8 grains of arsenic were found in the victim's body and a lethal dose was between 2 to 3 grains. He also said the registered dose diminishes with time, so the dose the deceased received would have been more arsenic than he found in the testing. The defense contended since the body of the victim had to be exhumed, the arsenic could have seeped into the body from the ground where he was buried.[36]

Inspector Bruce testified he found Obendoerfer's straw satchel in the check room at the Denver & Rio Grande railway station. When shown two salt shakers, he identified them as the ones he found in the victim's satchel and one of the shakers contained a white powder. Dr. Coghlan testified he discovered one of the salt shakers contained 82% arsenic trioxide and 14% table salt. The Denver pathologist testified Obendoerfer had died of arsenic poisoning. The same arsenic in the bottle of arsenic found in the home of Anna Hahn.[37]

On November 4, 1937, the jury began deliberations, twenty-four days after the beginning of the trial. After two days of deliberating the fate of Anna Marie Hahn, the jury came back with a verdict of guilty and sentenced her to die in the electric chair.[38] The following day her attorney filed a motion for a new trial on seven different grounds.[39] On November 27th, the new trial was denied and her execution was set for March 10, 1938.[40] Her case was sent to the Court of Appeals. December 1, 1937, she was transferred from the Hamilton County Jail to the Ohio Penitentiary in Columbus.[41] On February 7, 1938, the Court of Appeals affirmed her conviction. All that was left was to appeal to the State Supreme Court.[42]

Because of the appeal to the Supreme Court, her execution was stayed.[43] April 13, 1938, the Supreme Court refused to grant a new trial and ordered her execution to be May 4th. The lawyers applied to Governor Martin L. Davey to grant a stay of execution and commutation of her sentence.[44] A little over a day prior to Anna's scheduled execution, the Ohio State Supreme Court issued an indefinite stay of her execution.[45]

The case was sent to the United States Supreme Court for review.[46] On October 10, 1938, the court refused to review the case and the request to the governor was all that remained.[47] Her new execution date was set for December 7th.[48] Whimpering and unable to walk to the death chamber, the guards had to all but carry the "Blonde Borgia" to the electric chair.[49]

Hahn was the first woman executed in the State of Ohio. About an hour prior to Anna's execution, she confessed she gave Albert Palmer the poison that caused his death. She also did this to Jacob Wagner, George Gsellman and lastly, Johan Georg Obendoerfer.[50] Convicts made a small tombstone to mark the grave of Anna, where she was buried in Calvary Cemetery, in Columbus.[51]

Having only been in Colorado Springs but a few days, she left an impression and a dead body. If she had not stolen the jewelry of the proprietor of the Park Hotel, she might not have been caught for the murder of Obendoerfer.[52]

On December 8, 1938, the court dismissed the grand-jury indictment that charged Anna with the murder of Gsellman. Then in 1974, Judge Rupert Dean, presiding administrative judge, dismissed the fugitive from justice warrant and grand larceny charges filed by the Colorado Springs Police Department 37 years earlier. This was the final action of any kind in the case against Annie Marie (Filser) Hahn.[53]

Anna's son, Oscar, had his name changed and was sent to live with a family somewhere in the Midwest. There were a couple vague reports that Oscar served in the Navy and another that indicated he may have died in the Korean War.[54]

Notes

1   *The Good-Bye Door,*" By Diana Britt Franklin, 2006, published by Kent State University Press, Kent, Ohio, Pages 1-5.
2   *The Good-Bye Door,* Page 232.
3   Ibid.
4   *The Good-Bye Door,* Pages 18-19.
5   Ibid.
6   *The Good-Bye Door,* Page 11.
7   *The Good-Bye Door,* Page 11.
8   *The Good-Bye Door,* Pages 20-21.
9   *Cincinnati Post,* 16 Aug 1937, Page 1.
10 *The Good-Bye Door,* Page 232.
11 Ibid.
12 Ibid.
13 Ibid.
14 Ibid.
15 *The Good-Bye Door,*" Pages 6-7.
16 A bookmaker, bookie or turf accountant is an organization or a person that accepts and pays out bets on sporting and other events at agreed-upon odds.
17 *The Good-Bye Door,* Pages 38-39.
18 *The Good-Bye Door,* Pages 39-41.
19 *The Good-Bye Door,* Page 41.
20 Ibid.
21 Ibid.
22 *The Good-Bye Door,* Pages 42-43.
23 *Colorado Springs Gazette,* 11 Aug 1937, Page 1.
24 Ibid.
25 *Colorado Springs Gazette,* 12 Aug 1937, Page 1.
26 Ibid.
27 Ibid.

28 *Colorado Springs Gazette*, 14 Aug 1937, Page 1.
29 *Colorado Springs Gazette* & Telegraph, 15 Aug 1937, Page 1.
30 *Colorado Springs Gazette*, 17 Aug 1937, Page 1.
31 *Colorado Springs Gazette*, 18 Aug 1937, Page 1.
32 *Colorado Springs Gazette*, 24 Aug 1937, Page 1.
33 *Cincinnati Enquirer*, 12 Oct 1937, Page 1.
34 *Cincinnati Enquirer*, 15 Oct 1937, Page 1.
35 *Cincinnati Enquirer*, 19 Oct 1937, Page 1.
36 *Cincinnati Enquirer*, 20 Oct 1937, Page 1.
37 *Cincinnati Enquirer*, 23 Oct 1937, Page 1.
38 *Cincinnati Enquirer*, 07 Nov 1937, Page 1.
39 *Cincinnati Enquirer*, 09 Nov 1937, Page 1.
40 *Cincinnati Enquirer*, 28 Nov 1937, Page 1.
41 *Cincinnati Enquirer*, 02 Dec 1937, Page 6.
42 *Cincinnati Enquirer*, 08 Feb 1938, Page 1.
43 *Cincinnati Enquirer*, 05 Mar 1938, Page 1.
44 *Cincinnati Enquirer*, 29 Apr 1938, Page 1.
45 *Cincinnati Enquirer*, 04 May 1938, Page 1.
46 *Cincinnati Enquirer*, 28 Jun 1938, Page 5.
47 *Cincinnati Enquirer*, 11 Oct 1938, Page 1.
48 *Cincinnati Enquirer*, 18 Nov 1938, Page 1.
49 *Cincinnati Enquirer*, 08 Dec 1938, Page 1.
50 *Cincinnati Enquirer*, 19 Dec 1938, Page 1.
51 *Cincinnati Enquirer*, 11 May 1939, Page 1.
52 *Colorado Springs Gazette*, 08 Oct 2006, Page LIFE1.
53 *The Good-Bye Door*, Page 231.
54 *The Good-Bye Door*, Page 203.

Chapter 28

"The General"

HUGH D. HARPER; Colorado Springs Police Chief, a Foe of Outlaw Bands.
— Headline *New York Times* December 12, 1944

Two men were responsible for much of the modernization of the Colorado Springs Police Department. Both men were hired on April 1, 1913—April Fool's Day! The joke was on criminals from that time on. These two were both long serving officers and both of the longest serving chiefs the department ever had. The first of the two being appointed chief of police in 1917 was Hugh Davis Harper. The other was Irvin B. "Dad" Bruce.

Hugh Harper, a native of Duncanville, Illinois, arrived in Colorado Springs in 1898 and was employed as a streetcar motorman along with several other youths of Crawford County, Illinois, at the youthful age of 22.[1] On May 1st, 1903, the 27-year-old Harper became a police officer under the city's first police chief, Vincent King. Harper's beat was the near west side, from the Colorado Avenue bridge to the city limits of Colorado City.[2]

November of that year found Harper being removed from the police department by Mayor Ira Harris, ". . . to stop, if possible, the friction that to some extent is at present existing in the department."[3] Harper and another officer were let go because Harper exposed misconduct when he applied for a reward due the two officers. The department denied the reward. Harper told Chief King what he was doing was wrong. Officers were allowed to apply for rewards offered for the arrest of wanted persons. They could accept a portion of the offered reward, usually 50%, with the other half going to their employing agency. Harper moved to Seattle, Washington and took up farming until 1905, when he came back to Colorado Springs.[4]

While Harper was gone from the city, the police department moved into the new City Hall at Kiowa Street and Nevada Avenue during November 1904. The lower level, with entrance on Kiowa Street was the new police headquarters. With the move into new quarters the police officers had their own firing range located in the subbasement of City Hall. The officers were expected to use the range on a monthly basis. As an incentive Chief William Sullivan Reynolds proposed that a silver medal be given to the man with the best score.[5]

Returning to the CSPD in 1905, now under Chief Alexander Adams, Harper was assigned with Officer Stanley Dean Burno as detectives working at the railroad depots, trying to slow the work of pickpockets who worked among the throngs of people visiting Colorado Springs.[6] Harper stayed until 1908, when he again left the department and took up farming in Lincoln County, Colorado.[7]

On April 1, 1913, Hugh Harper, Job B. Adams, James Neff, and Albert Pulliam all were appointed to the ranks of police officers as probationary for a period of 60 days.[8] There was no explanation as to why Harper returned to the department for his third try at being an officer, other than maybe it was just "once an officer, it is in the blood." Interestingly, at this same time, an ordinance enacting a "day of rest," was started, where an officer would be provided one day of rest in every seven. Previously, the officers received one day a month off.

Following the city elections that April, newly appointed Police Chief Stanley Dean Burno, promoted Harper to city detective and assigned him with 18-year-old, Irvin B. Bruce.[9] Due to Bruce's youth, he wasn't taken seriously by the older detectives until they found that Bruce had begun making his own personal identity bureau of known miscreants. It was not long before officers were going to Bruce to see what information he might have in his records. The following May, Harper was appointed to police captain.[10] The ranking order was police officer, city detective, police sergeant, police captain, and finally chief of police.

When the new City Council was elected in April 1917, the position of chief of police sat unoccupied until July when Newton Hutchinson Haywood of Dayton, Ohio, was selected as the new chief. Still employed by the Dayton Police Department, he decided that it was in his best interest to return to Ohio where he would have a pension awaiting him which was worth more than staying in Colorado Springs. He lasted a little more than two months. With Haywood's rapid departure, Hugh Harper was made chief October, 1917.[11]

Hugh Davis Harper served as chief of the CSPD from 1917 to 1941.
Courtesy of Pikes Peak Library District, Special Collection, Irvin B. Bruce Collection.

Harper was the chief until 1919, when Commissioner of Public Safety Daniel G. Johnson, as noted in an earlier chapter, was up to his old tricks. For some reason Johnson decided he wanted Harper to resign, but was not able to produce any backing from the other council members or the mayor. His accusations against the chief were that he was not enforcing the ordinances regarding tourist drivers and speeding. Being unsuccessful at forcing a resignation, he suspended Chief Harper for 10 days.[12] Of course, Johnson's charges failed.

Trouble started in mid-January 1920, when the city auditor reported to City Council the positions of four employees of the police department had not been approved. Councilman Daniel G. Johnson, the Public Safety Commissioner who had to sign the payrolls, told council, because the records did not show they had been regularly appointed he had not approved their pay.[13] On the 28th of January, a petition from police and fire members, requested assistance from the City of Colorado Springs to help purchase one regulation uniform per year, at the City's expense. The matter was referred to the committee of the whole.[14] No record was found to indicate this requested action was approved.

By the last meeting of the City Council in February, a resolution was put forth (No. 1095) stating:

> WHEREAS, Albert Sidney Pulliam has rendered services to the City as Detective, Miles Burton Bright and William B. Smurdon have rendered services to the City as Patrolmen, and Mrs. F.W. Eagan has rendered services to the City as Police Woman, for which services they have not been paid; and
>
> WHEREAS, the following items upon the payroll of the City in the Department of Public Safety, to-wit:

A.S. Pulliam	Salary to Jan. 15, 1920	$67.50
M.B. Bright	" "	$58.40
Wm. Smurdon	" "	$52.50
Mrs. F.W. Eagan	" "	$50.00
A.S. Pulliam	from 1/15/20 to 1/31/20	$66.75
M.B. Bright	from 1/15/20 to 1/31/20	$59.25
Mrs. F.W. Eagan	from 1/15/20 to 1/31/20	$49.25
A.S. Pulliam	from 1/31/20 to 2/16/20	$67.50
M.B. Bright	from 1/31/20 to 2/16/20	$60.00
Mrs. F.W. Eagan	from 1/31/20 to 2/16/20	$10.35

Have not been approved, and the Commissioner of Public Safety has failed and refuses to approve each of said items:

BE IT RESOLVED BY THE City Council OF THE CITY OF COLORADO SPRINGS, That each of said items upon the payroll of said City in the Department of Public Safety, be and the same are hereby approved, and the City Auditor is hereby instructed to sign and issue the proper warrant to pay each of said persons the above named respective amounts;
RESOLVED FURTHER, That said amounts shall be paid from the appropriation for salaries in the Police Department of the Department of Public Safety.

Upon motion of Councilman Botts, seconded by Councilman Payton, the resolution was adopted by Councilmen Botts, Payton and Mr. President voting yea. Councilmen Chapman and Johnson voting nay.[15]

During the next meeting of City Council, Mayor Thomas called attention of Council that payroll of police department for the last half of February amounting to $1,849.35 had not been approved by the Commissioner of the Department. Councilman Botts introduced the following resolution which was read, and moved to its adoption, seconded by Councilman Payton;

R E S O L U T I O N (#1098)

WHEREAS, the various members of the Police Department have rendered services to the City for which services they have not been paid; and

WHEREAS, the items due upon the payroll in Police Department in the Department of Public Safety, for the last half of February, 16th to 29th, inclusive, amounting to $1,849.35 have not been approved, and the Commissioner of Public Safety has failed and refused to approve said payroll, therefore;

BE IT RESOLVED BY THE City Council OF THE CITY OF COLORADO SPRINGS, that each of said items upon the payroll of said City in the Department of Public Safety, be and the same are hereby approved, and the City Auditor is hereby instructed to sign and issue the proper warrant to pay each of said persons in the named respective amounts. RESOLVED FURTHER, that said amounts shall be paid from the appropriation for salaries in the Police Department of the Department of Public Safety.

Roll being called upon the resolution, Councilmen Botts, Payton, and Mr. President voted yea, and Councilmen Chapman and Johnson voted nay, and resolution was adopted.[16]

On March 12th, the police department payroll for March 1st through the 15th was passed by the council, since Commissioner of Public Safety Johnson refused.[17] Again, on April 2nd, it was required the council to pass the funding of the police department for the last half of March.[18] Since Johnson did not seem to get the hint, Resolution No. 1110 was passed by four members of the council stating that they were forced into the position of considering his removal from his office. Not only was he not signing the payrolls, as required, but he was also refusing to cooperate with the Civil Service Commission, plus he used vile, abusive and indecent language with citizens on official matters of the city. He was even investing Relief Association funds contrary to direction of the council. Therefore, on May 6, 1920, a hearing was scheduled to make a formal investigation into the Councilman Daniel G. Johnson's behavior and abuses.[19] After a lengthy hearing on the facts surrounding his conduct, he was removed from his office![20]

Chief Harper's expenses were approved by the City Council for him to attend the International Chiefs of Police Convention in Detroit, Michigan, early June of 1920.[21] Harper was able to attend the IACP convention in 1921 also, held at St. Louis, Missouri.[22]

From about 1895 through early 1920s, Denver's Louis Herbert

Blonger was in charge of confidence games throughout most of the western United States. His second in command, Adolph William Duff, plied the trade in Colorado Springs, Colorado City, and the mining district of Cripple Creek from 1901 through September of 1904, until he was convicted of operating a policy wheel in Colorado City and went to jail.[23] Upon his release in 1905, he left town. He was back in business by 1909, in the Portland, Oregon, area.[24] By the 1920s, Duff was installed in Denver, running the con games for Louis Blonger. He was basically, the equivalent of a business manager. He would hire, train and plan the operation of large con games in the Denver area. At the time Denver was so corrupt that much of the police department, judges, council members and others were on the payroll of Blonger. With the advent of a new district attorney, in 1920, Philip Van Cise, things would change. Van Cise praised the Colorado Springs Police Department as having an "excellent force, and its officers were honest. At their head was Chief of Police Hugh D. Harper, and his Captain of Detectives, Irvin B. "Dad" Bruce. They were relentlessly on the trail of the con-men, because Blonger's gang frequently dropped into town and picked up a sucker and then brought him to Denver to trim him."[25]

Colorado Springs, under the direction of Chief Harper, was reported as a city that had a rigid enforcement of the local laws. Colorado Springs "has become a byword not only for hobos who are 'floated' on sight but members of the underworld who are generally hustled from the railroad station to the city jail for investigation and then hastened on their way. Similarly, the percentage of recovery of stolen cars is unusually high, averaging around 95 percent for the last seven years, while automobile theft is comparatively slight," was reported by Stuart P. Dodge, in the *Police Officer Magazine*, February 1922, edition.[26]

The world operated a little differently in 1923, and attitudes of people were definitely more respectful. As an example, Chief Harper wrote a letter to Mrs. E.C. Bowen of Colorado Springs about her son Alex. The letter reported Alex had been driving in a reckless and dangerous manner on the streets of Colorado Springs. Because of his near miss in a traffic accident near the Broadmoor, his license to drive an auto in Colorado Springs had been indefinitely revoked. This was to be the situation until Alex learned to obey speed and traffic regulations.[27] It is hard to imagine a similar situation being handled this way in "modern" times.

The U.S. Congress passed what was known as the Sims Act, signed by President William Howard Taft, which became law on July 31, 1912, allowing the filming of boxing matches. It was still illegal to transport films across state lines. So, when a motion-picture of the Jack Dempsy-Tommy Gibbons boxing match was shown May 8, 1924, in a theater in Colorado Springs, it was quietly confiscated, at the direction of Chief of Police Harper.[28]

Harper was invited to speak in Washington, D.C., December of 1924 at the invitation of the Secretary of the Department of Commerce, Herbert Hoover. The conference was regarding what to do about auto deaths, and was described as a need to end the slaughter of motorists.[29] Upon returning, Harper was named as the chairman of a committee to draft legislation for accident prevention, since he was the representative of Hoover's Safety Committee.[30]

As part of the push to make the streets safer, 50 men were picked from the Colorado Springs Automobile Club to be an emergency traffic squad. A list of 200 names was submitted to the police department from which to select. Their purpose was to note and record violations of traffic laws. These violations were then sent to Chief Harper for action.[31]

During prohibition, the police were always on the lookout for "bootleggers." In July of 1925, Chief Harper reported the Department had been successful in the arrest of four members of a $2,000,000 national syndicate, which information was suppled to federal authorities.[32]

Often a speaker at national conventions, Harper was invited to speak before the International Association for Identification at Memphis, Tennessee, in August, 1927.[33] As reported earlier in this book, Chief Harper, was involved in the arrest of "Danny" Daniels, during an attempted burglary and shoot-out September 1927. Then in January Chief Harper was a speaker at the Wyoming Peace Officers' Association about "Up-to-Date Methods of Identification."[34]

During the end of May 1927, Harper was involved in one of the most challenging times in his career as a law enforcement officer. He was tasked by the Colorado Bankers' Association to assist in the solving of the Lamar, Colorado bank robbery and murder of four people.[35] After his solving the Lamar bank robbery case, Chief Harper was elected President of the International Association of Chiefs of Police in 1931.

The 1928 annual convention of the International Association of Chiefs of Police (IACP) was held at the Antlers Hotel in Colorado Springs during September.[36] Chief Harper was highly respected nationally, and brought light to the excellence of the Colorado Springs Police Department.

All was not smooth going for Chief Harper as he moved into the 1930s. The *Colorado Springs Independent*, editor, John Clark McCreary, 60,[37] was apparently not happy with the police chief, or two of the larger local newspapers. Of the ten local newspapers, the *Colorado Springs Independent* was the only one to have such strong opinions about fellow publications and the two leaders of the police department. The writer refers to the *Gazette* and the *Evening Telegraph*, as the 'Daily Twins' and wrote of *Associated Press* articles both papers covered regarding a federal liquor investigator in Colorado Springs. The writer accused the *Associated Press* of being on par with the 'Daily Twins' and wondered how any story they circulated could be believed. McCreary referred to Chief Harper, as "General Harper." He accused Harper of coming to the aid of the newspaper's management and getting their staff back to work by stopping their drinking. The bootlegger suppling the "150 bottles of beer" and the supplier of such, was fined merely $100 though. McCreary did not know what became of the "hooch," but thought someone could check with Dad Bruce.[38] It seems the editor was implying the chief was soft on liquor laws.

The *Independent* was published weekly, and McCreary followed in the next edition by asking the question "How to get rid of Harper?" The paper's answer was suggesting to get rid of the present City Council and accused them of knowing "what the chief was." But the paper was not clear on exactly what was the problem they had with Chief Harper.[39] Again, on the front page of the following week's edition, Harper was accused of outwardly wanting to enforce the laws against alcohol and its use, but the *Independent* thought Chief Harper had his fingers crossed behind his back.[40]

On May 4th, Harper left for Boulder where he was to be part of the University of Colorado extension department and lecture for three days about traffic conditions.[41] Harper was in demand for his knowledge and excellent record.

An article written by Courtney Riley Cooper, a one-time Colorado newspaperman, published in the *American Magazine's* December, 1934, edition, regaled "Dad" Bruce and Chief Harper. The article was titled: "Two Against the Underworld." Cooper provided monikers for the men: "The Dick with the Camera Eyes," for Bruce and "Old Stomach Pump," for Harper. Harper's nickname is said to be from underworld characters for the way Harper could get people to confess to their crimes. Basically, Bruce just produced the bad guys seemingly out of thin air, even though he had never met them before and then Harper pumped those captured until there was nothing more to give.[42]

During 1941, Chief Harper's health had declined to the point he was granted sick leave on May 17th, putting Irvin B. Bruce as acting chief during Harper's absence. When the attack at Pearl Harbor, Hawaii, on December 7th, 1941 occurred, Chief Harper told the City Council that considering the times and the United States entering into the fray of war, it was necessary the city have a full-time director with full powers. One week later, December 12th, Bruce was appointed to the position of chief of police.[43] Over his career of three service periods with the CSPD, Chief Hugh Davis

Harper served 32 years, one month and 17 days. He was chief for 24 years and two months.

Hugh Davis Harper died in Colorado Springs, Monday, December 11, 1944 and was laid to rest at Colorado Springs Evergreen Cemetery.[44]

Notes

1 *Colorado Springs Evening Telegraph*, 11 Dec 1944, Page 1.
2 *Colorado Springs Gazette* & Telegraph, 07 Jul 1929, Page 2.
3 Colorado Springs City Council Minutes, 07 Nov 1903, Book 9, Page 167.
4 *Colorado Springs Evening Telegraph*, 11 Dec 1944, Page 1.
5 *Colorado Springs Gazette* & Telegraph, 20 Nov 1904, Page 4.
6 *Colorado Springs Gazette* & Telegraph, 07 Jul 1929, Page 2. *Colorado Springs Gazette*, 02 Apr 1908, Page 2.
7 *Colorado Springs Gazette*, 30 Mar 1908, Page 5.
8 *Colorado Springs Gazette* & Telegraph, 07 Jul 1929, Page 2.
9 Colorado Springs City Council Minutes, 01 May 1914, Book 14, Page 218.
10 *Colorado Springs Evening Telegraph*, 12 Oct 1917, Page 5.
11 *Colorado Springs Gazette*, 22 May 1919, Page 1.
12 Colorado Springs City Council Minutes, 16 Jan 1920, Book 16, Page 73.
13 Colorado Springs City Council Minutes, 28 Jan 1920, Book 16, Page 76.
14 Colorado Springs City Council Minutes, 25 Feb 1920, Book 16, Page 96.
15 Colorado Springs City Council Minutes, 03 Mar1920, Book 16, Page 100.
16 Colorado Springs City Council Minutes, 12 Mar 1920, Book 16, Page 106.
17 Colorado Springs City Council Minutes, 02 Apr 1920, Book 16, Page 118.
18 Colorado Springs City Council Minutes, 05 May 1920, Book 16, Page 144.
19 Colorado Springs City Council Minutes, 28 May 1920, Book 16, Page 180.
20 Colorado Springs City Council Minutes, 04 Jun 1920, Book 16, Page 191.
21 Colorado Springs City Council Minutes, 25 May 1921, Book 16, Page 379.
22 *Colorado Springs Gazette*, 22 Sep 1904, Page 6.
23 *Portland Daily Journal*, 14 Nov 1909, Page 6.
24 *Fighting the Underworld*, By Philip S. Van Cise, 1936, Published by Riverside Press, Cambridge, Page 5.
25 "The Colorado Springs Police Department," The Police Officer Magazine, By Stuart P. Dodge, Feb 1922, Page 52.
26 Letter of Chief of Police Hugh D. Harper to Mrs. E.C. Bowen, 13 Jan 1923.
27 *Fort Collins Express Courier*, 11 May 1924, Page 7.
28 *Colorado Springs Gazette*, 02 Dec 1924, Page 14.
29 *Albuquerque Journal*, 19 Jan 1925, Page 3.
30 *Fort Collins Express Courier*, 21 Jun 1925, Page 13.
31 *Scottsbluff Daily Star Herald*, 23 Jul 1925, Page 2.
32 Memphis Commercial Appeal, 21 Aug 1927, Page 24.
33 *Casper Star-Tribune*, 16 Jan 1928, Page 8.
35 *Grand Junction Daily Sentinel*, 24 May 1928, Page 8.
36 *Colorado Springs Gazette*, 04 Oct 1927, Page 6.
36 1930 United States Colorado Census, 14 Apr 1930.
38 *Colorado Springs Independent*, 17 Apr 1930, Page 1.
39 *Colorado Springs Independent*, 24 Apr 1930, Page 1.
40 *Colorado Springs Independent*, 01 May 1930, Page 1.
41 *Colorado Springs Evening Telegraph*, 05 May 1930, Page 3.
42 *Colorado Springs Gazette*, 16 Nov 1934, Page 14.
43 *Colorado Springs Gazette*, 12 Dec 1941, Page 16.
44 *Colorado Springs Evening Telegraph*, 11 Dec 1944, Page 1.

Chapter 29

"Dad"

In a time of segregation in our country, "Dad" Bruce knew the Cotton Club, a highly respected nightclub for black entertainers, made everybody welcome. In a meeting with the owner, Bruce told Fanny May Duncan to make sure she only let in blacks. Fanny Mae said she only checked for age at the door not skin color. In a phone conversation Bruce changed his mind, "Whoever comes to the Cotton Club, you let 'em in. You're doin' a great job, and I WILL help you." — Everybody Welcome by Fannie Mae Duncan with Kathleen Esmiol

Born in Edgerton, Missouri, in 1893, Irvin B. "Dad" Bruce arrived in Colorado Springs with his parents and siblings in 1900. Eighteen-year-old Bruce graduated from Colorado Springs High School (now Palmer High School), in the spring of 1912. He played fullback for the school's football team and in the spring, catcher for the baseball program. Before graduation and sometime thereafter, he had a by-line in the *Gazette* newspaper reporting on the sports of the high school and Colorado College. His inclination was to become a journalist.[1]

After enrolling at Colorado College he was unable to complete his first year because of a shortage of funds. Having to leave school and unsure of his future, he met with former Police Chief William S. Reynolds, a family friend, and explained he did not know what to do with himself. Reynolds told him he should be a policeman. Although only nineteen, he spoke to then Chief Stanley D. Burno. Burno, impressed with the youth, decided to hire Bruce as a plainclothesman, but explained that since he was not twenty-one, he could only hire him as a temporary employee, and would have to lay him off at the end of every three months. And so it was, Bruce was employed beginning April Fool's Day, 1913, in three-month cycles until reaching the magic age of twenty-one.² Bruce & Harper both started work on the same day.

During the fall of 1914, Bruce was sent to Leavenworth, Kansas, to attend a school on fingerprinting.³ He receiving training from L.J. Fletcher, a former special agent in charge of the federal identification work at Leavenworth, George M. Sanders, then in charge of the Denver bureau, and Dr. A.L. Bennett, well-known criminologist in Denver.⁴

Thomas H. Reynolds (aka: Thomas H. Wilson) was arrested in April of 1915, suspected of stealing a saddle from the Alamo Ranch south of town. He was a long-time participant in larcenies. He was given the opportunity to be the first criminal identified through his fingerprints in Colorado Springs. This, by a young scientist, who had established the first fingerprint bureau in the State of Colorado, Irvin B. Bruce. The miscreant was not forthcoming about his identity. Bruce found his fingerprints were on file at the Idaho State Penitentiary, taken just months prior. This allowed Mr. Reynolds the chance to spend a three-year vacation in the lovely climes of Cañon City at the penitentiary. All with a reservation provided by the State of Colorado.⁵

By June of 1915, Bruce was appointed as Bertillon body measurement system and fingerprint specialist. The following year Bruce was sent to Leavenworth Penitentiary to study fingerprints over ten days in January of 1916.⁶ Until June of 1916, Bruce had been the temporary person in charge of the department's Bureau of Identification. He was then appointed as permanent head.⁷ He was tasked with establishing the fingerprint bureau of the Colorado State Penitentiary.⁸ Having become a member of the International Association for Criminal Identification, he was elected vice-president in 1918.⁹ April of that year, he received orders to report to the Secret Service Division of the Department of Justice for new work to serve during WWI.¹⁰

When the Frank Lewis-Dale Jones gang arrived in Colorado Springs on September 1918, Bruce was still in the service of the

Justice Department and not available to the CSPD. With the death of Chief of Detectives John William Rowan, the position was offered to Bruce. He turned down the offer. Because of his commitment to the Secret Service and contract, he would not be available for the position.[11] Bruce had to consider the offer something of which to be proud, because he was only twenty-six years of age.

With the conclusion of World War I, Bruce's commitment to the federal government was at an end. A letter from United States Attorney, Harry B. Tedrow, dated February 27, 1919, was given to Bruce as a strong recommendation letter. Bruce returned to the CSPD and took the position of captain of detectives.

A former Colorado Springs attorney, Rush L. Holland, an assistant United States Attorney General, wrote to Bruce asking if he would be interested in an appointment as division superintendent in charge of Bureau of Investigation Headquarters at Denver, with a salary of $9.00 per day and $4.00 subsistence when absent from headquarters.[12] Bruce thanked Mr. Holland, but believed he was where he belonged. The minimum wage in 1919 was $.28 per hour.

Chief of Detectives Irvin B. Bruce, nabbed Jimmy "Red" McCormick, known as "King of the Pickpockets," as he was leaving a vaudeville performance at the Burns Opera House. Bruce's seemingly photographic memory kicked in upon seeing the man after viewing a photograph from back east received by the police department several weeks earlier. McCormick admitted to Bruce his purpose for being in Colorado Springs was to find a way to get the four members of his gang the CSPD had arrested days earlier. McCormick, also known as Ed Deming, Thomas O'Toole, Red Deming, and Eddie Daly, had criminal records spread across the country in Newark, New Jersey; Cincinnati, Ohio; Buffalo, New York; Spokane, Washington; Pittsburgh, Pennsylvania; Omaha, Nebraska; Santa Monica, California; Kansas City, Missouri; Detroit, Michigan and San Francisco, California.[13]

The police department was known for their excellent work in all its operations, which included the Identification Bureau which received much attention when an article in a local newspaper described how the bureau operated and its capability. The bureau was described as the home where many Bertillon measurements and fingerprints of criminals were made and filed. It had almost 20,000 fingerprint cards on file, one of the best collections for a city the size of Colorado Springs. When a suspect arrived at the police headquarters, they were first photographed and Bertillon measurements taken. The system relied on defined body measurements and was a forerunner of the fingerprint system that was slowly supplanting the French anthropologist's system.[14]

In September of 1921, William J. Burns, head of the Bureau of Investigation (forerunner of the Federal Bureau of Investigation) and head of Burns National Detective Agency, addressed members of the International Association of Identification saying he wanted a fingerprint bureau established in Washington, D.C., run by the foremost expert in fingerprints. At that time federal fingerprint files were maintained at Leavenworth Federal Prison, in Leavenworth, Kansas. It was reported in the 1920s to have 412,000 prints on file.[15]

Rush L. Holland, Assistant United States Attorney General, wrote to the Colorado Springs City Council asking either Chief Harper or Chief of Detectives Bruce be sent to the International Chiefs of Police annual meeting to be held at Buffalo, New York, June of 1923. It was going to be proposed that the International Association of Chiefs of Police (IACP), turn their 50,000 fingerprint files over to the federal government in a proposed move to centralize their location.[16]

In June of 1923, Captain of Detectives Irvin Bruce traveled to Washington, D.C., where he would attend a conference where a plan for establishing a government fingerprint system would be discussed. This was the beginning of an effort to establish a central fingerprint bureau where police could go to ask for assistance in identifying criminals. By July 1924, the money had been appropriated by the Congress and a move had been completed to establish the fingerprint bureau. Burns had been replaced by John Edgar Hoover as its new director. The IACP fingerprints and those of the federal government were now intermingled into a central filing system.[17]

Irvin Bruce, known for his "camera eye," arrested many people he recognized from "wanted" posters during his career. In April, 1924, "Slippery" Dell Hanlon was being held in the Denver jail when he assisted thirteen people to escape. But, as many a wanted party, he made the mistake of traveling to Colorado Springs. Bruce, in a plaster cast because of a dislocated knee, was on a bench in front of the county courthouse with Officer George Emerick. A tall athletic man passed by the two plainclothes officers, and Bruce immediately recognized the man. Leaving his crutches on the ground, Bruce and Emerick quickly got control of Hanlon and jailed him in Colorado Springs—where he did not escape—and was returned to Denver.[18]

Police Chief I.B. "Dad" Bruce with pistol (left) and Captain Robert Wraith holding rifle taken from a shoot out with Delbert W. Snyder. Firing on two police officers, Snyder fled City Hall and was captured two hours later on the north edge of town. Snyder was reportedly angry over a recent arrest and traffic ticket.
Courtesy of Pikes Peak Library District, Special Collections
Photograph by Stanley L. Payne 004-343.

Another miscreant, Elgin Cole, wanted in Denver for robbing a woman in June of 1926, was arrested by Bruce while eating at McRae's restaurant. Bruce was walking past the restaurant, happened to look in, and immediately recognized Cole. He was shortly jailed by Bruce and held for Denver.[19]

Bruce, not one to "spill the beans," was off to the IACP convention in Chicago, July of 1926, and returned a changed man. While in Chicago, Bruce married Irene McCormick, 26, whose father was a Chicago police officer. Irene was a former secretary to William Pinkerton, head of the famous national detective agency. It seems that Miss McCormick and her mother had been visitors to Colorado Springs some time earlier where the couple met.[20]

Inspector Irvin B. Bruce, addressed the officers of the newly formed San Luis Valley Sheriffs and Peace Officers Association on the importance of preserving evidence and fingerprint methods for identification. On February 1, 1930, in Alamosa, Bruce used the example of how several exhibits of guns missing from evidence in the Lamar bank robbery case, were going to make the State's case against the Fleagles and the other two suspects, much harder to win.[21]

Badge presented to Inspector Bruce at the 1949 inauguration of President Harry S. Truman.

Inspector Bruce received an invitation from the Washington, D.C. Metro Police Department to aid in the guarding of Franklin Delano Roosevelt at his inauguration for President on March 4, 1933.[22] This was the first of these invitations issued to Bruce. Bruce, for the second and third time was invited to be a special police guard in Washington, D.C., for the inaugurations of President Roosevelt in

1937 and 1941. The special detail consisted of 65 men all invited from police departments throughout the country. Bruce known for his "eye" for criminals was always regarded as a valuable member of this group.[23] Bruce also was in this capacity during the inauguration of Harry S. Truman and both inaugurations of Dwight D. Eisenhower.

In an article for *American Magazine*, December, 1934 edition, Courtney Riley Cooper, wrote in the entitled article: "Two Against the Underworld," about Chief Harper and Inspector Bruce. Bruce had the instincts of a bird dog. Bruce seemed to have a passion for searching faces and did this constantly. The writer said one time Bruce was at a circus, left his seat to walk around to the other side of the hippodrome track and picked up a man on that other side who was a wanted criminal. Because of Harper's interrogating abilities and Bruce's tracking skills, the citizens of Colorado Springs surely enjoyed more safety than people living in other towns.[24]

A supposedly experienced burglar, while trying to sneak into an apartment at 2127 North Cascade Avenue, just prior to midnight on August 2, 1935, was attempting to jimmy the door. It was suddenly opened and the burglar found himself face-to-face with Police Department Inspector Irvin B. "Dad" Bruce—and a large revolver. Wearing sneakers at the time apparently was not enough to make Frank Reed a successful criminal.[25]

When Chief Harper had taken sick leave starting in May of 1941, he left Bruce as acting chief. Then the Japanese attacked Pearl Harbor, Hawaii, on December 7th, 1941, Harper resigned on December 12th and the following Tuesday, Bruce was sworn in as Chief of Police Bruce.[26]

In 1943, Bruce was made a life member of the IACP and was one of only 65 police chiefs to be so honored.[27] Elected president of the organization in 1954, he had been a member since 1920 and also a member of the Board of Officers since 1950.[28] During Bruce's tenure, he served on the executive and memorial committees and in March of 1947, also became a member of the education and training committee.²⁹ At the end of his term, the IACP presented Bruce with a gold badge to commemorate his time as president.³⁰ The IACP held their national convention in Colorado Springs in October 1950, at the Antler's Hotel, while the wives socialized at the Trianon at the Broadmoor. Bruce was the acting sergeant-at-arms during the convention as well as head of the hosting police department.³¹

Not everything was serious at the Police Department. In January of 1949, some offices in City Hall were in the process of being moved. One Wednesday morning, Bruce was busy for about 30 minutes interviewing a witness. As soon as he left the office, a sign painter went right to work. When Bruce returned to his office, he found the sign painter had completed the entry door to his office. However, Bruce was not happy with the result. The sign read in quite large letters:

PRESS ROOM and MAYOR and CHIEF

Bruce had a very good relationship with the press, who, along with the mayor were the instigators of this prank. Shortly, the sign was re-lettered more to the chief's taste.³² In fact, the chief's relationship with the press included his often picking up members and taking them to crime scenes with him.

November of 1951 had a good bit of excitement when actor Robert Mitchum was in Colorado Springs filming the movie "The Korean Story." Mitchum was involved in a fight in the then Fox lounge of the Alamo Hotel. Allegedly, the fight ended with Mitchum kicking a soldier in the head requiring the subject to be admitted to the Camp Carson hospital. Charges weren't filed in the matter.³³

During October 1954, Chief Bruce accepted an invitation from the United States State Department to travel to West Germany and assist in the organization of the West German police departments.³⁴ Bruce spent almost two months overseas before returning in January.³⁵ Bruce visited over a dozen cities, including West Berlin, where he spoke with and advised the many police organizations.[36]

Often people wondered where the nickname "Dad" was derived. He explained that one time while attending Colorado Springs High School he was a "big, bashful baseball and football star . . . pranksters planted baby clothes in his pockets" and then "while he was strolling with a girl, pulled the clothes" from his pockets. At first, he was referred to as 'The Father,' which became shortened to just 'Father,' and finally to 'Dad.' The name stuck and was very appropriate to his demeanor.[37]

On February 6, 1960, Dad was taken to Penrose Hospital after suffering gall bladder problems.[38] Two days later, the chief's condition was listed as improved, but he was kept in the hospital for observation.[39] By the 12th, improvement in his condition allowed him to go home, with the expectation of surgery in the near future.[40] Suffering further pain, Bruce was returned to the hospital two days later, with surgery being conducted on the 17th. Following the surgery, it was reported that his condition had greatly deteriorated.[41] Thursday, February 18, 1960, Irvin B. "Dad" Bruce died at the hospital at the age of 66.[42]

Chief Bruce had been a police officer in Colorado Springs, serving for 46 years, 10 months and 19 days. He was the chief for 18 years, 2 months and 1 day. For 43 years, just two men led the department: Hugh Davis Harper and Irvin B. Bruce. They were two of the longest serving police officers on the department. Dad never served in uniform, being hired as a detective from the first day. He also did not drive.

Notes

1. *Colorado Springs Free Press*, 28 Feb 1970, Page 6.
2. *Colorado Springs Free Press*, 28 Feb 1970, Page 6.
3. *Colorado Springs Free Press*, 25 Feb 1947, Page 1.
4. *Colorado Springs Gazette*, 02 Apr 1922, Page 1.
5. *Colorado Springs Advertiser*, 14 Oct 1935.
6. *Colorado Springs Gazette*, 21 Jan 1916, Page 10.
7. *Colorado Springs Gazette*, 08 Jun 1916, Page 6.
8. *Colorado Springs Free Press*, 28 Feb 1970, Page 6.
9. *Routt County Sentinel*, 08 Feb 1918.
10. *Colorado Springs Gazette*, 18 Apr 1918.
11. *Colorado Springs Evening Telegraph*, 19 Oct 1918, Page 3.
12. Letter to I.B. Bruce, 04 Jan 1920.

13 *Colorado Springs Gazette*, 29 Mar 1921, Page 1.
14 *Colorado Springs Gazette*, 02 Apr 1922, Page 2.
15 *Washington Herald*, 24 Sep 1921, Page 9.
16 Letter to Colorado Springs City Council, from Rush L. Holland, 08 May 1923.
17 *Bureau, The Secret History of the FBI*, By Ronald Kessler, 2002, Published by St. Martin's Press, New York, Page 21.
18 *Denver Post*, 28 Apr 1924, Page 1.
19 *Colorado Springs Gazette*, 03 Jul 1926, Page 1.
20 *Colorado Springs Gazette*, 26 Jul 1926, Page 1.
21 *Denver Post*, 01 Feb 1930, Page 16.
22 *Colorado Springs Gazette* & Telegraph, 12 Feb 1933, Page 5.
23 *Colorado Springs Gazette*, 07 Jan 1941.
24 *Colorado Springs Gazette*, 16 Nov 1934, Page 14.
25 *Colorado Springs Gazette*, 03 Aug 1935, Page 1.
26 *Colorado Springs Gazette*, 12 Dec 1941, Page 16.
27 *Colorado Springs Gazette*, 24 Aug 1943, Page 10.
28 Law & Order Magazine, Nov 1954, Pages 8 & 20.
29 *Colorado Springs Gazette* Telegraph, 21 Mar 1947, Page 1.
30 *Colorado Springs Gazette* Telegraph, 10 Oct 1955, Page A1.
31 *Colorado Springs Gazette* Telegraph, 08 Oct 1950, Page C1.
32 *Colorado Springs Gazette* Telegraph, 12 Jan 1949, Page A9.
33 *Colorado Springs Gazette* Telegraph, 08 Nov 1951, Page A1.
34 *Rocky Mountain News*, Oct 1954.
35 *Colorado Springs Gazette* Telegraph, 06 Jan 1955, Page A1.
36 *Colorado Springs Gazette* Telegraph, 10 Jan 1955, PageA1.
37 Empire Magazine, Sunday *Denver Post* — Supplement, 08 Nov 1953, Page 4.
38 *Colorado Springs Gazette* Telegraph, 06 Feb 1960, Page A1.
39 *Colorado Springs Gazette* Telegraph, 08 Feb 1960, Page A11.
40 *Colorado Springs Gazette* Telegraph, 12 Feb 1960, Page A11.
41 *Colorado Springs Gazette* Telegraph, 17 Feb 1960, Page A1.
42 *Colorado Springs Gazette* Telegraph, 18 Feb 1960, Page A1.

Chapter 30

OFFICER RICHARD STANLEY BURCHFIELD COLD CASE

Experience shows cold case programs can solve a substantial number of violent crime cold cases. Advances in DNA technologies have increased the successful DNA analysis of aged, degraded, limited, or otherwise compromised biological evidence. The National Institute of Justice seeks to assist law enforcement agencies by developing their knowledge base, affording them opportunities to use forensic laboratories for DNA analysis, and aiding in investigation to solve cold cases. — National Institute of Justice https://nij.ojp.gov

By the 1950s, the population of Colorado Springs was pushing 50,000 souls. Growth was not very fast as the town had only added about 30,000 people in fifty years. Not reflected in these totals was Camp Carson, the U. S. Army camp located just south of the city, consisting of a large contingent due to the end of World War II and the Korean conflict being in progress. The Colorado Springs Police Department had 48 men in 1951 which grew to 75 men by 1954. They were patrolling over 30 square miles within the city limits. Crime was not a significant problem during this time period and as for major crimes, the city had experienced 15 homicides from 1950 through 1955. The 50s had much lower homicide rates than in the Great Depression years.

However, during 1953, the city experienced a homicide that remains unsolved 70 years after the deed.[1] This case started with a series of personal robberies that began during October of 1953. Women were initially being targeted. Apparently, the robber was watching women take a city bus from their employment around the downtown area and then following the bus until the women reached their stop. The first robbery occurred on Friday evening, October 23rd, in the Knob Hill area, east of downtown Colorado Springs at the intersection of Sunset and Monument Streets. In the 1950s the Knob Hill area was outside the city limits of Colorado Springs and fell under the jurisdiction of the El Paso County Sheriff's Office.

Mrs. Martha Claire Needles, age 45, rode a city bus to the intersection of Monument Street and Iowa Avenue, and walked east on Monument where she was accosted by a man armed with a handgun. He held a handkerchief over his face and ordered the woman to drop her pocketbook. She described the man as being in his early 20s, about 5 feet 9, and 130 pounds. She related it was dark and foggy that evening which made it difficult to get a clear look at the suspect. She reported to sheriff's deputies she only had between $3 and $4 in her handbag.[2] Mrs. Needles purse was recovered by a woman on Iowa Avenue, half-a-block south of Platte Avenue and four and a half blocks south of the robbery.

The following Monday, Anna Mae Carthwright, age 24, a waitress at Ruth's Oven Restaurant located across the street and west of Acacia Park in downtown Colorado Springs, boarded a city bus to go home. Miss Carthwright rode the bus to West Colorado Avenue and 21st Street, then walked north up 21st Street the five blocks to her home. As she was walking near an alley about 8:30 p.m. a man's voice from behind made her stop. When she turned there was a man with a handgun holding a light-colored cloth over his mouth. He told her to drop her purse and run. She only had about $4 in change in her purse. Having no phone at her home, she ran four blocks west to a friend's home to notify police. The victim described the robber as being a white male, about 5 foot 11, slim, wearing blue jeans, and a dark colored top. His handgun was long barreled, about five to six inches.[3] This crime occurred in the Old Colorado City area, approximately 42 blocks west of the first robbery in the Knob Hill area.

Just over a week later, about 7:15 p.m., on Monday, November 2nd, at 400 North Nevada Avenue, just a half block north of Colorado Springs High School (now Palmer High School) another incident occurred. As Martins Licis, age 50, walked south on the west side of the street, a man approached him from behind. He suddenly felt something pushed against his back which he thought to be a gun. He was told to stop and look at the ground. The robber took 60 cents in change and the man's hat. It was believed to be the same robber of the two previous crimes. The victim described this robber as a white male, 20-22 years old, 5'6" to 5'8" in height, about 155-160 pounds, wearing jeans, dark shirt and jacket.[4]

About a quarter hour after the robbery of Licis, Emma Cara Cantrell, age 75, was waiting for a city bus at the northwest corner of Monument and Weber Streets when a man wearing a brown hat, grabbed the woman's coat sleeve and demanded her purse. No weapon was displayed. She said the robber was wearing something that looked like a carpenter's apron under his jacket. She described him as about 20-25 years old, brown eyes, dark hair, wearing blue jeans and a dark jacket. The robber obtained $5.50. This robbery went unreported because she feared publicity. Later it would be reported after the death of a police officer.[5]

Four days later on the evening of Friday, November 6th, a man described as youthful robbed Helen Rose Riepl as she was walking home to 600 East Espanola Street a block west of the Patty Jewett Golf Course. She had attended a meeting at Glockner-Penrose Hospital, 2200 North Nevada Avenue, and was in the process of walking to her home about nine blocks distant. As she was nearing the alley, she realized that a man was following her. She described him as a young white man, about 17-18 years old, 5 foot 6, 140 pounds, slim build, with light brown hair, wearing blue jeans and a brown jacket. The youth held a cloth over his face, and pointed a handgun at her. He took her purse and about $10.00 in cash. The next day the purse was recovered by a woman on 800 North Logan Street about sixteen blocks southeast of the robbery location.[6]

Monday, November 9th, Grace D. Johnson, who worked in the offices of the Chamber of Commerce, 200 North Tejon Street, in the downtown area, rode a bus toward her residence. She exited the bus on North Tejon Street and was starting to enter her yard on 1700 Wood Avenue just after 7 p.m. A man stepped from the bushes and ordered her to drop her handbag. She said the man had a long-barreled blue revolver and a dirty handkerchief over his face. The robber obtained a check for $24, a cameo ring, plus a dollar in change. She said the man was a white male, 25-30 years old, 6 foot 2, slim build wearing tight fitting blue jeans, dark jacket and a cap. The man had a long-barreled gun, possibly a .22-caliber. After the robbery the man ran to an old model car, somewhat square shaped.[7]

Almost two weeks passed before another robbery was reported. Saturday, November 21st, Marguerite Alice Barngrover, 52, after getting off the Palmer Park route city bus at Willamette and Wahsatch Avenues, walked west to Weber Street, just about a block and one-half from her home. As she turned into the yard of her home around 6:00 p.m., at 711 North Weber Street, a man with a pistol threatened her when she would not relinquish her purse. She said that her handbag contained papers she did not want to lose. The bandit told her she would get them back. Giving in, she gave the red plastic purse to him which she thought had about $5 in it. She described the man as about 20-years of age, tall and slender, 5 foot 8 to 10, slim build, dark complexion, dark hair that was combed back tightly with a low-pitched voice. He was wearing a tan or khaki belt length jacket, darker trousers, neatly pressed. A couple of hours later, her purse was found just east of Prospect Street on High Street.[8]

Five days later, Thanksgiving, a man pursued Maude M. Gardner, 65, on the west side of Colorado Springs. She had just gotten off a city bus a little after 6:00 p.m. when a man stepped from an alley and started following her. She began to run and eluded the man by running into the yard of a neighbor, 2400 West Willamette Avenue. Her description of the culprit resembled that of the man conducting the earlier personal robberies.[9]

Approximately an hour later, Alton Leroy Peterson, an employee of the Internal Revenue Bureau, 201 East Pikes Peak Avenue at Nevada Avenue had been at his office catching up on some work between 4 and 6:30 p.m. He was walking back to his home on 1500 North Cascade Avenue, around 7:00 p.m., on the west side of the street, when he noticed a man rapidly approaching him from behind. This man was described as being 25-30, about 6 foot, 150 pounds, long black hair, a handkerchief held over his face. The man pointed a handgun at Peterson and informed him that he was being robbed. He was told to throw his wallet on the sidewalk, to which Peterson complied. He asked that he be allowed to take some of his papers, but the robber demanded Peterson to leave. The robber was wearing tight-fitting cowboy overalls, a dark shirt and a light jacket. The bandit netted between $5 and $6 dollars.[10]

That evening, Officer Eldon Barley, using police cruiser No. 3, was ending his afternoon shift. The normal practice was the off-going officer would pick up his oncoming replacement at the officer's home and both would return to police headquarters. This day, Barley drove to the home of Officer Richard Stanley Burchfield. On their way to headquarters, at 7:10 p.m., they were dispatched to the home of Alton Peterson, 1611 Wood Avenue, to help investigate a robbery. The officers were soon relieved by Detective Jess Garred and Chief of Police I.B. "Dad" Bruce. After dropping Barley off at his home about 7:45 p.m., Burchfield started patrol of his northeast district.[11]

At 7:55 p.m., Officer Burchfield radioed the police dispatcher and asked if any detectives were available. This was the last communication with the officer before he was found shot to death in his southbound facing police car on El Paso Street, north of Bijou Street. The officer had been shot by a person from the right front seat of the police car, with a .22-caliber semi-automatic pistol. The holster of the officer did not show any indication that he tried to draw his weapon, as his holster was still snapped.[12]

Robert McVay, who lived at 540 East Bijou Street, was on his way home from his parents where he and his wife had celebrated the Thanksgiving holiday. Just after 8:00 p.m. he drove west along Platte Avenue, where he stopped at the dead-end above the Platte

Avenue overpass and turned south on El Paso Street. As he and his wife were approaching Bijou he saw a marked police car, pulled into the west curb at somewhat of an angle, just before Bijou Street and the driver's door glass was cracked. A man was seen stooped down, looking on the floorboard on the passenger side of the police car. McVay turned west at the corner, then made a U-turn and drove back past the police car. His wife saw the man get in a car parked north up the street, a 1940 or '41 Ford.[13] McVay, drove north on El Paso Street to the dead-end north of Boulder Street. He turned around and drove south again on El Paso. On the way back the unknown man was sitting in the car where they had last witnessed his location, but still no police officer was seen. After turning the corner onto Bijou, instituted a second U-turn and drove back to the intersection. At this time the unknown man was again looking on the floorboards of the police car. McVay stopped and hollered at the man to inquire if he needed any help and was told rudely, no. At that point McVay went home and tried to call the police station. The incoming telephone line was busy, so he decided to drive three blocks to police headquarters. After reporting what he saw to the police, he followed two policemen who found Burchfield had been killed. Several pieces of identification, that belonged to Alton Peterson, the employee of the IRS that had been earlier robbed, were found on the floor of the police car. Robert McVay, an employee of the *Gazette Telegraph* was the only known person to see and talk with the killer of Officer Burchfield.[14]

Officers and *Free Press* reporter Charles Carte rushed to the scene and found Officer Burchfield dead, slumped over in the front seat. Of nine shots fired, seven struck the officer.[15] Cooperation was soon evident from all the regional law enforcement agencies, including the military. The fire department set up lighting at the crime scene so officers could look for clues. Roadblocks were soon in operation around the city. Denver police offered men if needed. Pueblo sent four officers to help. The police dispatch center was crewed by Officers George Follmer and Vern Wilson, who worked all night.[16]

The last police officer killed in the line of duty was Chief of Detectives John William Rowan on Friday, September the 13th, 1918, when he was killed in a shoot-out with Dale Jones, his wife and Roscoe "Kansas City Blackie" Lancaster, at Colorado and Nevada Avenues as reported earlier.[17]

Nine cartridges from the Burchfield crime scene and other materials were sent to the FBI laboratories for testing.[18] Examination of recovered bullets were identified by the FBI as having been fired from a Colt Woodsman .22-caliber automatic pistol.[19] After the type of weapon had been identified involved in the killing of Officer Burchfield, several citizens voluntarily took their Colt .22-caliber semi-automatics to the CSPD for test firing.[20]

Homicide investigation, November 1953, Marked police car No. 3. Courtesy of CSPD.

According to former retired Lieutenant Kenneth Beery, when he was interviewed by Detective John W. Anderson in 1985, Beery related, because of the personal robberies that had been occurring around town, Chief Bruce was anxious to catch the man before he hurt someone. Bruce offered to the officer that caught the bandit a full week's vacation, with pay. In those days an officer worked 21-days straight, then got seven off and vacations were few and far between. Beery said since the crime was during hunting season, everyone was trying to make the arrest. He recalled that Burchfield said a couple days prior to Thanksgiving, he had an idea who the robber was and was already planning how to use the extra vacation to go deer hunting.

With the offer of extra vacation, every officer was working hard to find the bandit, but the down side was officers were not sharing information with each other, because they all wanted the vacation. This meant that no one else knew what Burchfield had learned about the suspect. By the Saturday following the homicide, over 100 people had been questioned. Burchfield's body was sent to Yakima, Washington for burial.[21]

At the time of Burchfield's death officer's badges were numbered and his was No. 19. The department retired that badge from service. The badge was mounted on a plaque. The number on the badge signified his position in seniority. It was a pride thing to be badge one.[22]

Interestingly, on Monday, October 19, 1953, Howard DePew Breeden reported to police that his car had been vandalized while parked at the rear of his business, the Gambles Store on 116 North Tejon Street. Breeden's 1947 Dodge, parked for a 20-minute period after 10:25 p.m., had a gun stolen from inside. The gun was identified as a Colt Woodsman semi-automatic, .22-caliber pistol.[23] During an interview with former CSPD Retired Detective John Wesley Anderson, it was learned that when the gun was taken there was also a sock full of odd brands of ammunition missing. This coincides with shell casings that were recovered from the police car after the homicide.[24] It was very possible the weapon stolen from Mr. Breeden was used in the killing of the police officer. Although numerous weapons were sent to the FBI for testing, the weapon used on the police officer has never been located.

In April of 1966, Peggy Gottfried reported to the Denver Police Department that her former brother-in-law was the man who killed Officer Burchfield.[25] In May 1966, CSPD Detectives Richard C. Ballard and Thomas Kosley learned the Belmont Motel, 1501 South Nevada, had been owned by Earl A. Johnson and his wife Willa from 1953 through 1957.[26] Willa was the mother of Peggy's brother-in-law. Identified as William Dwight Gottfried, it was noted he spent weekends often at the motel, but would not be seen during the week.[27] During June, Peggy Gottfried was interviewed by CSPD detectives and told of Dwight Gottfried's propensity of stealing. She had warned Dwight he would get caught if he continued to deal in crime. Dwight said to her, "What deal? When I killed that cop?"

Dwight was involved in several crimes and had been arrested in Illinois in 1955 and sent to prison.[28] In 1967, Detective's Kosley and Ballard traveled to the Colorado State Penitentiary to interview William Dwight Gottfried. He told officers he had been a patient in the Porter Sanatorium in Denver until his release on November 6, 1953, but denied ever being in Colorado Springs prior to 1955. Also, he said that he had only been a free man five months out of the previous ten years.[29]

Peggy Ann Mutchie (formerly Gottfried), in 1974, was interviewed with regards to her former brother-in-law. CSPD Detective Sergeant Norman Short and Chief Deputy District Attorney Ron Rowan met with her in Denver, where she lived. Peggy related that on Thanksgiving, 1953, Dwight and his mother, had an argument and he did not wish to have dinner that evening with the family and left. After his return to the Denver address a day or two later, another big argument occurred between Dwight and his mother about his not attending the Thanksgiving Day dinner with the family. While this was going on, Peggy overheard talk about the police officer that had been killed in Colorado Springs, but could not hear all the details. The following weekend, she overheard Dwight and his brother Gary, discussing getting rid of something that Dwight "had used."[30]

Gottfried, was born in Kansas on February of 1936, so he would have been 17 years of age at the time of Burchfield's death. In September of 1958, Gottfried, who had been living in Pueblo, was dating a beauty queen, Dixie Ann Dikes, 18. The couple married in New Mexico that month.

Gottfried was involved in several crimes over the years, including the September of 1957 kidnapping of a police officer in Illinois.

Arrested in the company of another man, Everett Foster, they were picked up by two special deputies for taking gas from a filling station without paying. After the deputies arrived at the sheriff's station, the two arrested men pulled guns and kidnapped Deputy Ernie Davis and took his patrol car. It was believed that these were the two men who had robbed a service station in Hamilton, Illinois.[31] The kidnapped deputy was released at Niota, Illinois and the two youths escaped. Nine days after the kidnapping, Everett Foster, 22, was stopped at a roadblock near Williams, Arizona and while reaching for a gun was shot and killed by an Arizona deputy sheriff. Meanwhile, the search continued for Gottfried in the Denver area.[32]

Ironically, the same day that Foster was killed, Gottfried was arrested in a hotel in downtown Denver.[33] Gottfried was then returned to Illinois to face charges.[34] Having pled guilty to the kidnapping charge, he was sentenced from one to five years in the Illinois penitentiary.[35] Shortly after being released from Joliet Prison in January of 1962, Gottfried and James Srbinovich, were being sought for the killing of Louis Prince in Denver. Pursued to California, the men were arrested in San Leandro after a struggle and chase with the local police. Both men were returned to Colorado to face the murder charges.[36] After serving time in the Colorado State Penitentiary, Gottfried was released in December of 1968.[37] He returned to California, where he and two companions were arrested trying to rob a pharmacy in Monterey Park.[38] While being held in Los Angeles jail, Gottfried and two others managed to escape.[39]

Turning up in 1974 in Colorado Springs, Gottfried was arrested at the home of his sister for possession of a weapon of a previous offender. He was found to be wanted for the escape in California and a warrant had been issued in the State of Iowa for bond jumping.[40] October of 1974 Gottfried was charged with possession of a weapon and ten other charges. He was considered a habitual criminal, which meant he could be sent to prison for life. Some of the previous charges were a Denver murder, kidnapping in Illinois, armed robberies in Iowa and California, and the jail escape.[41] Sadly, due to evidence problems, the case was dismissed in December.[42]

Gottfried's life of crime came to an end on Friday, July 28, 1978, when he was killed in the front yard of his Newton Street apartment in Denver by two shotgun blasts. Police found his apartment contained chemicals which evidenced the start of a lab for the manufacture of speed, an amphetamine.[43] In May of 1979, Robert Witz, a former private investigator was found guilty of Gottfried's murder.[44]

It was just after the death of Gottfried that his former sister-in-law made her second report to police that Gottfried was responsible for the death of a policeman in Colorado Springs. There were several reviews of the murder of Officer Burchfield over the years and in 1985 the department thought they might have solved the killing.[45] However, knowing and being able to prove was the problem.

January 2020, after reviewing the newspaper articles about the homicide of Officer Burchfield, it was noted a personal robbery occurred just over two weeks after the homicide. This time the bandit, took a purse from Katherine Harrison. As in the past, he held a handkerchief in front of his face for disguise, but upon escaping the handkerchief was dropped. This handkerchief was picked up by the police and examined.[46]

This information was taken to the CSPD cold case officers in January 2020. If it was possible to obtain DNA from the handkerchief, it could provide a needed lead in solving the killing of the police officer if the crimes were connected. A check of the retained evidence was made, but the handkerchief had not been retained. This was the last known robbery that fit the previous pattern.

The seventieth anniversary of Officer Burchfield's demise was 2023. No arrests of a person or persons committing this crime will happen as too much time has passed. It is regrettable that unless there is some kind of miracle, this will remain in an "officially unsolved" state.

Two questions remain. Was the person who killed the police officer the man who committed ten robberies in Colorado Springs? Who was picked up by Officer Richard Stanley Burchfield?

Notes

1 *Colorado Springs Free Press*, 27 Nov 1953, Page 1.
2 CSPD Homicide Investigation, Case 53-3232, 22 Feb 1957, Interview.
3 CSPD Homicide Investigation, Case 53-3232, 25 Oct 1953, Interview.
4 CSPD Homicide Investigation, Case 53-3232, 02 Nov 1953, Interview.
5 *Colorado Springs Gazette* Telegraph, 02 Dec 1953, Page A1.
6 CSPD Homicide Investigation, Case 53-3232, 07 Nov 1953, Interview.
7 CSPD Homicide Investigation, Case 53-3232, 09 Nov 1953, Interview.
8 CSPD Homicide Investigation, Case 53-3232, 21 Nov 1953, Interview.
9 *Colorado Springs Gazette* Telegraph, 27 Nov 1953, Page A9.
10 CSPD Homicide Investigation, Case 53-3232, 26 Nov 1953, Interview.
11 *Colorado Springs Free Press*, 29, Nov 1953, Page 1.
12 *Colorado Springs Gazette* Telegraph, 29 Nov 1953, Page A1.
13 CSPD Homicide Investigation, Case 53-3232, 1953, Document 19-0022.
14 *Colorado Springs Gazette* Telegraph, 27 Nov 1953, Page A1.
15 *Colorado Springs Free Press*, 27 Nov 1953, Page 1.
16 *Colorado Springs Gazette* Telegraph, 27 Nov 1953, Page A1.
17 *Colorado Springs Gazette* Telegraph, 27 Nov 1953, Page A9.
18 CSPD Homicide Investigation, Case 53-3232, 1953, Document 19-0022.
19 *Colorado Springs Gazette* Telegraph, 01 Dec 1953, Page A1.
20 *Colorado Springs Gazette* Telegraph, 08 Dec 1953, Page A1.
21 *Colorado Springs Gazette* Telegraph, 28 Nov 1953, Page A1.
22 *Colorado Springs Gazette* Telegraph, 02 Dec 1953, Page A5.
23 CSPD Homicide Investigation, Case 53-3232, 19 Oct 1953, Interview.
24 Personal interview with Retired Detective John Wesley Anderson, 01 Apr 2023.
25 CSPD Homicide Investigation, Case 53-3232, 29 Apr 1966, Interview.
26 CSPD Homicide Investigation, Case 53-3232, 02 Jun 1966, Interview.
27 CSPD Homicide Investigation, Case 53-3232, 23 May 1966, Interview.
28 CSPD Homicide Investigation, Case 53-3232, 18 Jun 1966, Interview.
29 CSPD Homicide Investigation, Case 53-3232, 16 Mar 1967, Interview.
30 CSPD Homicide Investigation, Case 53-3232, 20 Dec 1974, Interview.
31 *Rock Island Argus*, 16 Sep 1957, Page 1.
32 *Moline Daily Dispatch*, 23 Sep 1957, Page 9.
33 *Rock Island Argus*, 24 Sep 1957, Page 4.
34 *Lewistown News*, 02 Oct 1957, Page 1.
35 *Rock Island Argus*, 19 Oct 1957, Page 3.
36 *Oakland Tribune*, 29 Jan 1962, Page 3.
36 *Colorado Springs Gazette* Telegraph, 18 Sep 1974, Page A6.
38 *Pasadena Star-News*, 12 Jan 1970, Page 20.
39 *Long Beach Press Telegram*, 22 May 1970, Page A3.
40 *Colorado Springs Gazette* Telegraph, 18 Sep 1974, Page A6.
41 *Colorado Springs Gazette* Telegraph, 26 Oct 1974, Page A6.
42 *Colorado Springs Gazette* Telegraph, 07 Dec 1974, Page A4.
43 *Denver Post*, 28 Jul 1978, Page 2.
44 *Rocky Mountain News*, 24 May 1979, Page 10.
46 *Colorado Springs Gazette* Telegraph, 30 Oct 1985, Page B2.
46 *Colorado Springs Free Press*, 13 Dec 1953, Page 1.

Appendix

INCORPORATING THE TOWN OF
COLORADO SPRINGS

Special Meeting of the Board of County Commissioners.
CLERK'S OFFICE.
COLORADO CITY, September 2, 1872.
 Full board in attendance.

Commissioner France presented a petition signed by two-thirds of the citizens of Colorado Springs, asking that the town of Colorado Springs be incorporated under the statute in such case made and provided; therefore, on motion, it was

Ordered, That the town of Colorado Springs be, and hereby is, declared duly incorporated under the laws of the Territory of Colorado, and that said incorporated town shall included all the lots and lands within the following described boundaries, to-wit:

> Commencing at the center of section five (5), township fourteen (14), range sixty-six (66), running thence westerly to the center of section one (1), township fourteen (14), range sixty-seven (67) west; thence southerly to the center of section twenty-four (24), township fourteen (14), range sixty-seven (67) west; thence easterly to the center of section twenty (20), township fourteen (14); range sixty-six (66) west; thence northerly to the place of beginning; and the following named persons, viz: R.A. Cameron, William B. Young, Edward Copley, Matt. France and John Potter, are hereby appointed trustees to manage the affairs of said town until an election be held as provided by law.

D. MCSHANE, Chairman.
IRVING HOWBERT, Clerk.

TERRITORY OF COLORADO)
) ss.
COUNTY OF EL PASO.   )

I, Irving Howbert, County Clerk within and for said county, do hereby certify that the foregoing is a true and correct copy of the order made by the Board of County Commissioners in incorporating the town of Colorado Springs, according to the records on file in my office.

Witness my hand and official seal, this 29th day of November, A.D. 1873.

                                      Irving Howbert,
 [seal]   *County Clerk.*

SOURCE: *City of Colorado Springs Annual Reports and Financial Statements, 1901-2.* Edited and Arranged by L.S. Harris, City Auditor

CITY ORGANIZATION

On the 16th day of March, 1876, a meeting of the Board of Trustees of the town of Colorado Springs was held to consider the question of assuming a city organization. All the members of the board were present, viz;

> Henry McAllister, Jr., president of the board; G.H. Stewart, Lewis Whipple, C.H. White, G.S. Barnes, N. Hodgmen and H.A. True.

It was shown that a census had just been completed and the population of the town found to be three thousand one hundred and three, more than enough to entitle the town to a city organization.

Whereupon G.H. Stewart offered a resolution which was adopted by a unanimous vote that the town of Colorado Springs assume a city organization under the corporate name of The City of Colorado Springs.

SOURCE: *City of Colorado Springs Annual Reports and Financial Statements, 1901-2*
Edited and Arranged by I.S. Harris, City Auditor.

COLORADO BECOMES A STATE

1875 brought about an act of Congress enabling Colorado to become a state which was approved by President Grant on March 3, 1875. A constitutional convention met to produce a state constitution December 20, 1875. The constitution was then adopted on March 14, 1876. This was then put in front of the Territory's citizens and it was adopted by the people on July 1, 1876. With this passage, a proclamation was made by President Grant on August 1, 1876, making Colorado the 38th state of the Union.

SOURCE: *Civil Government of Colorado,* by Dorus R. Hatch, Herrick Book & Stationery Co., Denver, CO, 1924, pages 2-3.

CITY REORGANIZATION – 1878

The Town operated under the City system until 1878 when:

A petition was next read signed by 79 citizens of the City asking the Board to submit to the legal voters of the City the question of re-organizing the City under the act of the General Assembly of the State of Colorado, entitled, "An act in relation to municipal corporation," approved April 4, 1877. After some discussion the petition was on motion of Alderman Bradbury laid on the table.

The following Resolution was then offered by Alderman Morley who moved its adoption. That, whereas a petition has been presented to the City Council signed by the requisite number of legal voters of the City of Colorado Springs asking the Council to call an election to re-organize under the new laws of the State of Colorado of 1877, Section 88 of Chapter on Towns and Cities: <u>Resolved</u>: That a special election be held on the Third day of March 1878 between the hours of 8 O'clock in the morning and 7 o'clock in the afternoon at the Engine House in the City of Colorado Springs. The resolution was adopted.[1]

After due examination of the election returns said committee reported as follows:
That we find the whole number of votes cast to be 383.
    For - Municipal organization under General Laws — 241.
    Against - Municipal organization under General Laws - 142.
    The report was received and committee discharged.[2]

Monday, the first of April, 1878, a special election was held and with the reorganization of the City:

Under the new form there will be a Mayor elected annually, and one Alderman for each ward, holding office for two years — these to receive no compensation except by direct vote of the people. A Treasurer, whose term is one year, is also elected by the people. The City Clerk, City Marshal (Constable), Solicitor, and Police Judge are elected by the Council, and hold office during their pleasure.

In addition the Constable will receive a commission on taxes this year amounting to $500, and fees $200, and the Attorney receives $5 per day in case of conviction.

The City Marshal can well perform the duties of Constable and Street Commissioner, combined, and certainly the Ditch Commissioner, if a necessary officer, need not be paid $75 per month, especially during the winter months.[3]

Endnotes

1   Colorado Springs City Council Minutes, 04 Feb 1878, Book 1, Page 210.
2   Colorado Springs City Council Minutes, 06 Mar 1878, Book 1, Page 215.
3   *Colorado Springs Weekly Gazette* & *El Paso County News*, 09 Feb 1878, Page 2.

CLASSIFICATION, CITY OF THE FIRST CLASS

STATE OF COLORADO.
SECRETARY OF STATE'S OFFICE.

DENVER, COLORADO, February 16th, 1901.

    I, David A. Mills, Secretary of State of the State of Colorado, do hereby certify that heretofore, to-wit, and on the sixth day of February, A.D. 1901, there was filed in the office of the Secretary of State, of the State of Colorado, the returns of the Twelfth Census of the United States, showing the number of inhabitants of the City of Colorado Springs, according to said enumeration, to be twenty-one thousand and eighty-five (21,085).
    I do further certify that the Governor, Auditor of State and the Secretary of State, met at the Executive Office in the Capitol Building, at Denver, Colorado, on the 8th day of February, A.D. 1901, and ascertained that said City of Colorado Springs was entitled to become a city of the First Class;
    And I further certify that James B. Orman, Governor of the State of Colorado, did, by Executive Order bearing date of February 8th, A.D. 1901, cause this instrument to be prepared by the Secretary of State pursuant to the statute in such case made and provided, and did by said Executive Order also direct the publication of the same in some newspaper published in Denver, the State Capitol, and also some newspaper published in the City of Colorado Springs.
    IN WITNESS WHEREOf, I David A. Mills, Secretary of State of the State of Colorado, have hereunto set my hand and affixed the Great Seal of the State.
    Done at Denver, Colorado, this 16th day of February, A.D. 1901.

                                             (Signed)   David A. Mills,
                                                                       Secretary of State.

CITY OF COLORADO SPRINGS,   )
) ss.
COUNTY OF EL PASO.   )

    I, I.S. Harris, City Clerk within and for said city, do hereby certify that the foregoing is a true and correct copy of statement, to the City Council of the City of Colorado Springs, made by the Governor, Auditor of State and the Secretary of State in the matter of classification of the City of Colorado Springs from a City of the Second Class to a City of First Class, according to the records on file in the office of the City Clerk.
    Witness my hand and official seal, this 18th day of February, A.D. 1901.

                                                                                  I.S. Harris,
                                                                                  City Clerk.

SOURCE: *City of Colorado Springs Annual Reports and Financial Statements, 1901-2*
                    Edited and Arranged by I.S. Harris, City Auditor.

Officers List - The Nineteenth Century

While researching the history of the Colorado Springs Police Department and its history, the following are the names of the officers recorded. I cannot guarantee that every person serving the City as a law enforcement officer was located, but here is what was compiled below in order of their service.

CONSTABLES
Delos Durfee	Constable — 1875
Frank P. Lombard	Constable — 1876
Joshua Sumner	Constable — 1877
James Lazear Parker	Deputy Constable — 1877
John Wilson	Deputy Constable — 1877
G.M. McClure	Deputy Constable — 1877
James Russell Millard	Deputy Constable — 1877

MARSHALS
1878
Loren C. Dana	First City Marshal
John N. Beall	Police Officer

1879
John Emory Clark	City Marshal
John N. Beall	City Marshal
H.S. Clement	Police Officer
James McCabe	Police Officer

1880
John N. Beall	City Marshal
T.C. White	Police Officer
H.S. Clement	Police Officer
L. J. Tell	Police Officer

1881
John N. Beall	City Marshal
H.S. Clement	Police Officer
L. J. Tell	Police Officer
William Saxton	Police Officer

1882
John N. Beall	City Marshal
James McCabe	Police Officer
William Saxton	Police Officer

1883
John N. Beall	City Marshal

1884
Amos E. Hart	City Marshal
William Clark	Police Officer
William S. Saxton	Police Officer
Elias Johnson	Police Officer
John Chapman	Police Officer

1885
Chester Hubbill Dillon	City Marshal
William S. Saxton	City Marshal
E.W. Frost	Police Officer
C.H. Burritt	Police Officer
M. Stewart	Police Officer
William S. Saxton	Police Officer
L.J. Tell	Police Officer
Q.L. McCreery	Police Officer
J.C. Duncan	Police Officer

1886
William S. Saxton	City Marshal
Q.L. McCreery	Police Officer
Clem Williams	Police Officer

1887
William S. Saxton	City Marshal
Joel Atkinson	Police Officer
John W. Chapman	Police Officer
Granville Alsbury	Police Officer
A.E. Hicks	Police Officer
John W. Garthright	Police Officer
James Duncan	Police Officer
Clem Williams	Police Officer

1888
Loren C. Dana	City Marshal
Thomas M. Michael	Police Officer
Joel Atkinson	Police Officer
John W. Garthright	Police Officer
John W. Chapman	Police Officer
Joseph Ballou	Police Officer
Delos Powell	Police Officer
Horace Shelby	Police Officer
A.L. Bainter	Police Officer
C.F. Taylor	Police Officer

1889
John Simmons	City Marshal
Loren C. Dana	City Marshal
M.J. Wilson	Police Officer
John W. Chapman	Police Officer
Al.L. Bainter	Police Officer
O.H. Davis	Police Officer
Scott Jackson	Police Officer
Horace Shelby	Police Officer
A.L. Hunter	Police Officer
C.E. Woods	Police Officer
C.F. Taylor	Police Officer

1890
Loren C. Dana	City Marshal
John W. Garthright	Captain
John W. Chapman	Officer No. 1
M.J. Wilson	Officer No. 2
Joel Atkinson	Officer No. 3
C.F. Taylor	Officer No. 4

C.E. Wood   Officer No. 5
U.C. Unnsell   Officer No. 6
Horace Shelby   Officer No. 7
Robert Martin   Officer No. 5

1891
Loren C. Dana   City Marshal
John W. Garthright   Captain
John W. Chapman   Officer No. 1
M.J. Wilson   Officer No. 2
Joel Atkinson   Officer No. 3
C.F. Taylor   Officer No. 4
Robert Martin   Officer No. 5
Stephen Harlan   Officer No. 6
Horace Shelby   Officer No. 7
Henry Cornell   Officer No. 7

1892
Loren C. Dana   City Marshal
John W. Garthright   Captain
M.J. Wilson   Officer No. 1
Joel Atkinson   Officer No. 2
C.F. Taylor   Officer No. 3
Robert Martin   Officer No. 4
Stephen Harlan   Officer No. 5
Henry Shank   Officer No. 6
Horace Shelby   Officer No. 7
Henry Cornell   Patrolman
Granville Alsbury   Patrolman
Clem Williams   Patrolman
Harvey Gillingham   Patrolman

1893
Loren C. Dana   City Marshal
John W. Garthright   Captain
Joel Atkinson   Officer No. 1
C.F. Taylor   Officer No. 2
Robert Martin   Officer No. 3
Stephen Harlan   Officer No. 4
Thomas Sullivan   Officer No. 5
L.E. Curtright   Officer No. 6
Horace Shelby   Officer No. 7
Henry Cornell, mounted   Officer No. 8

1894
Loren C. Dana   City Marshal
John W. Garthright   Captain
K.E. McMillen   Patrolman
Joel Atkinson   Officer No. 1
Charles F. Taylor   Officer No. 2
Stephen Harlan   Officer No. 3
Thomas Sullivan   Officer No. 4
John Henry   Officer No. 5
Granville Alsbury   Officer No. 6
W.B. Edwards   Officer No. 6
Horace Shelby   Officer No. 7
Henry Cornell, mounted   Officer No. 8

1895

Loren C. Dana	City Marshal
John W. Garthright	Captain
Joel Atkinson	Officer No. 1
R.M. Martin	Officer No. 2
Stephen Harlan	Officer No. 3
Samuel Agard	Officer No. 4
John Henry	Officer No. 5
W.B. Edwards	Officer No. 6
Horace Shelby	Officer No. 7
Henry Cornell, mounted	Officer No. 8

1896

Loren C. Dana	City Marshal
John W. Garthright	Captain
Joel Atkinson	Officer No. 1
Samuel Agard	Officer No. 2
John Henry	Officer No. 3
Horace Shelby	Officer No. 4
Henry Cornell, mounted	Officer No. 5
William Barr	Officer No. 6
Frank Bish	Officer No. 7
J.H. Elliott	Officer No. 8
Sherman McNew	Officer No. 9
J.E. Birch	Officer No. 10

1897

Loren C. Dana	City Marshal
John Walter Garthright	City Marshal
John Henry	Captain
Joel Atkinson	Officer No. 1
Sherman McNew	Officer No. 2
Samuel Agard	Officer No. 3
J.E. Birch	Officer No. 4
Horace Shelby	Officer No. 5
O.E. Rickerson	Officer No. 6
Henry Cornell, mounted	Officer No. 7
H.H. Rodney	Officer No. 8
William Barr	Officer No. 9
Ackley	Officer No. 10
J.H. Elliott	Officer No. 11
George H. Sixt	Patrolman

1898

John Walter Garthright	City Marshal
John Henry	Captain
Joel Atkinson	Officer No. 1
H.H. Rodney	Officer No. 2
Horace Shelby	Officer No. 3
G.H. Sixt	Officer No. 4
Henry Cornell, mounted	Officer No. 5
Thomas J. Fair	Officer No. 6
William T. Barr	Officer No. 7
Samuel Agard	Officer No. 8
J.H. Elliott	Officer No. 9
F,C, Rulison	Officer No. 10
Sherman McNew	Officer No. 11
Jacob Greenwaldt	Officer No. 12

1899
John Walter Garthright	City Marshal — 1899
Thomas J. Fair	Night Captain
Joel Atkinson	Detective
Horace Shelby	Patrolman
Henry Cornell, mounted	Patrolman
Sherman McNew	Patrolman
HA. Rodney	Patrolman
G.H. Sixt	Patrolman
F.C. Rulison	Patrolman
Jacob Greenwaldt	Patrolman
John E. Schofield	Patrolman
O.E. Bishop	Patrolman
D.H. Bennett	Patrolman
C.E. Knapp	Patrolman
George F. Dayton	Patrolman
John Oliver Henry	Patrolman
F.G. Hughes	Patrolman
H.A. Wilkinson	Patrolman

1900
John Oliver Henry	City Marshal — 1900
Sherman McNew	Night Captain
Joel Atkinson	City Detective
Horace Shelby	Patrolman
W.D. Thomas	Patrolman
Isaac Hatler	Patrolman
D.H. Bennett	Patrolman
C.E. Knapp	Patrolman
John E. Schofield	Patrolman
F.G. Hughes	Patrolman
George F. Dayton	Patrolman
Charles A. Dutton	Patrolman
George H. Sixt	Patrolman
D.F. Gaines	Patrolman
Thomas J. Fair	Patrolman
J.E. Burch	Patrolman
William Calvert	Patrolman

Glossary of Terms Used by the Underworld

Accident	When crook is arrested.
Badger game	Entrapment of victim by woman and her alleged husband.
Ballyhoo	The come-on talk.
Big Store	A protected town.
Blow-off	Stealing a victim's money.
Blow-off wire	Last telegram from mob.
Blow-up	When victim gets wise.
Boodle	Crooked money package at exchange.
Bookmaker	Clerk in a fake exchanged or race parlor.
Booster	Extra man in charge.
Break-down	Fake telegram to start sucker into raising money.
Bunco-game	Con-game.
Con-man	Confidence man.
Convincer	Initial winning.
Dick	Detective.
Dope	Narcotics; also information.
Entertain	To interest a sucker.
Firm	Fixer.
Fisherman	Con-man.
Fishing-season	When it is safe to pick up suckers.
Fixer	Man behind the scenes who handles police and public officials.
Frail	Woman.
Gang or mob	Con-men in a town.
Goods	Fake stock.
Grafters	Con-men's name for themselves.
Grand	One thousand dollars.
Honkey-tonk	Combination dance hall and saloon.
Hopped up	Under influence of narcotic drug.
In the hospital	In jail.
Kick	Complaint to police.
Lay-out	Paraphernalia.
Lookout	The center of activity of a pay-off game gang, where one man watches for the steerer's signal.
Lookout, the	The watcher against the Law.

Manager	Active head of a gang.
Moll	Woman of underworld.
Mug	To take the picture of a criminal.
Nut	Expense in running the game, including protection.
Office	Underworld sign for an officer.
Pay-off game	Swindle in which the victim is twice paid off before losing his money.
Play to the wall	Simulated stock exchange.
Putting the bee	Making a crook pay for protection.
Rap	Complaint against a crook.
Retie	Trimming a victim for a second time.
Sale, or beat	Trimming a sucker.
Salted-mine	Mine with ore fixed to resemble high grade.
Score	Amount of the swindle.
Show-up	Exhibition of arrested men before the detectives.
Slicker	Con-man.
Spieler	Second inside man, or mysterious stranger.
Spring	Get out on bond.
Squealer	One who talks to the Law.
Steer, steerer or salesman	Pick-up man.
Stir	Penitentiary.
Stool-pigeon	Police spy.
Store or joint	Fake stock exchange or race parlor.
Store-booster	Shoplifter.
Store-men	Con-men.
Straw-bond	Bail bond with worthless signers.
Sucker, boob, chump, egg, customer	The victim.
Tailer	The man who follows the victim.
Take for a ride	Convey a man to an out-of-the-way spot and kill him.
Tied	When victim sends for money
Tied-up	When victim enters stock exchange.
Tip-off	Underworld surveillance on police.
Work the streets	Street-walking.[1]

Endnote
Fighting the Underworld, by Philip s. Van Cise, Houghton, Mifflin Company, 1936, Pages 355-357

Police Chief List

Name:	Dates of Service:
Vincent King	04/15/1901 to 07/31/1903
William Sullivan Reynolds	08/01/1903 to 05/02/1905
Alexander "Alec" Adams	05/02/1905 to 04/01/1907
William Sullivan Reynolds	04/15/1907 to 05/01/1909
Stephen Armstrong	08/15/1909 to 08/15/1911
Stanley Dean Burno	10/26/1911 to 03/11/1914
James Howard Stark	03/16/1914 to 04/15/1917
Newton Hutchinson Haywood	07/10/1917 to 09/28/1917
Hugh Davis Harper	10/12/1917 to 12/15/1941
Irvin B. "Dad" Bruce	12/16/1941 to 02/18/1960
Cecil James McKissick	03/09/1960 to 06/01/1966
Oren Ellis "Cooley" Boling	06/01/1966 to 06/30/1976
John Lincoln Tagert	07/07/1976 to 02/28/1985
James Dewey Munger	11/04/1985 to 11/15/1990
Luis Velez	05/13/2002 to 09/01/2006
Richard W. Myers	01/12/2007 to 10/11/2011
Peter Timothy Carey	01/24/2012 to 03/01/2019
Vincent Benedict Niski	02/12/2019 to 03/04/2022
Adrian Gray Vasquez	04/26/2022 to

Note: Reynolds was chief twice.

Colorado Springs First Police Department 1901

Monday, April 15, 1901, the City Council met and formed the Colorado Springs Police Department.

Vincent King's name was put before the council as being a recommendation of the Mayor J.R. Robinson for the position of police chief.

A motion was made and seconded to act on the mayor's recommendation and after a roll call vote he was elected on a nine to one vote.

Thursday, April 18, 1901, the mayor made his recommendations for the men to be appointed as police officers, which were unanimously approved and thereby elected:

Detective:	George F. Dayton
Detective:	Joel Atkinson
Captain:	Thomas J. Fair
Sergeant:	Sherman McNew
Patrolman:	Charles Williams
Patrolman:	Clyde Hall
Patrolman:	William Calvert
Patrolman:	Horace Shelby
Patrolman:	James Edmund Burch
Patrolman:	Darius H. Bennett
Patrolman:	Stephen Armstrong
Patrolman:	Charles Edwin Knapp
Patrolman:	Harvey Gillingham
Patrolman:	Frank Gardner Hughes
Patrolman:	William James
Patrolman:	I.L. Hatler
Patrolman:	Clyde C. McReynolds
Patrolman:	Daniel F. Gaines

Source:

Colorado Springs City Council Meeting April 15, 1901, Book 8, Page 2

Colorado Springs City Council Meeting April 18, 1901, Book 8, Page 12

Colorado Springs Police Department Firsts

02 Sep 1872	Town Board of Trustees appointed Smith C. Foote as its first constable.[1]
08 Apr 1878	First appointed Marshal - Loren C. Dana.[2]
18 Apr 1888	First minority Black officer - Horace Shelby appointed.[3]
18 Apr 1890	First captain was appointed - John W. Garthright.[4]
15 Apr 1901	First police chief appointed - Vincent King.[5]
18 Apr 1901	Patrol wagon was delivered to the CSPD.[6]
	First sergeant was appointed - Sherman McNew.[7]
01 Jan 1904	Six patrol boxes were installed around the city.[8]
20 Nov 1904	Regular target practice for officers was scheduled in the sub-basement of City Hall.[9]
19 Dec 1904	Red lights were added to the patrol boxes.[10]
03 Oct 1907	Inaugurated Bertillon System of identification.[11]
01 Jan 1909	Officers were greeted with an 8-hour workday from the current twelve.
29 Jun 1910	Motorcycle purchased with a speedometer for detection of speeders.[12]
23 Dec 1914	CSPD requested to be allowed to purchase two automobiles.[13]
30 Jun 1915	Georgia S. Easley was appointed as the first woman social investigator.[14]
13 Jul 1917	First chief hired from outside Colorado Springs—Newton Hutchinson Haywood.[15]
23 Mar 1924	With the opening of the new City Auditorium, the officers had a new pistol range in its basement.
28 Oct 1927	Hand grenades added to police artillery.[16]
09 Nov 1930	Tear gas gun ordered for the department.[17]
06 Sep 1931	Detective Sergeant George C. Emerick, made the department's first bullet comparison.[18]
10 Dec 1935	Deputy Chief Earl Cleo Boatright - First CSPD officer to attend the FBI training academy.

31 Jan 1937	The department purchased its first 3-wheel motorcycle for meter patrol.[19]
15 Mar 1941	Police 2-way radio system installed - call sign KPCS.[20]
20 Aug 1941	First police call was made using the 2-way radio system.[21]
27 Jan 1942	Council authorized the spending $60.00/year to purchase uniforms for police officers.[22]
Jun 1949	Purchase polygraph machine.[23]
27 Nov 1953	First lieutenant appointed - Kenneth C. Beery.
02 Aug 1954	Purchase radar speeding equipment.[24]
24 Aug 1954	Purchase an alcometer breath testing device.[25]
01 Aug 1966	First female sworn police officer - Charlotte Ann (Mahan)(Wittges)(Morris) Buckley.[26]
01 Feb 1967	First corporal appointed - Jerome Paul Busemeyer.
13 Nov 1972	First Black male cadet was hired - Ronnie Stallworth.[27]
16 Jul 1973	First female cadet was hired - Lois E. Ellsworth.[28]
28 Sep 1973	First Black female cadet was hired - Delorise J. (Channell) Brown.[29]
16 Aug 1974	First Black female sworn police officer - Rosemary G. Williams.[30]
01 Apr 1975	First female sergeant - Charlotte Ann (Mahan)(Wittges)(Morris) Buckley.[31]
05 Jan 1979	First female lieutenant - Charlotte Ann (Mahan)(Wittges)(Morris) Buckley.[32]
15 Feb 1984	First Black sergeant was promoted - Robert Malcom Sapp.
04 May 1986	First female captain - Charlotte Ann (Mahan)(Wittges)(Morris) Buckley.[33]
07 Aug 1989	First female to retire from the CSPD - Charlotte Ann (Mahan)(Wittges)(Morris) Buckley.[34]
03 Jan 1992	First Black Lieutenant - Arthur N. Sapp.
11 Jul 1999	First female member of the SWAT team - Brenda

	Michelle (Day) Whitlock.
24 Dec 2000	First female member assigned as a motor officer - Julie L. Angene.
13 May 2002	First Hispanic police chief - Luis Velez.[35]
10 Jul 2008	First Black commander promoted - Fletcher Howard.[36]

Notes

1 "City of Colorado Springs Annual Report and Financial Statements, 1901-02,"
2 Colorado Springs City Council Minutes, 08 Apr 1878, Book 1, Page 224.
3 Colorado Springs City Council Minutes, 30 Apr 1888, Book 3, Page 123.
4 Colorado Springs City Council Minutes, 18 Apr 1890, Book 4, Page 5.
5 Colorado Springs City Council Minutes, 15 Apr 1901, Book 8, Page 2.
6 Colorado Springs Gazette, 19 Apr 1901, Page 5.
7 Colorado Springs City Council Minutes, 18 Apr 1901, Book 8, Page 12.
8 Colorado Springs Gazette, 01 Jan 1904, Page 29.
9 Colorado Springs Gazette & Telegraph, 20 Nov 1904, Page 4.
10 Colorado Springs Gazette & Telegraph, 04 Dec 1904, Page 9.
11 Colorado Springs Evening Telegraph, 03 Oct 1907, Page 2.
12 Colorado Springs City Council Minutes, 29 Jun 1910, Book 12, Page 275.
13 Colorado Springs City Council Minutes, 23 Dec 1914, Book 14, Page 313.
14 Colorado Springs City Council Minutes, 30 Jun 1915, Book 14, Page 407.
15 Colorado Springs City Council Minutes, 13 Jul 1917, Book 15, Page 207.
16 Colorado Springs Evening Telegraph, 28 Oct 1927, Page 8.
17 Colorado Springs Gazette & Telegraph, 09 Nov 1930, Section II, Page 2.
18 Colorado Springs Gazette & Telegraph, 06 Sep 1931, Page 4.
19 Colorado Springs Gazette & Telegraph, 31 Jan 1937.
20 Colorado Springs Evening Telegraph, 15 Mar 1941,
21 Colorado Springs Evening Telegraph, 20 Aug 1941,
22 Colorado Springs City Council Minutes, 27 Jan 1942, Book 21, Page 365.
23 Colorado Springs Free Press, 29 Jun 1949, Page 3.
24 Colorado Springs City Council Minutes, 02 Aug 1954, Book 24, Page 393.
25 Colorado Springs City Council Minutes, 24 Aug 1954, Book 24, Page 405.
26 Police Officer Oath of Office, 966, 1972, 1973, 1974, 1975.
27 Police Officer Oath of Office, 13 Nov 1972.
28 Police Officer Oath of Office, 16 Jul 1973.
29 Police Officer Oath of Office, 28 Sep 1973.
30 Police Officer Oath of Office, 16 Aug 1974.
31 Police Officer Oath of Office, 01 Apr 1975.
32 Colorado Springs Gazette Telegraph, 06 Jan 1979, Page A5.
33 Police Officer Oath of Office, 04 May 1986.
34 Colorado Springs Gazette Telegraph, 04 Aug 1989, Page B6.
35 Colorado Springs Gazette, 14 May 2002, Page METRO1.
36 Colorado Springs Gazette, 09 Jul 2008, Page METRO1.

Fallen Officers

Earlier the death of three police officers that died violent deaths on-duty were reported. Following is a short synopsis of remaining ten officers that have died on-duty:

Thursday, June 12, 1941
GEORGE KALTENBERGER
DETECTIVE SERGEANT

Retired badge of Officer Richard Stanley Burchfield

Officer while using the men's room in City Hall/Police Station, 212 East Kiowa Street, hung his gun belt and holster with a semi-automatic pistol on a hook in the bathroom stall. The gun fell to the floor, fired; the bullet struck the officer in the abdomen on Saturday, May 31, 1941, but he survived until June 12, 1941.

Wednesday, May 14, 1975
BERNARD LIVINGSTON CARTER
CORPORAL

Officer was the pilot of the CSPD's Bell 47 helicopter when it crashed in the intersection of Carefree Circle South and North Murray Boulevard. The fuel tanks tore loose, striking the ground, causing a fire, which killed the officer and his passenger, Carl Welsh, regional director of the Colorado Division of Wildlife.

Thursday, August 7, 1975
DENNIS JOHN IVES
UNIFORMED MOTORCYCLE OFFICER

Officer was on his way to work on a CSPD motorcycle southbound on Interstate 25, when it went off the right side of the roadway, striking a curb, brushing a light pole, traveling about 175 feet before coming to rest against a chain link fence where the officer died.

Monday, December 22, 1975
HARRY LEE ALLEN
UNIFORMED OFFICER
Officer was investigating a traffic accident about 10 p.m., 5600 East Platte Avenue, near Powers Boulevard. He was taking measurements for the investigation when he was struck by the right front fender of a vehicle driving by. The officer died at the scene.

Saturday, April 12, 1980
AUGUSTUS JOSEPH PERREIRA, JR.
UNIFORMED OFFICER

Officer assigned to southeast Colorado Springs was flagged down by the clerk of the 7-Eleven Store at Delta Drive and Hancock Expressway about 7:45 p.m. The Officer parked in front of the store and walked to a man that the clerk had complained had been loitering in the store. The officer approached the man, Seth Andrew Buckmaster, Jr., took the man out into the parking lot and told him he had to leave or would be arrested. Buckmaster yelled at the officer, "You ain't gonna throw my ass in jail." He pulled a gun, firing at the officer 3 times before the officer could react. After the officer fell to the ground the suspect emptied his gun at the officer. The officer fired at the suspect two times injuring the suspect.

Friday, March 27, 1981
MICHAEL F. HURLEY
OFF-DUTY OFFICER

Officer made contact with a vehicle near Cimarron Street and Nevada Avenue, which he followed to the 700 block of Winnipeg Drive, where he was involved in a disturbance with Jimmy W.

Brown. When the fight was finished, the officer had been stabbed in the upper left chest. Officer died at the hospital.

Monday, December 6, 1982
Mark Layne Dabling
Uniformed Officer

Officer in a marked police car stopped a vehicle about 6:30 p.m. for a traffic violation, and pulled into the parking lot of a Long John Silver's Restaurant, 315 West Fillmore Street. The driver, Vernon Wayne Templeman, was a wanted man who had escaped from the jail in St. Petersburg, Florida. As the officer approached the suspect's car, Templeman raised a double-barreled .44-caliber rifle that had the stock and the barrel sawed off. The officer saw the rifle and tried to get to cover, but was shot in the back and later died at the hospital. The officer never had a chance to defend himself.

Wednesday, February 22, 2006
Jared Scott Jensen
Detective

Officer assigned to the Metro Vice, Narcotics and Intelligence Unit, received a tip that a fugitive had been seen in the area of Costilla Street and Hancock Avenue. At 10:40 a.m., Officer radioed that he found the suspect, Jereme Alexander Lamberth, at a bus stop 1000 East Costilla Street. Officer attempted to arrest the suspect, and was shot in the head. The officer was found lying on the ground, handcuffs in his right hand, and his weapon was still in his holster.

Tuesday, December 5, 2006
Kenneth Chua Jordan
Uniformed Officer

Officer was dispatched to assist officers with a drunk driver on Fountain Boulevard near Jet Wing Drive about 11:30 p.m. Monday. As officer approached the suspect's vehicle, Marco Reiner Lee, exited his car and shot the officer 5 times. Two other officers fired at the suspect, who was wounded but lived.

Tuesday, July 24, 2012
Matthew Robert Tyner
Motorcycle Officer

Officer was riding the CSPD motorcycle on Austin Bluffs Parkway, when he observed a vehicle speeding in the other direction. Officer made a U-turn and started pursuit when he struck the side of a vehicle that turned in front of him. The collision occurred near Oro Blanco Drive. Officer died later at the hospital.

Index

Symbols

1900 United States Census 11, 57

A

Abshier George Johnson 199-205
    Aka: William C. Messick
Adams, Alexander 50, 100, 228, 273
Adams, Job 228
Adams, William Herbert 203
Agard, Samuel 36, 37
Ahern, Philip, 105
Albin, Carl 30
Alderman, Lloyd Earl 195, 197, 199
Aldrich, Charles F. 91
Aleshire, Arlo 61, 63
Allen, Harry Lee 279
Allward, Harry C. 60, 106
Althouse, William 161
Ammons, Governor Elias Milton 100
Anderson, Carl 171
Anderson, Harry 195
Anderson, John Wesley 255, 256
Anderson, William J. 141
Andrews, Jennie 84
    aka: Jennie Walsh
Andrews, Milton Franklin 83-85
    aka: Milton Franklin; George Bouton; George Barnett; William Brush; William Curtis; Clayton Hill
Angene, Julie L. 277
Anthony, William C. 97
Armstrong, Stephen 273, 274
Arnold, Frederick G. 161,
Arnold. Mary 218
Atkinson, Joel 16, 22, 24, 37, 61, 63-68, 267-270, 274
Atkinson, Jesse 67
Atkinson Merchant's Police & Fire Patrol 67

B

Baggs, Charles 90
Baily, Joe 61
Baker, Frank J. 59
Ballard, Richard 256, 257
Ballard, Robert 73
Ballistics 43
Balthazard 46
Bank of Manitou ix, 165, 174, 195
Bank Robbery ix, 20, 23, 143, 165, 193
Banning, William M. 66
Barley, Eldon 253
Barngrover, Marguerite Alice 252
Barrett Drug Store 1
Barrett, Regis 203
Beall, John N. 15, 17, 266
Beery, Augustus Eden 134
Beery, Kenneth 255, 276
Behrer, Dr. Otto 223
Belle of the East 6
Bennett, Dr. A.L. 240
Bennett, Darius H. 274
Berry 100
Bertillon 240, 242, 275
Bertillon, Alphonse 11, 121, 147, 240, 242
Bernard, Douglas 97
Best, Roy 152, 203
Billy the kid 133
Binger, William F. 121
Birdsall, George G. 67, 68, 160
Bish, Benjamin Franklin 35, 37-40, 269
Bland-Allilson Act 43
Blonger, Louis Herbert 72, 74, 232, 233
Boatright, Earl Cleo 275
Boatright, William 16
Boehme, Dr. Gustav 213
Boling, Oren Ellis 273
Bonbright, George Dana Boardman 97
Bootlegger 235
Botts, Councilman 231, 232
Botts, Frank H. 188
Bouton, Bessie 82-84
    aka: Bessie Franklin; Bessie Kempter
Bowen, Alex 233, 234
Bowen, Mrs. E.C. 233
Bowerman, Dr. David 9
Bowers, F.M. 23
Boynton, Winfield Scott 45
Breeden, Howard DePew 256

Bright, Miles Burton 230
Broad, Jr., Richard 44
Brown, Delorise 276
Brown, Ray 189
Bruce, Irene 244
    Aka: Irene McCormick
Bruce, Irvin B. "Dad" 72, 74, 147, 148, 150, 152, 153, 165, 167, 170, 185, 186, 221-223, 227-229, 233, 235, 236, 239-247, 253, 255, 273
Bubb, Martha 138
    aka: Martha Humphrey; Martha Lewis
Bubb, John 138
Buckley, Charlotte Ann 130-132, 276
    aka: Charlotte Ann Nolan; Charlotte Ann Mahan; Charlotte Ann Wittges; Charlotte Ann Morris
Buckley, George 105
Buckwald Jewelry Company 184
Buckwalter, Harry H. 97
Burch, James Edmund 274
Burchfield, Richard Stanley x, 249, 253-257, 259, 260
Bureau of Investigation 143, 241, 242
Burnham, Arthur J. 120, 122
Burnham, Alice 119
Burno, Stanley Dean 65, 100, 115, 228, 239, 273
Burns National Detective Agency 242
Burns, William J. 242
Burton, Olin 117, 184
Busemeyer, Jerome Paul 276

C

Cable, Stina 218
Cabler, Edward J. 95-97
Café Royal 21
Caldwell, Cecil 117
Calvert, William 274
Campbell, Charles P. 107
Campbell, John 184
Campbell, Nealie A. 119
Cantrell, Emma Cara 251
Carbolic acid 83
Carey, Peter Timothy 273
Carpenter, George 100, 115
Carrel, Gilbert R. 153

Carte, Charles 254
Carter, Bernard Livingston 278
Carthwright, Anna Mae 250
Cassidy, Butch 133
Cerva, Gene 166
Chamberlain, Dr. Frank 81
Chapin, Roy 117
Chapman, Councilman 231, 232
Chapman, John 16
Chezum, Mrs. J. 135
City Hall 18, 35
Clancy, Ed 61
Clark, John E. 12, 13
Clark, William H. 36
Clinton, Chester Charles 145, 146-149
    aka: J.C. Clark; Frank Green; H.I. Stewart; H.W. Carter; Jim Katz; Frank Allen; George Dixon; William Green; J.B. Williams; Charles Morris
Clinton, Josie May 146, 147
    aka: Josie May Morris; Mrs. J.C. Clark; Josie May Clark Clopp, Henry Estine 170, 171, 172, 174, 175
    aka: William H. Clopp; Ernest Clopp; John Clott; John Clopp Coghlan, Dr. J. Thomas 221, 223, 224
Cole, Elgin 244
Cole, Frank 138
Coleman, W. 99
Clow, Merle 180
Collins Grocery 119
Colorado City 20-22, 25, 27, 39, 60, 61, 66-68, 70, 77-79, 104,107, 108, 113, 133, 227, 233, 250, 262
Colorado College 17, 98, 166
Colorado Springs Automobile Club 102, 103, 234
Colorado Springs Company 19, 20, 49, 54-56
Colorado Springs Opera House ix, 43-45, 57, 241
Colorado Springs Power Plant 77-79
Colorado State Penitentiary (Prison) 42, 74, 148, 152, 153, 188, 203, 205, 240, 258
Colorado Supreme Court 19
Conley, Louis 171
Cook, George T. 139
Cook, Reverend Dr. George 90
Cooper, Courtney Riley 236, 245

Cooper, John C. 31
Cornell, Henry 29-31, 109, 268-270
Cowell, David A. 19, 20, 54, 55
Cowell v. Springs Company 19
Coyne, Patrick 36, 37, 39, 40
Craig, Sam Herman 171
Crapo, Alton Frank 168-173
Crapo, Opal 169, 170
Crawford, Francis E. 190
Crooks, Mrs. H.R. 83
Crowell, Miss M.E. 97
Cripple Creek 47, 58, 59, 60, 68, 69, 77-80, 96, 104, 233
Crissman, Eva 175
Cunningham, Judge 61, 66
Cunningham, Thomas 110

D

Dabling, Mark Layne 280
Dalton gang 133
Dana, Loren C. 15-22, 24, 29, 35, 37, 97, 185, 266-269, 275
Daniels, Albert A. "Danny" ix, 183-191, 235
    Aka: T.F. Dailey
Dasey, C.V, 108
Davidson 5
Davidson, John W. 171
Davie, Jr., Robert Parsell 99
Davis, Alfred 189, 190
Davis, Arthur E. 89-91
    aka: Robert Edward Piper
Davis, Ernie 258
Davis, John 79
Davey, Martin L. 224
Dayton, George F. 274
Dean, Rupert 225
Decker, Mathew J. 161
DeMoss, George Washington 199
Dempsy, Jack 234
Deskin, D. F. 67
Dickerson, Red 168
Dillinger Law 174
Dodge, Stuart P. 233
Doeschel, Max 217

Downing, Commodore Perry 4, 11-15
Drake, Martin 160
Duff, Adolph William ix, 57, 59-66, 68, 71-74-76, 233
Duncan, Fannie Mae 4, 239
Duncan, Marvin 188
Dunnington, Orville R. 91
Durfee, Delos 15
Dyer Act 170, 172, 173

E

Eagan, Mrs. Frankie W. 128, 129, 230
Easley, Georgia S. 126-128, 275
Eastman, E.E. 6, 7
Edwards, Ford 59
Eeles, John J. 190
Eisenhower, Dwight D. 245
Elbert County State Bank 144
Elks Club 107
Ellis, William E. 85
Ellsworth, Lois E. 276
El Paso County Bank 23
Emerick, George C. 243, 275
Erb, J. Ward 122
Erickson, Walter 75
Erwin, Elmer George 188, 189
Espinosa gang 133
Essick, Charles Harrison 87, 88
Essick, Charles Pittman ix, 87-91
Essick-Davis, Ella W. 90
Essick, Flora Ina 90
Essick, Paul S. 90
Eudaley, George 137
    aka: Ray Long; Jesse Morgan; George Snyder
Exchange National Bank 23, 24

F

Fair, Thomas J. 274
Fargo, Charles 171
Federal Bureau of Investigation (FBI) 87, 171, 172, 248, 255, 256

Ferguson 189
Fingerprint 121, 151, 198, 240, 242, 244
First National Bank of Colorado Springs 23
First National Bank of Lamar ix, 148, 193, 199, 205
Fitts, Buron 210, 212, 213
Fleagle, Frederick Earl 199-206, 244
Fleagle gang 196
Fleagle, Jacob Booth 199
Fleagle, Jacob Harrison 198, 199, 200, 203, 204
    aka: Little Jake Fleagle; William Harrison Holden; James Reed; Joseph Reed; Joe Baker; Clarence Warren; Henry Warren
Fleagle, Ralph Emmerson 199-201, 203
Fleagle, Walter Howard 199
Flanagan, Frank 12
Flynn, Katleen A. 131
Follmer, George 255
Foote, Smith C. ix, 1, 2, 4-9, 11, 275
Foote's Hall 1, 2, 4, 6
Forensic dentistry 81
Foster, Everett 258
Foster, Orion Lawrence 98
Frank Lewis-Dale Jones gang 134, 135, 142, 240
Francisco, Leslie 87
    aka: Leslie Foster
Fricke, Charles William 215
Fusion 44

G

Gaines, Daniel F. 274
Galton, Francis 92
Gandy, Newton S. 64, 65
Gardner, Maude M. 252
Garred, Jesse 253
Garthright, John Walter 16, 22, 29, 37, 43, 45, 57, 151,257, 258, 267-270, 275
George, Fred 23
Gibbons, Tommy 234
Gibson, Charles 180
Giddings & Kirkwood ix, 177
Gieseker, Norman 130

Gillingham, Harvey 274
Gilmore, Dr. George Benjamin 211
Gladson, Albert C. 171-174
Goddard, Henry 43
Goldman, Ron 95
Goodwin, Harry Hall 204
Goodwin. Myron H. 189, 190
Gottfried, Dixie Ann 257
    aka: Dixie Ann Dikes
Gottfried, Gary 257
Gottfried, William Dwight 256-259
Grant, Michael 178
Graves, Britton L. 105
Gray, Vernon 209
Great Depression 165
Great Falls, Montana 14
Greg, James B. 67
Gregory, James R. 65
Grey, John S. 105
Ground, Albert Bradford 198
Gsellman, George G, 218, 222, 224

H

Hahn, Anna Marie Filser 217-225
    aka: Marie Fisher; Blonde Borgia
Hahn, Margaret 218
Hahn, Oscar 217, 220, 225
Hahn, Philip J. 218
Hall, Clyde 274
Hall, Mrs. Thomas 91
Halstead, Mrs. Alfred 91
Hamlin, Clarence C. 105
Hammond, Earl C. 61
Hammond, Luther B. 97
Hanlon, Dell 243
Harley-Davidson 115
Harmon, Mary B. 134-136
Harper, Hugh Davis 72-74, 101, 103, 118, 132, 135, 136, 142, 144, 147, 150-152, 160, 167-170, 175, 176, 178, 181, 184-186, 195, 199, 203-206, 211, 222, 227-230 232-238, 240, 242, 245, 247, 273

Harris, Charles E. 45
Harris, Ira 62, 65, 66, 160, 227
Harrison, Katherine 259
Hatler, I.L. 274
Haverkorn, Dwight v, vi, 245, 257
Hayes, Captain 222
Haywood, Newton Hutchinson 229, 273, 275
Heis, George E. 218
Heizer, David N. 105
Heller, Dorothy M. 129, 130
    aka: Springer, Dorothy M.
Heller, Lawrence Glenn 129
Henderson, Frank 134
Henry, John Oliver 57, 58
Heron, Ed 24
Herzberger, Barbara J. 130
Higgins, Hugh Y. 117, 185
Hill, John H. 107
Hill, William H. 194
Hiller, Clarence 151
Hilyer, E.C. 122
Himebaugh, James A. 100, 115, 122
Hissong, John Douglas 197
Holden, William Harrison 198, 199, 205
Holland, Rush L. 241, 242
Holloway, William 145
Holmes, Oliver Wendell 46
Hope, Charles 211-214
Hoover, Herbert 234
Hopkins, Richard J. 172
Hoy, Carson 222, 223
Hueftle, Nora 175
Houston, Grant 7, 8
Howard, Fletcher 277
Hughes, Frank Gardner 274
Hughes, Thomas 15
Hurley, Michael F. 279
Hutchinson, Edward 23, 24I

I

International Association of Chiefs of Police (IACP) 151, 152, 232, 235, 242, 244-246
Ives, Dennis John 278

J

Jack, Ellen E. 82
Jackson, Len 58, 59
Jackson, Robert M. 167, 211
Jacobs, Mrs. 91
James, Jesse 143
James, Mary Emma 208-211, 213-215
    aka: Mary Emma Busch
James, Ruth 210
    aka: Ruth Thomas
James, Vera May 209
    aka: Vera May Vermillion
James, William 274
James, Winona 207, 208, 210-214
    aka: Winona P. Wallace 210
Jardine, Douglas C. 161
Jennings, Thomas 151
Jensen Jared Scott 280
Johnson, Daniel G. 14, 55, 116, 126, 127-129, 199, 205, 229-232, 251, 256, 266
Johnson, Earl A. 256
Johnson, Grace 251
Johnson, Willa 257
    Aka: Willa Gottfried
Jones, Dale Dean 2, 134, 135, 139-142, 160, 240, 255
Jones, Margie 1354, 135, 139, 141
    aka: Marjie Celano
Jones, W.C. 160
Jordan, Kenneth Chua 280
Joyce Hotel 121

K

Kaltenberger, George 184, 185, 278
Kansas City Nut & Bolt Company 139
Kasiah, Foster Paul 186
Keener, Joseph M. 68
Kelleher, Larry 117
Kelly, Rankin Scott 1
Kelly, William O. 180
Kemp, Dorothy J. 129
Kempter, Charles R. 83
Kennedy, Mike 23, 24

Kesinger, Everett Asa 194, 198, 200, 201
Killion, Willard 209
Kimball, Otis S. 37
Kinney, William Palmer 125
King, Alfred Lavan 204
King, Vincent 58, 59, 61-68, 70, 157, 204, 227, 241, 273-275
Kirkendall, Omar 180
Kirkwood, T.C. 160
Kitterman, Archie 145, 146
    aka: Cyrus Maddox; George H. Brown; Charles Seitz
Kline, E.H, 204
Kline, Robert 173
Knapp, Charles Edwin 274
Kohler, Ernst 218, 222
Kohler, Olive Louella 218
Klowen, William 12
Klug and Smith Manufacturing Company 101
Koehler, Olive Luella 218
Kosley, Thomas 256, 257
Kresckay, Julia 218
Kruger, James Everett 173
Ku Klux Klan 155-163
    aka: KKK; White Rose; The White Caps; White League; Palefaces, White Brotherhood; Knights of the Ku Klux Klan
Kunz, Arthur 199

L

Lake City 5-10, 148, 178
Lamont, Duncan 161
Lancaster, Roscoe Conkling 134, 139, 141
    aka: Kansas City Blackie
Lane, Harry 138
Law, David Freeman 81, 87, 105
Law, Russell 180
Leech, J.A. 38
Levins, Peter 207
Lewis, Bessie 138
    aka: Bessie Rogers; Bessie Clayton; Bessie Goetz Lewis, Eva 137, 138
    aka: Eva De Morris; Eva De Orman

Lewis, Frank 12, 14, 69, 134, 137-142, 240, 263
    aka: Henry J. Clayton; Fred Rogers; Frank De Morris; James Clayton; Frank Rogers; Frank Grey; Frank De Orman
Lewis, Ora Otis 140, 141
Licis, Martins 250
Lindstrom, William 175
Lisenba, Major Raymond 207-215
    aka: Robert Sherman James; Joseph Wright
Lisenba, Maud 210
    aka: Maud Duncan
Lloyd, Chester Alvin 204
Locke, Dr. Charles E. 158, 159
Locke, Dr. John Galen 159, 160
Lombard, Frank P. 12, 15
Lowell-Meservey Hardware 90
Lowell, Ray 90
Lucas Sporting Goods Company 116
Lulu Belle's Sporting House 22
Lundgren, Eskel A. 194, 201

M

Manitou Park 12
Manley, Belle 175
Marksheffel, Albert W. ix, 105-112
Marksheffel Motor Company 110
Marksheffel, Dr. Zeo Zoe 110, 111
    aka: Zeo Zoe Wilkins; Zeo Zoe Cunningham
Marlowe, Walter D. 107
Martin, Robert 16, 185
Mason, Gene 178-181
    aka: Gene Logan
Matscheki, Dr. 222
McCabe, James 16
McCartin, Patrick Daniel 136
    aka: Patty McCartin
McConnell, Dr. Frances 222
McCormick, Jimmy 241
    Aka: Ed Demming; Thomas O'Toole, Red Demming; Eddie Daly
McCreery, H.C 38
McCreery, John Clark 235, 236
McFarland, Bob 23, 24

McFerran, James H.B. 6
McGee, Roscoe 79
McGenty, Leo 189
McIntyre, W,H. 38
McKinney, Cheryl E. 131
McKissick, Cecil James 273
McMahon, Benjamin H. 185
McMahill, Luther 138
McNellis, Patrick 63, 64, 65
McNew, Sherman Ellsworth 65, 274, 275
McReynolds, Clyde C. 83, 99, 274
McVay, Robert 253, 254
Meistrell, John 173
Michaels, Thomas 16
Merritt, Anna 119
Miller, Arthur 88
Miller, Joseph F. 134
Mine Owners Association 79
Mitchum, Robert 246
Morley, Clarence J. 159
Morris, Wesley, S. 107
Morse, Elizabeth S. 129
Mosley, E.L. 129
Mount Cutler 81
Mowry, A.L. 160
Munger, James Dewey 273
Munger, Hurbert 171
Mutchie, Peggy Ann 256, 257
  aka: Peggy Ann Gottfried
Myers, Richard W. 273

N

National Association for the Advancement of Colored People 157
  aka: NAACP
National Café 184, 187
National Firearms Act 172
Nebraska City National Bank 148
Needles, Martha Claire 250
Neff, James 228
Neil, James 60
Nelson 204

Nelson, Mrs. Charles 83. 84
Niski, Vincent Benedict 273
Nitsche, E. 73
Norlin, James E. 172
North End Addition 17
Nye, Simeon Nash 44

O

Obendoerfer, Johan Georg 218-225
Olivia, Nulta 85
Oppenheimer, Joe 21
Oppenheimer, William 21
Oregon Boot 169
Orr, Sr., James Alexander 92
Osgood, Perry 67
Osswald, Charles "Karl" 217, 218
Owens, Marie 125

P

Palmer, Albert J. 218, 224
Palmer, General William Jackson 27, 97
Pardue, James 188
Peabody 79
Pardue 188, 189
Parham, Joe 204
Parrish, Amos Newton 193, 194, 201
Parrish, John Festus 193, 194, 201
Patach, Edward J. 173
Patton, Albert L. 65
Payton, Councilman 231, 232
Pease, John 188, 190
Perreira, Jr., Augustus Joseph 279
Pershing, William Samson 136, 137
Peterson, Alton Leroy 252-254
Peyton Farmers State Bank ix, 144
Pinkerton National Detective Agency 121, 122, 134, 141, 169, 244
Pinkerton, William 244
Pittock, Charles R. 187
Pope, Augustus 15
Pray, Dr. J. Parker 83
Price, William Wells 99

Prince, Louis 258
Pritchard, Rex B. 148
Pulliam, Albert Sidney 228, 230
Purcell, Michael William 92

R
Raley, David D. 167
Ralston, William H. 105
Reavis, Carlos 197
Reed, Frank 245
Reed, Midge 214
    aka: Midge Wright
Reilley, Red 190
Reserved Watch 137, 138
Revere, Paul 81
Reynolds, Thomas H. 240
    aka: Thomas H. Wilson
Reynolds, William Sullivan 65, 83, 84, 87, 89, 99, 105, 151, 228, 239, 240, 273
Richardson, Dr. Harry L. 89
Richardson, Lee Clement 168, 197
Richardson, R,S. 71
Riley, John Dolan 134, 136, 138, 236, 245
Risc, M.L. 117
Riepl, Helen Rose 25
Rinker, Walter 189
Robinson, S, P. 8
Robinson, John R. 58, 274
Robinson's Drug Store 12
Rogers, Gerald D. 211
Rogers, James A. 213
Roosevelt, Franklin Delano 244
Roosevelt, Theodore 21
Rose, J.R. 161, 162
Rose, R.R. 61
Rose, William 137
Ross, James 83
Roswell City 17
Rowan, John William 133-136, 138, 143, 241, 255, 257
Rowan, Ron 257
Rowton, V. Eleverton 160

Royston, Howard Lester 199-203, 205
    aka: Walter W. Adams
Ruby, William N. 106
Ruth, June 119
Rutledge, Dr. James A. 120

S
Sandell, Edward C. 15
Sanders, George M. 240
Sanders, J.E. 117
Sapp, Robert Malcom 276
Sapp, Arthur N. 276
Saxton, William 17, 266
Schillo. Joe 190
Schisler, Jesse 144
Schultz, Charles 85, 100
Scofield, John E. 106
Scott, Frank L. 87
Scott, Ralph 186, 187
Seeds, Wiliam P. 63, 65, 66
Serial killer ix, x, 119, 217
Seymour, L. 121
Shea, Jack J. 191
Sheafor, John Weller 110, 148, 180
Shelby, Anna 30
Shelby, Horace 16, 18, 27-30, 267-270, 274, 275
Sherman Silver Purchase Act 43
Sherrill, LeRoy Dale 137, 138
    aka: Gabe Price; George Ryan; Charles D. Gillings; Charles A. Rollings
Shockley, Thomas 135, 136
Short, Norman 257
Silver Republican 44, 58
Silver World 7
Simmons, William Joseph 156
Simpson, Orenthal James (O.J.) 95
Sims Act 234
Smith, Soapy 133
Smith, Walter 17
Smurdon, William B. 230
Snyder, Delbert W. 243
Snyder, Walter William 170
Southard, John Clair 210, 211

Spears Frank 31
Sprague, Charles S. 44
Springer, Fred H. 117, 120
Srbinovich, James 258
Stalcup, Charlie 184
Stallworth, Ronnie 276
Stark, James Howard 5, 273
Starr, Henry George 20-23, 25, 142
    aka: Frank Jackson
Starr, Hulda 23
Starr, Mary 21, 22
    aka: Mary Jackson
Starr, Roosevelt 21
Starrett, Clyde I. 105
Sterling, William W 146, 147
    Aka: Bill Starling; Joseph Yale; Will Verdue; Will Sterling; J.W. Sterling
Stauffacher, Walter A. 67
Stetson, Louise D. 127, 128
Strawn, Ben 168
Swain, George 5

T

Taft, William Howard 234
Tagert, John Lincoln 273
Taylor, George L. 116-118
Taylor, George M. 160, 185
Taylor, James B. 134
Tedrow, Harry B. 241
Teeple, Earl E. 60
Tear gas 176, 183
Teller, Henery Moore 44
Tellerites, 44
Temple, Robert 95
Terrill, Ray 187
    aka: George R, Dyer
Terwilliger, Roland S. 168, 198
Thaw, Lewis E. 12-14
Thiel Detective Agency 121
Titus, L.B. 175
Thomas, Charles E. 127, 129
Tobins, Thomas Tate 133
Toppan, Jane 217
    aka: Jolly Jane
Touzalin, Lydia M. 128
Trip, George B. 78
Trowbridge, Henry 62, 64
Truman, Harry S. 244, 245
Turner, Mrs. 221
Tyner, Matthew Robert 281

U

Union Ice & Coal Company 58, 66
United States Supreme Court 19, 46, 55, 56

V

Van Cise, Philip Sidney 70, 72-76, 159, 162, 233, 237, 272
Van Hook, Glenn 171, 72
Van Vliet, George 141
Vasquez, Adria Gray 273
Velez, Luis 273, 277
Vindicator Mine 78
Volstead Act (Prohibition) 143
Vos, Dr. Arthur 222

W

Wade, Burt 99
Wagner, Dr. Andrew F. 213
Wagner, Jacob 218, 222, 224
Walston, Ike B. 168, 169
Wandel and Lowe Transfer & Storage Company 115
Ward, Frank H. 105, 110
Warren, Dr. Joseph 81
Washburn, R.S. 60
Wayne, Blanche 120
Wayne, Henry F. 119-121
Webb, Reuben 135
Weedman. Ira 121
Western Automobile and Supply Company 106, 107
Western Federation of Miners 79
Wheelock, Addison N. 105
White Oaks Filling Station 141
Whitlock, Michelle 277

Wiggins, Robert A. 191
Wilbur Dry Goods 35
Wilde, Harry Norman 204
Williams, Charles 274
Williams, Rosemary G. 276
Williams, Dr. Sherman 84
Wilson, Carl 138
Wilson, Kid 21
    John Willison
Wilson, Vern 255
Winbourn, Robert Emmett 200
Wineinger, Dr. William Wesley 196, 197, 200
Witz, Robert 259
Wolcott, Edward Oliver 44
Woodland 57
Woodland Park 12
Woodman of the World 91
Woodman Sanatorium 120
Woodside, William P. 81
Woolworth, Allen 171, 172, 243
Wraith, Robert Hope 145, 167, 178, 191, 195, 221
Wright, Lois 209, 210

Y

Yarnell, Grace 214

www.ingramcontent.com/pod-product-compliance
Lightning Source LLC
Chambersburg PA
CBHW070737170426
43200CB00007B/549